Myanmar

Towards Sustainable Development

Nay Pyi Taw, Myanmar's modern, sprawling capital of grand, imposing buildings and expansive highways rises abruptly out of what was once a sleepy rural area. The scenes it provides are often those of quaint juxtapositions; an ox-drawn cart rattling down the shoulder of an eight-lane highway while a motorcade of black government SUVs speeds past is not an unusual sight.

While Nay Pyi Taw is not yet a magnet for conventional tourists—though this is something that the government is hoping to change—serious business travellers will undoubtedly find themselves making their way to the capital during their visit to Myanmar.

In the wake of the comprehensive economic reforms undertaken by the government, representative offices of companies interested in operating or already based in the country have begun to open in Nay Pyi Taw. They are often housed at offices in one of the city's upscale hotels.

The offices provide businesses with access to key ministers and government officials and invaluable opportunities for face-to-face meetings.

The degree of access that business people are granted can be a welcome surprise to those used to dealing with governments that include expansive public relations divisions and bureaucratic stepping stones needed to reach decision makers. Meetings with high-level government officials are certainly obtainable, though the increased demands for their time means that flexibility is essential and last-minute schedule changes may be necessary.

Nay Pyi Taw was not designed for pedestrians and a car is essential for any type of travel within the capital as some Ministry buildings are located some distance from the hotel zone.

Business travellers will find that hotels are geared to their needs. Wireless internet is widely available in hotels and better than average mobile phone coverage means that staying in touch is easier in Nay Pyi Taw than in the rest of the country.

While hotels include conference facilities there is also the expansive Myanmar International Conference Centre (MICC) that opened in 2010. This 30,000 square foot building, set on a 16-acre site, has a main hall capable of seating about 1,200 people.

BACKGROUND

Myanmar's political and economic reforms, undertaken since President U Thein Sein's reformist government took power, have attracted the world's attention. The country has taken a series of bold steps to reengage with members of the global community following President U Thein Sein's commitment to, "clean government and good governance."

These continuing reforms, coupled with Myanmar's large population, its geographic position between super consumers India and China and the easing of economic sanctions have helped to make it one of the world's most intriguing and sought after emerging markets.

In the 1960s Myanmar's per capita income was one of the highest in the region. But economic mismanagement constrained the economy and Myanmar then fell behind most of it's neighbours. Today it has Southeast Asia's lowest per capita GDP, according to the Asia Development Bank.

But the steps being undertaken by the current government hold promise that the country could return to prosperity with a projected growth of around 8% if reforms continue to be enacted and are managed carefully.

ECONOMICALLY A NUMBER OF IMPORTANT STEPS HAVE ALREADY BEEN TAKEN

In April 2012, the central bank announced that it would use a managed float for the country's currency, kyat, to help modernize the economy. Visitors no longer have to grapple with black-market money exchangers or subject themselves to Myanmar's once eccentric exchange rate, which was pegged to the International Monetary Fund's Special Drawing Rights (SDRs) of 6.4 kyat to the US dollar. For companies looking to invest, it removed a serious barrier.

The move was followed a year later in March 2013 with the announcement of the abolishment of the Foreign Exchange Certificate (FEC) a US dollar proxy currency, a further sign of confidence in the Kyat.

The country's long-awaited new Foreign Investment Law was approved in November 2012, replacing an outdated law from 1988. The law drew criticisms for being overly protectionist. The Ministry of National Planning and Economic Development responded to criticisms with further clarifications and amendments in January 2013 making Myanmar a much friendlier environment for foreign investors.

Foreign companies are now allowed to have 100pc of ownership in non-restricted sectors, a change that would have been unthinkable a short while ago.

Myanmar signed into the New York Convention in March 2013, which could further encourage investors by bolstering their confidence that foreign arbitral awards will be enforceable in Myanmar.

Social and political reforms such as the freeing of political prisoners, including opposition leader Daw Aung San Suu Kyi, and easing of press censorship, have been recognized by other nations as the pathway to a more stable democratic nation.

These countries have responded enthusiastically. Sanctions by the United States, Australia, the European Union and other countries have been substantially eased, allowing companies to work more freely and grant them greater access to financial institutions within Myanmar.

A massive debt clearance of around US$6 billion has made the way for the World Bank and Asia Development Bank to resume much needed international aid and development funding.

While the economic reforms must be lauded, it is still necessary to understand that many changes have not touched the majority of the country's population. Reforms must continue and it is important that policies enacted from the top down reach their intended audience.

TELECOMS

The mobile network has been a monopoly by the state-run Myanmar Posts and Telecommunications (MPT) and currently Myanmar has some of the lowest mobile phone penetration in the world with only around 5.4 million mobile subscribers in the country. Additionally, mobile coverage is limited in rural areas, where the majority of Myanmar's population resides.

But President Thein Sein's government has set an ambitious goal of raising the penetration rate to 80 percent by 2015. Closer to the level found in neighboring Thailand and nearby Cambodia. To achieve this government has announced a comprehensive overhaul of the telecoms sector from infrastructure to operators.

The Ministry of Communications and Information Technology has launched an international tender process for two of the four telecoms-operators licenses up for bid. The ongoing tender has received considerable interest from some of the sector's leading companies, and selection of winning tenders is imminent.

Mobile internet usage is also set to rise with new networks utilizing 3G and 4G connectivity.

While this process is being undertaken, a limited number of low cost SIM cards have been released for sale. The SIM cards will look to relieve some of the current demand without overloading the aging and already stressed network.

A new Telecommunications Law is being drafted to couple changes with a strong regulatory framework that will increase freedom for private service providers in the market.

ENERGY

None of Myanmar's sectors have attracted the same amount of attention and excitement as the energy sector since reforms were undertaken. The country holds tremendous potential for oil and gas as well as hydropower production. But despite these abundant natural resources to date most are sold abroad leaving Myanmar with an energy deficit that leaves one in four of the population without access to electricity and frequent power cuts, especially during the dry season, remain a reality. However with additional foreign investment and technical expertise Myanmar has every chance to correct these historic problems.

In 2012 oil and gas was the largest sector for foreign direct investment, amounting to US$366.6 million according to the Union of Myanmar Chambers of Commerce and Industry.

Gas has long been the country's largest moneymaker, constituting around 30 to 40 pc of exports from the country annually. Larger growth is expected when the China-Myanmar pipelines go online. The gas pipeline will be capable of carrying around 12 billion cubic metres of gas a year to southwest Yunnan province in China from the Bay of Bengal off Myanmar's western coast. Myanmar will use no more than 2 billion cubic metres domestically.

A parallel pipeline carrying crude oil will carry 22 million tonnes a year of imported crude to China. The pipeline will provide China with a welcome alternative route to the Strait of Malacca, were around 80 percent of China's crude oil must transit at present. No more than 2 million tonnes will be used in country.

The Ministry of Energy and its subsidaries including the Myanma Oil and Gas Enterprise (MOGE) has shown a real commitment to improving its transparency over the past year. MOGE delayed an oil and gas block tender in September 2012 to improve the process at the urging of international oil and gas companies. The additional time gave MOGE the opportunity to meet with company officials and ensure that the process was carried out in a transparent manner.

Myanmar has also begun the process of entering into the Extractive Industries Transparency Index (EITI) to report revenues from extractive processes, with the expectation of submitting an application by the end of 2013.

In addition to oil and gas. The Ministry of Electric Power has identified around 200 possible hydropower sites through out the country. Dams however, must be approached in a manner that takes into account the environmental impacts and the impact on local communities. As the suspended Myitsone Dam projected showed, the government will take into serious consideration the opinions of citizens, activist groups and environmentalists when assessing the viability of future projects.

AGRICULTURE/LIVESTOCK

Myanmar has a rich agricultural history that has long hinged on the country's staple product, rice. Its decades of prodigious rice output earned the country the distinction of "a rice bowl of the world," and is a title the nation is eager to regain.

Myanmar was the world's largest rice exporter from 1960 to 1963, with shipments of 1.6 million to 1.7 million tons a year. It shipped a record 3.4 million tons in 1934 while under British rule. But lack of sufficient agricultural development since the 1960s left Myanmar behind whiles its fellow Southeast Asian nations continued to grow. Thailand held the position of the world's top exporter from 1983 until 2012.

Today the bulk of the rice trade takes place over the border with China. Myanmar exports generally low quality, broken rice that does not demand top price. Yields per hectare also remain low compared to neighbouring countries. However, the country's fertile soil, access to water for upgraded irrigation systems, use of hybrid seeds, mechanization of farming techniques and abundant workforce along with new interest from foreign investors are reasons to believe that the historic output of rice could be reached again.

Development of special economic zones at Thilawa and Dawei could further boost exports by providing an alternative to the antiquated Yangon port, which struggles to handle about 90 percent of the nation's trade. These ports, if developed correctly, could better handle an increase in rice volume.

Despite the slowdown from its historic highs, the agricultural sector as a whole remains a main sector for the Myanmar economy, accounting for around 36% of GDP and more than half of the country's employment.

Aside from rice, Myanmar is one of the world's largest producer of sesame seeds. The country is also a major producer of fresh fruits and vegetables, but limited transportation options keep most of consumption within country.

Small numbers of cattle, goats, pigs, buffaloes and various poultry are still kept by most rural families. While most are still used in a relatively unchanged traditional manner, like buffaloes for farming practices, there has been some industrialization of commercial chicken farms.

MEDIA

Myanmar's high literacy rate, believed to be around 90%, has aided in the creation of a media sector that is set to thrive once unburdened by regulations.

After taking office President Thein Sein, in June 2012, began to ease press restrictions that had been some of the toughest in the world since the passing of the 1962 Printers and Publishers Registration Act. Journalists were given greater freedom to cover political topics and articles with nonpolitical focus, like sports and health, were no longer subject to pre-printing censorship.

In August 2012 The Press Scrutiny and Registration Division was suspended. The division, under the Ministry of Information, was the responsible for the censorship and editing of printed publications ranging from books to magazines to newspapers and journals.

Furthermore in late January 2013 the government took the action further and the division was completed disbanded, ending what had been nearly 50 years of strict press censorship. Both the Committee to Protect Journalists reported that the country has zero journalists imprisoned.

The country announced that it would allow for the printing of independent daily newspapers starting in April 2013. Exiled media groups that were not permitted to report from within Myanmar such as the Democratic Voice of Burma and The Irrawaddy Magazine have returned to the country, opening offices in Yangon and work freely to cover the news.

A temporary setback came in March 2013 with the announcement of the Draft Press Bill. Media officials and journalists inside the country, as well as international watchdog groups criticised the government for back sliding on what had been promising momentum towards a truly open press.

But the government quickly acknowledged the concerns and decided to put the Draft Press Bill on hold less than a month later, with plans to revisit it after meeting with journalists and industry professionals to gather further input.

Use of the Internet including access to social media platforms is not blocked or inhibited by the government. The government has upgraded ministry websites and created accounts on popular social media websites including Facebook and Twitter to engage with citizens and deliver important information in a more timely and effective manner. The Korean International Cooperation Agency has helped the government to further develop e-governance practices through its third national ICT Master Plan.

Fisheries

Over 1,900 miles of coastline stretching along the Bay of Bengal and Andaman Sea, coupled with inland lakes and large rivers like the Irrawaddy, Chindwin and Thanlwin make Myanmar a premier site amongst Asian nations for fisheries and aquaculture.

The country's appeal is further boosted by its location between three of the top export destination for fisheries, Thailand, Bangladesh and China and that fish are a staple food in the Myanmar diet.

There are 13 European Union certified processing plants for aquaculture in Myanmar, with the bulk located in Yangon. Marine capture fisheries are divided into three areas; costal, offshore and deep sea.

A major setback to the industry came in 2008 when Cyclone Nargis extensively damaged large and productive fishing grounds in the Ayeyarwady Delta region. In addition to the natural environment suffering, fishermen's homes, vessels and other equipment were destroyed and many lives lost. Through continued relief work and development efforts the region shows signs of rebounding.

The export of saltwater shrimp to the United States in March 2013 marked a key step forward in the warming of Myanmar-US business relations and re-entry into a large market.

The sector will need to be closely monitored and developed in a sustainable manner that takes into account the delicate balance of Myanmar's marine environments, which will come under increased pressure from both man made and natural elements. The education of local communities will be needed too as development of more efficient and mechanized fishing techniques increase hauls and potentially threaten fishing stocks.

Mining/Gems

While Myanmar is rich in mineral resources and they are one of the country's largest earners, the nation remains greatly unexplored by major international mining firms, something that the government is hoping to change. There is optimism that the current Mining Law, enacted in 1994, will be widely reworked in the near future, making the sector more attractive to international firms.

The government is keen to use Myanmar's strategic geographic location to export to its large, populous neighbors and there is hope that further development of the mining sector will increase job opportunities for Myanmar's citizens.

While the country has a variety of minerals, its gems have been historically noted for their exceptional quality. Myanmar is particularly known for its dark red, "pigeon's blood" rubies largely considered to be the finest in the world. The rubies are mined in Mogok a region north of Mandalay in an area that is often referred to as the Valley of Rubies. One of the finest examples of a Myanmar ruby, the 23.1-carat the Carmen Lúcia Ruby, mined in the 1930s, is prominently displayed in the Smithsonian's National Museum of Natural History in Washington, DC.

The country's vivid green jade is equally as renowned. The mines in Hpakant produce huge slaps of uncut jade that is carved into high quality jewellry, Buddha images and numerous desirable ornamental items.

Forestry

A draft forestry law is currently being worked on by the Ministry of Environmental Conservation and Forestry (MOECAF) aiming to restore Myanmar's once stringent forestry management systems that have become increasingly lax.

The government has announced that unprocessed logs will no longer be exported from the country starting April 1, 2014. The European Union has also become increasingly interested in working with Myanmar authorities to modernize the sector for future exportation.

Further developments will be needed with an emphasis on reforestation efforts, the prevention of widespread environmental degradation and the stemming of illegal logging in border areas.

Tourism

2012 marked a tourism milestone for Myanmar as the country welcomed over a million tourists for the first time. It was a jump of around 200,000 from the previous year. With positive reviews from the media and multiple appearances on top destination lists, the country attracted a broad range of travellers from multiple countries.

The once burdensome visa process for tourists has been streamlined in an effort to make the country more accessible. Citizens from almost 50 countries are now eligible to obtain visas on arrival at the international airports in Yangon and Mandalay. Additional immigration officers have been added to the staff to help relieve lengthy waits for documents and customs clearance.

The one time limited travel agenda that included only a hand full of pre-approved tourism destinations has been greatly expanded. Travelers are allowed greater freedom to see more of the country, like western Chin State and the southern islands of the Megui Archipelago. Package tours are no longer necessary for travel and the bulk of tourists in 2012 were independent travellers.

The arrival of major electronic payment companies has made using credit cards possible at a number of hotels, restaurants and shops. ATMs now accept major bankcards ending the need to carry large amounts of cash into the country and the often-troublesome situations of cash only travel.

Both Yangon International Airport and the under used Mandalay International Airport have been scheduled for major overhauls to handle the increased demand. The long delayed Hanthawaddy International Airport, located about 50 miles north of Yangon near Bago, is also moving forward.

The influx has been the quickest and most visible boom since Myanmar began its reforms process, increasing revenues 70 percent in 2012, but has put considerable strain on Myanmar's underdeveloped hotel sector. In tourist destinations like Yangon, Bagan and Inle Lake, high season travellers often find themselves struggling to find suitable rooms or available rooms at all.

Foreign investment in the sector, though it has risen dramatically, lags behind especially in hotel construction. Yangon, the country's main entry point for foreign travellers, has less than 9,000 hotel rooms in around 200 hotels of varying quality. The country has about 28,000 hotel rooms total, not enough to meet the increased demand inevitably sending room prices soaring. Nevertheless the potential for this sector too is immense.

Since the new government took office in 2011, tremendous reform processes have been implemented. Such processes signal the seeming good intentions of the incumbent government which in turn hopefully reflects the will of many of the people of Myanmar.

Myanmar is now back on the international stage and countries around the world are coming to recognize these energetic reforms.

The holding of the World Economic Forum on East Asia in Myanmar's capital Nay Pyi Taw in June 2013 is a resounding acknowledgement of Myanmar's ongoing reform processes.

And through 2014 Myanmar is the Chair of the Association of Southeast Asian Nations.

INTRODUCTION TO NAY PYI TAW

Myanmar is full of surprises and Nay Pyi Taw is one of them. Nay Pyi Taw, its name translates as 'Royal City' or 'Seat of Kings', is a young capital which, contrary to belief, has much to offer a visitor whether on business or on holiday. Built on a plain which sits between two ranges of hills, the Bago Yoma and Shan Yoma, on a clear day the city has a marvellous backdrop.

For the visitor who arrives at the gleaming new airport the drive into the city is first through beautiful lush farmland, dotted with small white pagodas, and if not too hazy you may spot the lofty Uppatansanti Pagoda off to your right.

On nearing the city that all changes; the road becomes a multi-lane highway the central reservation is planted with oleander and tumbling bougainvillea, with light traffic on the road a relief after Yangon's dense traffic. The highways which criss-cross the city are interspersed with stately roundabouts, a huge sculpted red rose sits atop one such well-planted roundabout.

The first impression of the city is its scale—huge spaces and substantial but mostly low-rise buildings. The majority of buildings are painted soft colours with intricate traditional-style Myanmar roofs. There is still much construction under way but all that is needed in a capital city is now in place; the government buildings, housing, schools, hospitals, markets, hotels and for both residents and visitors recreational things to do (including several golf courses).

One of the pleasures for the visitor is that surrounding the modern city are several old towns such as Pyinmana and Lewe, these have a wealth of treasures to explore, old pagodas, teak monasteries, traditional markets.

HISTORY AND CONSTRUCTION

Historically there is a tradition of moving the capital for each new dynasty—for instance around Mandalay, the last royal capital, are three former capitals, Ava, Amarapura and Sagaing. However in 2005, the seat of administration was moved 230 kilometres north from Yangon, then the capital to newly constructed Nay Pyi Taw there was certain speculation, both national and international as to why the move. The main reason was that Yangon was becoming too crowded, which to anyone recently stuck in a downtown Yangon traffic jam makes sense. And crucially the location of Nay Pyi Taw is geographically much more central.

Nay Pyi Taw is a Union Territory with its administration in the remit of the President. He in turn has appointed members of the Nay Pyi Taw Council who run the city. Nay Pyi Taw is arranged into 8 townships, 5 new ones and 3 original townships. This means that all the government ministries are found in one area, all the hotels together in two specific zones and so on. Again the residential areas are zoned hence the government ministers and employees live in a certain area depending on seniority—indeed the roofs of some apartment buildings are colour-coded to indicate in which ministry the inhabitants are employed (Ministry of Agriculture employees have green roofs). The landscaping throughout the city is good; it is well tended and watered. Luckily the area is surrounded by three reservoirs so there is no water shortage, this also means, due to hydro-electricity that power is not a problem.

Because the footprint of the city is so huge transport is challenging. There is as yet apparently no good bus service, only one taxi company and the proposed Metro service has been shelved. For residents and visitors alike it can present problems as you cannot just leave your office, home or hotel and walk to the market, a restaurant or indeed for an evening stroll in the Zoological Gardens.

HIGHLIGHTS OF NAY PYI TAW

Of all the sights in Nay Pyi Taw the golden Uppatansanti Pagoda is the most spectacular. It was opened in 2009 and is a replica of the great Shwedagon Pagoda; it sits on a hill looking down on the city with a large monastery complex below. The stupa is 325 feet tall so a mere 12 inches shorter than the Shwedagon. A long staircase leads up onto the wide marble terraces which encircle the pagoda. Unlike the Shwedagon it is possible to walk into the stupa, a large space with marble slabs along the walls on which are carved the Jataka stories. Around the centre on golden thrones sit four jade Buddha images; they depict the four phases of his life; birth, enlightenment, the first discourse, and attaining Nirvana. The relic chamber holds a tooth of the Lord Buddha.

In the gardens below the pagoda live seven White Elephants, at any one time two will be on show. To possess a white or albino elephant has been all important in the history of Myanmar; they are supposed to bring 'peace, stability and prosperity'. Until recently there were five white elephants housed below the Uppatansanti Pagoda. There is a charming story about the capture of the 7th elephant from the Pathein area. This 15 year old female elephant was first spotted in 2006 but the story goes she was protected by her herd who covered her in mud. Unfortunately one rainy day in 2011 she was spotted again as the rain had washed off the muddy disguise.

THE GEMS MUSEUM

Two sculptures of white elephants stand guard outside the entrance to the museum. The ground floor is arranged like a market with different merchants selling their wares. The majority of gems have already been set into

Statue of Aung San Suu Kyi's father, General Aung San, in Pyinmana Township, a short drive from the centre of Nay Pyi Taw

a piece of jewellery although there are some raw stones available. Upstairs is the museum which houses some startlingly large stones—a dragon of rubies guarding a vast pearl. A star sapphire which the label proclaims is the world's largest though it looks a little boring as it is unpolished. A piece of jade intricately carved to the shape of the Shwedagon Pagoda.

Nay Pyi Taw hosts the Gem Emporium now in its 50th year, before it was held in Yangon. It takes place once or twice a year in another purpose built centre with a vast helmet-like roof, which glistens in the sun as you drive past. The Emporium attracts gem merchants from around the world as Myanmar is known for producing the world's best rubies and jade, fine pearls and many other precious and semi-precious stones.

PARKS AND GARDENS

Nay Pyi Taw is well catered for with public gardens; the Jade Garden, the Water Fountain Garden, Zoological Gardens, Safari Wildlife Park, National Herbal Garden and the National Landmark Garden are all to be found in and around the capital. Every one of these gardens is worth a visit and several are open at night with attractive lighting. The zoo is now home to some 430 animals many of whom were moved to their specially created new home from the former capital Yangon. The 200 acre Herbal Garden boasts 353 species of herbal plants, many indigenous. It is run by the Health Ministry hence there is much information on the use of herbs in medicine. The National Landmark Garden features mini versions of the country's famous sights. This includes a model of Nay Pyi Taw so for anyone interested in the development and architecture of the city a must to visit.

Again for those interested in architecture several of the government buildings are worthy of a visit. The Myanmar International Convention Centre is a grand colonnaded building in front of which is a large, reflective pool. Behind the vast marble clad entrance hall is the auditorium which seats some 1,900 people. Very tastefully decorated, comfortable red velvet seats, teak walls, and the stage is equipped with all the latest technology for presentations. The Centre was a gift from China and was originally planned for Yangon but then with the shift of capital it was built in Nay Pyi Taw. The various smaller meeting rooms and offices are separated from the main spaces by some internal gardens all well-kept.

The Hluttaw (Parliament) complex is made up of 31 buildings, with the Presidential Palace nearby. The significance of 31 is said to refer to the 31 'planes of existence' in Buddhist cosmology. Set in 800 acres of land this highly decorated statement building with traditional Myanmar-style roofs is home to the 664 members of parliament. The Hluttaw is made up of an Upper House (House of Nationalities) and a Lower House (House of Representatives) with all members elected save 25% reserved for the military. Hluttaw is the word which was used for the Council of Ministers under the King of Myanmar.

The City Hall built in the same style, though not so ornate, is nearby. Other buildings of interest are the Railway Station, which has several old engines parked out front plus a charming topiary engine. The entrance to the station is a triple height space with a grand double staircase. But once on the platform the normal humdrum of a station is safely in place—groups of all ages waiting for trains, the bustle, the food hawkers advertising their wares and the noise of the trains. The International Airport is another impressive building; designed by a Singaporean architect it has the capacity to welcome 3.5 million passengers a year. Major buildings still to be finished are the National Library and the National Museum.

For those wanting some night life the Myoma Market is a lively spot—a multitude of stalls including some good food stalls. Here it is possible to sample some delicious Shan dishes, Nangyi Salad or coconut noodles. It is open during the day but comes to life in the early evening.

AROUND NAY PYI TAW

Some twenty minutes' drive from Nay Pyi Taw is the town of Pyinmana, the car leaves the broad highways of the city onto a tree-lined avenue bordered by teak houses interspersed with a few larger ones of brick and mortar. At the centre of this busy town is Lake Mingalar Shan-Kan one side of which stands a handsome statue of Bogyoke Aung San in his army 'great coat'. The statue was erected in 1948 as, during World War II, the General spent time here. Around the shore of the lake are various fine heritage buildings, some wooden some brick. The Cyber House Internet café sits alongside a lovely old teak house its shutters open, on the benches in the forecourt sit several people reading their newspapers. Delicious Shan mohingha is served in the cafés for breakfast. This town has a feeling of a vibrant community, local music heralds a Hindu ceremony further around the lake, and it is full moon so festivals are never far away.

At one corner of the lake is Pa-Ya-Koe Suu Pagoda, this compound with nine small stupas built in the Shan style, dates from around CE (AD) 1305. Originally the nine stupas were built by nine devotees from nine surrounding villages. Not far away is another fine pagoda complex Koe Khan Gyi. Up some steps with gardens either side where a mixture of birdsong and chattering babes punctuate the silence of the pagoda. In the centre of the building is a large seated

Buddha image made of bronze whilst the perimeter of the complex is decorated with 264 paintings of Buddha's former life, the Jataka stories. This is a popular place for astrologers (and given the queues at several astrologers some are more popular than others!).

Next door is a marvellous complex of old teak buildings which form the Lawka Yan Hnein monastery, this is home to some 10 monks. The central stupa was built by King Theebaw, whilst the mixture of wooden and brick buildings surrounding the main stupa date from different times. A place with a wonderfully calm feeling, it would be so easy to spend time at this monastery imbibing the atmosphere.

In a nearby village is Aung Kone monastery which is a real treasure. At the end of a village track sits this beautiful teak building on stilts, shaded by fine old Acacia trees. The main building is one big room with a few wooden cubicles where the older monks sleep. The Abbot himself has a bed next to the annexe containing a Buddha image in the Mandalay style. A few punkahs hang from the carved ceiling. Around the old central building are various modern ones where the some 25 monks sleep.

Lewe is another small town next to Nay Pyi Taw—more beautiful trees line the road into town. At the centre stands the heavily restored 1,200 year old Phaung Taw Chat Ma Pagoda, a large golden stupa topped off with a beautiful gem encrusted *hti* or umbrella. An ancient, but very healthy looking, Banyan fills one corner of the surrounding terrace. Sitting at the base of the tree is a Buddha image surrounded by five disciples.

Lewe like Pyinmana has a mixture of fine old shop-houses displaying their wares; rice in huge black lacquer containers alongside wooden residences with balconies displaying flower filled pots. A general buzz of life fills the streets, a motorcyclists passes with a laptop bag slung over his shoulder—a mixture of old and new. This is a snapshot of things to do and see in and around the capital of Nay Pyi Taw, but there is plenty more.

NAY PYI TAW AS A STOP-OVER

While Nay Pyi Taw is primarily a diplomatic and business destination leisure vistors who may wish to include "NPT" in their itineraries can consider a stop-over travelling to or from Yangon or Mandalay. Luxury buses make for a comfortable journey up from Yangon on the excellent Yangon–Nay Pyi Taw–Mandalay Expressway. "NPT" being located quite close to the half-way point about four and a half hours out of Yangon, with Mandalay around three and half hours further north. A nice and indeed interesting way to break the all-day ride northward or southward.

Myanmar
Burma in Style
An Illustrated History & Guide

Dedication

The Burmese are a curious crew
The boys wear skirts, the girls do too.
The boys wear hats, the girls refrain
And view such things with much disdain.

By the late U Myint Thein, or Uncle Monty (1900–1994)
as he was known by his host of worldwide friends.

Author and Editor's Notes

When referred to in an historical context, Myanmar's place names retain their original, pre-1989 form. See the end of the History section for a list of place-name changes.

Transliteration from the Burmese does not conform to a single system; one comes across the same word spelled in a multitude of ways. To avoid confusion we have tried to be consistent in the spelling of place names and Burmese terms.

The publishers wish to make it clear that any opinions expressed in this book are exclusively those of the authors and not those of the citizens of Myanmar who have helped to provide and check factual information.

A word about the title—*Myanmar: Burma in Style*

We have included both country names in the title because the majority of people outside Asia are not familiar with the name Myanmar. For further comment on the challenge relating to name please refer to our editor Caveat Emptor (inside back cover).

Style because Myanmar is a country of tremendous natural style, both the physical country and the people exude grace and elegance. Lastly the text we hope, will appeal to the traveller who appreciates style.

MYANMAR
BURMA IN STYLE

BY

CAROLINE COURTAULD

(top) Uppatasanti Pagoda; (bottom) City Hall. Both located in Myanmar's capital city, Nay Pyi Taw

Odyssey Books & Maps is a division of Airphoto International Ltd.
1401 Chung Ying Building, 20–20A Connaught Road West, Sheung Wan, Hong Kong
Tel: (852) 2856 3896; Fax: (852) 3012 1825
E-mail: magnus@odysseypublications.com; www.odysseypublications.com
Follow us on Twitter—www.twitter.com/odysseyguides

Distribution in the USA by W.W. Norton & Company, Inc. 500 Fifth Avenue, New
York, NY 10110, USA. Tel: (800) 233-4830; Fax: (800) 458-6515; www.wwnorton.com

Distribution in the UK and Europe by Cordee Ltd. 11 Jacknell Road, Dodwells Bridge
Industrial Estate, Hinckley, Leicestershire LE10 3BS, UK. Tel: (1455) 611-185
info@cordee.co.uk; www.cordee.co.uk

Distribution in Australia by Woodslane Pty Ltd. Unit 7/5 Vuko Place, Warriewood,
NSW 2012, Australia. Tel: (2) 9970-5111; Fax: (2) 9970-5002; www.woodslane.com.au

Myanmar: Burma in Style, An Illustrated History & Guide
ISBN: 978-962-217-832-8
Library of Congress Catalog Card Number has been requested.
Copyright © 2014, 2013 Airphoto International Ltd.
Based upon Caroline Courtauld's **Burma** **(Myanmar)** Copyright © 1999, 1988 Odyssey
Publications Ltd.

Grateful acknowledgment is made to the following authors and publishers:
Asia 2000 Ltd. for *Burma's Golden Triangle* © 1992 André and Louis Boucaud; Eland
Books for *Golden Earth—Travels in Burma* by Norman Lewis © Norman Lewis 1952;
Macmillan and Co., Limited for *The Burman: His Life and Notions* by Shway Yoe; Martinus
Nÿhoff and Yale University for *Aung San of Burma*, compiled and edited by Maung Maung
© 1962 Martinus Nÿhoff, The Hague, Netherlands; Michael Joseph Ltd for *The Road Past
Mandalay* by John Masters © 1961 Bengal-Rockland Inc.; Penguin Books for *Burmese Days*
by George Orwell © 1934 Eric Blair, 1986 the Estate of the late Sonia Brownell Orwell;
Penguin Books for *Letters from Burma* by Aung San Suu Kyi © 1996, 1995 Aung San Suu
Kyi; Peter Owen Publishers for *The Changing of Kings: Memories of Burma 1934–1949* by
Leslie Glass © 1985 Sir Leslie Glass; Virago Press Limited for *The Lacquer Lady* by F.
Tennyson Jesse © 1929 F. Tennyson Jesse, 1979 The Public Trustees, The Harwood Will
Trust; Quadrille Publishing © 2010 for *Orchards in the Oasis, Recipes, Travels & Memories*
by Josceline Dimbleby.

My numerous trips to Burma, or Myanmar, the name by which the country now prefers to be known, have been made possible by the help and support of many dear friends. To mention but a few, Kenneth Maung Maung Pa, oriental Renaissance Man, introduced me to the magic of his country, beguiled me with legends and historical anecdotes and told me about Buddha. The diplomatic prowess and endless sense of humour of the late U Tin Tun has guided me. Among many excellent British ambassadors, Martin Morland's great love for and profound knowledge of the country have stood out and been a constant inspiration. The Ministry of Hotels and Tourism (Myanmar Travel and Tours), until recently under the helpful day-to-day stewardship of U Myo Lwin, also Daw Kyi Kyi Aye, Kyi Thein Ko, and Geoffrey Goddard. My late husband William, ever enthusiastic, loving and supportive. To all these and many others, I express my warm gratitude. However, perhaps it is to the people of Myanmar as a whole that I am in deepest debt. For as observed by the 19th-century colonial Sir George Scott, 'it is their natural kindness and that first of all qualifications for the title of gentleman, consideration for the feelings of others, which make the Burmese such general favourites with all who come across them.'

Photography by Caroline Courtauld unless otherwise specified below:
Additional photography/illustrations courtesy of Peter Arnold 279; Magnus Bartlett 3 (top), 22, 131–8, 149, 185 (top), 188, 189, 190, 295; Roger Brumhill 2; Clara Courtauld 1, 228, 232, 237, 240, 246, 247; Creative Commons Attribution 187; John Colling 65; Josceline Dimbleby 96, 254, 255; EPA (European Press Photo Agency) 50; The Hongkong and Shanghai Banking Corporation Limited 6–7; Nick Garbutt 291 (middle); Maximilian Horsley cover spine, 14–5, 243; William Hurst 30–1, 185 (bottom), 187 (insert), 250, 277; Image Science and Analysis Laboratory, NASA-Johnson Space Centre 186–7; The Illustrated London News Picture Library 37, 45, 167; Bagan Min Min Oo Front cover & back cover (bottom); Ministry of Hotel and Tourism 54, 302–3; Steve Winter/National Geographic 291 (top & bottom); V&A Picture Library 56, 129, 155, 271.

Essays:
Timothy McLaughlin *Myanmar Today* pages i–ix.
Email: timothy.mclaughlin3@gmail.com

Bagan Min Min Oo *Photo Essay*, follows page 240.
Email: minminoobagan@gmail.com

Maximilian Horsley & William Hurst *Photo Essay*, follows page 256.
Email: maximilianhorsley@gmail.com, www.arakantravel. com
Email: whurst@netvigator.com

Mark Stroud *Atlas*, follows page 272.
www.cartography.net

Editor: Geoffrey Goddard   Maps: Tom Le Bas
Designer: Au Yeung Chui Kwai   Remote sensing: Martin Ruzek
Index: Don Brech, Records International Management, Hong Kong

Production by Twin Age Ltd, Hong Kong. Email: twinage@netvigator.com
Printed in Hong Kong

CONTENTS

A panoramic view of Rangoon 1828, painted by William Prinsep

The moment the fisherman spies bubbles, he plunges his conical-shaped net into the water, pushing it home with his leg. He then attempts to spear the ensnared fish

FOREWORD: THE NEW SILK ROAD

Dr Thant Myint-U

Over the next few years, Asia's geography will see a fundamental reorientation, bringing China and India together as never seen before across what was once a vast and neglected frontier stretching over a thousand miles from Kolkata (Calcutta) to the Yangtze River basin. And Burma, long seen in Western policy circles as little more than an intractable human rights conundrum, may soon sit astride one of the world's newest and most strategically significant crossroads. Mammoth infrastructure projects are taming a once inhospitable landscape. More importantly, Burma and adjacent areas, which had long acted as a barrier between the two ancient civilisations, are reaching demographic and environmental as well as political watersheds. Ancient barriers are being broken, and the map of Asia is being redone.

For millennia, India and China have been separated by near impenetrable jungle, deadly malaria, and fearsome animals, as well as the Himalayas and the high wastelands of the Tibetan plateau. To reach India from China or vice versa, monks, missionaries, traders, and diplomats had to travel by camel and horse thousands of miles across the oasis towns and deserts of Central Asia and Afghanistan, or by ship across the Bay of Bengal and then through the Straits of Malacca to the South China Sea.

But as global economic power shifts to the East, the configuration of the East is changing too. The continent's last great frontier is disappearing, and Asia will soon be woven together as never before.

At the heart of the changes is Burma. Burma is not a small country; it is as big in size as France and Britain combined, but its population of 60 million is compared with the 2.5 billion combined populations of its two massive neighbours. It is the missing link between China and India.

China's leadership has written about its "Malacca dilemma". China is heavily dependent on foreign oil, and approximately 80 percent of these oil imports currently pass through the Strait of Malacca, near Singapore, one of the world's busiest shipping lanes and just 1.7 miles across at its narrowest point. An alternative route needed to be found. Again, access across Burma would be advantageous, lessening dependence on the strait and at the same time dramatically reducing the distance from China's factories to markets in Europe and around the Indian Ocean. That Burma itself is rich in the raw materials needed to power industrial development in China's southwest is an added plus.

Meanwhile, India has its own ambitions. With the "Look East" policy, successive Indian governments since the 1990s have sought to revive and strengthen age-old ties to the Far East, across the sea and overland across Burma, creating new connections over once impassable mountains and jungle barriers. Just north of where China is building its pipeline (across Burma to south-western China), along the Burmese coast, India is starting work to revive another seaport with a special road and waterway link to Assam and India's other isolated and conflict-ridden northeastern states. There is even a proposal to reopen the Stilwell Road, built by the Allies at epic cost during World War 11 and then abandoned, a road that would tie the easternmost reaches of India with China's Yunnan province. Indian government officials speak of Burma's importance for the security and future development of their country's northeast—while also keeping a cautious eye on China's dramatic push into and across Burma.

Watching these developments, some have warned of a new Great Game, leading to conflict between the world's largest emerging powers. But others predict instead the making of a new Silk Road, like the one in ancient and medieval times that coupled China to Central Asia and Europe. It's important to remember that this geographic shift comes at a very special moment in Asia's history: a moment of growing peace and prosperity at the conclusion of a century of tremendous violence and armed conflict and centuries more of Western colonial domination. The happier scenario is far from impossible.

But is a modern-day Silk Road really in the making? Until recently it was difficult to be optimistic, but in March 2011 the Burmese junta was formally dissolved and power handed over to a quasi-civilian government headed by a retired general, U Thein Sein. President Thein Sein quickly began to exceed expectations, speaking out against graft, stressing the need for political reconciliation, appointing technocrats and businessmen to key positions, inviting exiles to return home, announcing fresh talks with rebel groups and reaching out to Aung San Suu Kyi. Poverty reduction strategies have been formulated, taxes lowered, trade liberalised, and a slew of new laws on everything from banking reform to environmental regulation prepared for legislative approval. The new Parliament, after a shaky start, began to take a life of its own. Media censorship has been significantly relaxed, and opposition parties and Burma's burgeoning NGO community have been allowed a degree of freedom not seen in half a century.

It's a fragile opening......

By kind permission, *Foreign Affairs* 2011

Hill tribe family in the Shan hills near to Kyaukme

Phaung Daw U Pagoda on Inle Lake, Shan State

The Amarapura Palace with the Sacred White Elephant. The albino beast was considered one of the prized possessions of the monarch. 'Every Burmese king longed for the capture of such a treasure during his reign as a token that his legitimate royalty is recognized by the unseen powers,' wrote colonialist Sir Henry Yule

Myanmar (Burma)

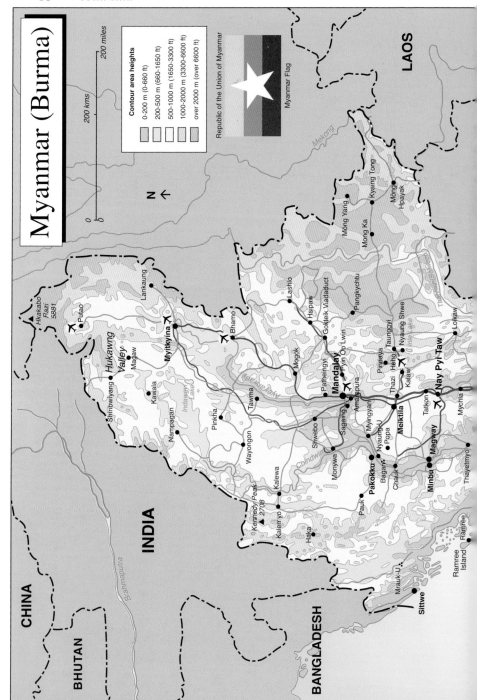

200 miles

200 kms

Contour area heights

0-200 m (0-660 ft)
200-500 m (660-1650 ft)
500-1000 m (1650-3300 ft)
1000-2000 m (3300-6600 ft)
over 2000 m (over 6600 ft)

Republic of the Union of Myanmar

Myanmar Flag

N

CHINA

BHUTAN

INDIA

BANGLADESH

LAOS

Brahmaputra

Mekong

Hkakabo Razi 5681

Putao

Lankaung

Hukawng Valley

Magaw

Myitkyina

Shinbwiyang

Indawgyi Lake

Kawala

Nampagan

Pinkha

Tawma

Chindwin

Bhamo

Lashio

Hsipaw

Gokteik Viadaduct

Mogok

Mong Yang

Mong Ka

Kyaing Tong

Mong Hpayak

Pangkychtu

Pyin Oo Lwin

Patheingyi

Mandalay

Amarapura

Sagaing

Shwebo

Monywa

Wayongon

Kalewa

Kaleryo

Kennedy Peak ▲ 2708

Haka

Mrauk-U

Sittwe

Ramree Island

Ramree

Pauk

Chauk

Bagan

Nyaung-U

Popa

Pakokku

Myingyan

Minbu

Magway

Meiktila

Thazi

Kalaw

Heho

Pindaya

Taunggyi

Nyaung Shwe

Inle Lake

Nay Pyi Taw

Tatkon

Mychla

Thayetmyo

Lokaw

Thanlwin/Salween

Ayeyarwady/Irrawaddy

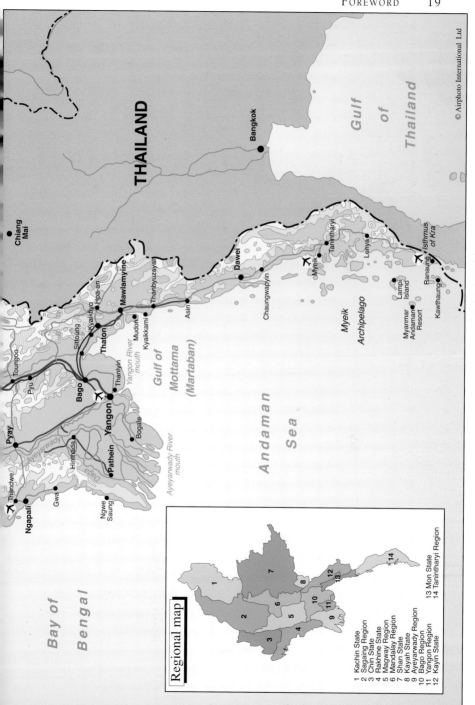

© Airphoto International Ltd

THAILAND

Bangkok

Chiang
Mai

Gulf
of
Thailand

Isthmus
of Kra

Tanintharyi

Dawei

Myeik

Lenya

Ranaung

Kawthaung

Chaungwa Pyin

Myanmar
Andaman
Resort

Lampi
Island

Myeik
Archipelago

Andaman
Sea

Gulf of
Mottama
(Martaban)

Hpa-an

Mawlamyine

Thanbyuzayat

Kyaikto

Thaton

Mudon

Kyaikkami

Asin

Sittoung

Toungoo

Pyu

Bago

Thanlyin

Yangon River
mouth

Yangon

Bogale

Pyay

Hinthada

Pathein

Ayeyarwady

Dala

Ayeyarwady River
mouth

Thandwe

Ngapali

Gwa

Ngwe
Saung

Bay of
Bengal

Regional map

1 Kachin State
2 Sagaing Region
3 Chin State
4 Rakhine State
5 Magway Region
6 Mandalay Region
7 Shan State
8 Kayah State
9 Ayeyarwady Region
10 Yangon Region
11 Yangon Region
12 Kayin State
13 Mon State
14 Tanintharyi Region

INTRODUCTION

It is still true to say that Myanmar, until recently known in both English and Burmese as Burma, is a country of a different age, where time itself moves at a different speed; a country of quiet eccentricity and gentle charm.

Today the country is on the threshold of great change so at last its citizens have the opportunity to join the modern world. The easy indicator, the mobile telephone and internet café are much in evidence. The change of regime, the release of Aung San Suu Kyi from house arrest, the relaxation of sanctions by America and the European Union have all had a huge impact on the numbers of visitors to Myanmar in the past year or so. Hotels that stood empty for years are now jam packed and it can be difficult to find rooms in Yangon during the high season. To visit Myanmar is still a delight for the genuine traveller, but tourists who expect an air-conditioned bus to whisk them from clinical airport to sanitized hotel room may even now find it not quite so.

The drive into the capital, Yangon (formerly Rangoon), is a feast for the eye: men and women dressed elegantly in longyis (sarongs) go about their business; elders, sitting in front of their criss-cross mat houses—as U Thein Sein the President tells us "more than half of the city's population lives in a house built from bamboo or wood". Survey the scene, maroon-robed monks wander quietly along the road while a gang of chattering children follow behind, endlessly tying and retying their longyis. But the true enchantment of the country is experienced with the first glimpse of the hauntingly beautiful Shwedagon Pagoda. Its golden spire towers over the city like a glittering flame, inviting all who look to make a pilgrimage up the long stairways to its marble terraces. Kipling was right: 'This is Burma, and it will be quite unlike any land you know about.'

Sipping your rum sour, a delicious concoction of fresh lime and Mandalay rum, under a swirling fan in the Strand Hotel bar or on the terrace of one of the new hotels, the spell of Burmese calm will begin to fall. Perhaps there is more ozone in the air; more likely it is the aura of Buddhism which permeates almost the whole of Burmese life.

One of the great charms of visiting Myanmar is the melting of tensions as one is inexorably drawn into the Burmese way of relaxation; even the most jaded are not exempt. Adding to this air of different calm, or rather not distracting from it is a lack of tourists. For although the tourist numbers have now escalated enormously as a result of the endorsement to visit Myanmar by both Aung San Suu Kyi and Secretary of State Hillary Clinton, the country is large enough to absorb the new influx. In the past few years all facilities have greatly improved.

No longer is it necessary to queue for hours to get air or rail tickets, there is now a crop of good and efficient travel agents in Yangon with offices around the country, plus the majority have websites and are on e-mail. Until recently the Burmese authorities had looked around at their neighbours and witnessed the impact an influx of tourists had wrought, and opted to remain secluded. It appears, however, that they would now welcome a significant increase in the tourist industry. Foreign and Myanmar hoteliers and property developers have built some beautiful hotels. A host of excellent restaurants have opened in recent years.

Yangon is a handsome city, with a history spanning more than two millennia, though it was the capital for just 120 years—newly built Nay Pyi Taw usurping its role in 2005. The city was rebuilt on a grid plan in the 1850s, its wide, tree-lined boulevards are bordered by fine stone and brick buildings—some of the finest in Asia. In the 1880s Yangon was renowned as 'Queen of the East'. Such were her prospects, forecast the 19th-century colonialist and writer, Sir George Scott, that her trade would outstrip that of Calcutta before the end of the century and 'hitherto the progress made will compare with the most vaunted American city successes'. How wrong he proved to be. Today, Yangon bustles without urgency, numerous high-rise buildings, endless traffic jams or vast shopping malls like other Asian cities. This is now bound to change and the traffic jams are already in evidence, as are supermarkets and internet cafés. The majority of shops are small, selling everything from antique lacquerware and silver-backed dressing table sets, left over from colonial days, to plastic buckets and second-hand Dorothy L Sayers novels. There is no forest of television antennae cluttering up the skyline but many buildings sprout satellite dishes. Flashy billboards promote products ranging from mobile phones to health tonics, but there are still some stylish hand-painted movie posters.

Visually Myanmar is unique: in no other land is the eye so constantly delighted by scenes of casual, almost unintended beauty. There is no better way to enjoy this picture than to travel by train. Myanmar is an agrarian society, and from the anonymous vantage point of your compartment, you can absorb the essence of the country: a background of soft browns, wooden ploughs following patient oxen across broad fields, the dazzling green paddies, noble tamarind trees, and above all, white and golden pagodas gracing hills and plains like a cascade of jewels. Myanmar's chief beauty, however, lies in her people, who exude style, grace and vivacity. Both men and women wear the traditional *longyi* with blouse or shirt, the jet-black hair of the women often adorned with fresh flowers. The person and clothing alike are washed obsessively often, and a finishing touch to the toilette is frequently provided by patterns of powdered, fragrant *thanaka* wood on ever-smiling faces.

Long-distance buses at a 'pit stop' on the expressway between Yangon and Nay Pyi Taw, good food at reasonable prices and impressively clean amenities

The intrepid traveller will soon want to venture beyond 'metropolitan' Yangon. To the north, on a bend of the Ayeyarwady River (formerly Irrawaddy River) you discover Bagan, once the capital of Myanmar and a marvel of the Buddhist world, now an arid plain thickly studded with pagodas of all shapes and sizes, their magnificence a testament to Bagan's former greatness. The Ayeyarwady is and always has been Myanmar's main artery. Its banks have provided sites for royal capitals, and boats laden with cargo have plied the river from the Ayeyarwady delta port of Pathein to Bhamo near the Chinese border for centuries. Countless soldiers travelled her length during the three Anglo-Burmese Wars. Perhaps the most bizarre of war vehicles was a steam vessel named Diana, a 60-horsepower paddle wheeler with a funnel nearly as tall as a mast. She was the first to be used by the British forces and 'the very sight of her created more consternation than a herd of armed elephants'.

Some 160 kilometres (100 miles) upstream from Bagan, the Ayeyarwady glides past 'the gilded spires of Mandalay and the pagoda-sprinkled heights of Sagaing'. These places, with their romantic names, have all hosted capitals, and the buildings they have to show today document their magnificent past. Of Myanmar's last great palace, the Gem City of Mandalay, little remains except the crenellated outer brick walls and the 70-metre- (230-foot-) wide moat where, 140 years ago, the royal barges, each manned by as many as 60 paddlers, floated among the lotus blossoms.

South-east from Mandalay, high up on a plateau in the Shan Hills, sparkles Inle Lake, a place of dazzling beauty and possessed of its own separate, magical quality. It is inhabited—literally, since their homes float upon the lake itself—by the Intha people who are renowned for their delightfully eccentric leg-rowing. Here there are no great ruins or former capitals, just breathtaking scenery. Market day in Nyaung Shwe, the small town on the northern shore of the lake, is a visual delight—the costumes of the local minorities, with vibrant colours and sparkling jewellery are, as Sir George Scott suggested, reminiscent of 'wind-stirred tulip beds or a stir about of rainbows'.

So here we have a brief glimpse of Myanmar as the traveller will see her, an enchanted country of enchanting people imbued with other-worldliness and an inherent sense of style. What is the source of this special Burmese timelessness? The answer seems to lie in the arrival and influence of Buddhism and its interaction with the country's geographic and ethnic circumstances.

It is easy to be misled by the apparent gentleness of this Buddhist country which nonetheless abounds with contradictions. Myanmar has a bloodcurdling history and even today the country is unsettled.

However long the visit, the traveller will quickly absorb and delight in some of Myanmar's magic, and wonder at its contradictions. Relax with the Burmese in a land of long-suffering acceptance of one's fate, a land of making do. Here, in their softness and fluidity, even the colours and contours of the countryside conform to the ideals of Buddha's Middle Way.

A bamboo raft transporting some straw downstream. The Ayeyarwady River, navigable for some 1,610 kilometres (1,000 miles), is a much-used artery for the country's trade

HISTORY

SOME BASIC THEMES

Myanmar's history would be complex enough, but making matters even more difficult for those who try to grasp it is the fact that the country itself kept changing shape. Kingdoms were created, broke up, mutated and occasionally coalesced approximately into its present-day form. 'Geography, that great moulder of history' has undoubtedly been one of the key influences in Myanmar's development. The country is bounded on three sides by mountains and jungle, and on the fourth by the sea. The peoples who penetrated this enclosed space found themselves in a fertile land with a clement climate. They stayed and put down roots.

This geographic insulation also served to intensify the influence of Buddhism. Its rapid acceptance as a predominant religion after 1056 is perhaps explained in part by the fact that Theravada Buddhism had a captive audience. It was often fervent religious belief which led the different kingdoms to split and reform; they were fighting religious wars, but for the same religion.

A fundamental theme in modern Burmese history is the impact of the West. Beginning in the 15th century, Western merchants primarily attracted by the gem trade arrived at Burmese ports. But somehow Burma—'tucked away on the right of the Bay of Bengal not on the way to anywhere'—never became a major trading arena. By the 19th century, however, both Britain and France realized that Burma was indeed on the way to somewhere. She held the key, in the form of the Irrawaddy River, to the back door into China. Fear that this key might fall into the hands of the French resulted in the Third Anglo-Burmese War and, in 1886, complete absorption of Burma into the British Empire.

EARLY MISTS

Very little is known of Burma's early history, and most of what 'information' is available is hard to distinguish from the fabric of myth and legend into which it is woven.

Various stone and petrified wooden implements provide evidence of man living in the Irrawaddy valley some 5,000 years ago. The major migrations began around the beginning of the Christian era: the Mons came from present-day Thailand to settle in lower Burma; the Burmans (originally known as the Mramma or Bamars) grew tired of their aggressive Chinese and Tibetan neighbours and fled the arid plains of south-east Tibet. The Pyus, who had in fact been at the front of this stream of migration, were pushed gradually southward by the Burmans and founded a kingdom at Srikshetra (near present-day Pyay). To the west, peoples from India had pushed into Arakan, where they remained until CE 957, when they were overrun by the Burmese and absorbed into the Kingdom of Pagan.

There are few if any documentary references to travellers visiting Burma prior to the second century BCE. During his lifetime (*c.*566 BCE–486 BCE) Gautama Buddha is said to have spent a week preaching on a hill near the Arakanese city of Dhannavati (some of the city's wall can still be seen today). The story goes that at the end of Buddha's stay, his host King Candrasuriya begged him, 'Lord of Three Worlds, when you go from us we shall have no one to whom we may pay homage. Will you not leave us the shape of yourself?' The Buddha consented and so the Mahamuni Image (now in Mandalay) was cast by a 'heavenly sculptor'. These legendary events are minutely described in the ancient palm-leaf manuscript, *Sappadanapakarana.*

Arakan also possesses a 'formal list' of kings from 2666 BCE to CE 1784. King Ashoka of India, a dedicated follower of the Buddha and convenor of the Third Buddhist Synod in 235 BCE (the second had been held near Wethali in the Arakan), is said to have visited the great Shwedagon Pagoda in Rangoon around 260 BCE to pay homage to the relics of the four Buddhas interred there. Then in 128 BCE, the Chinese emperor Han Wudi sent his emissary Zhang Qian to Central Asia in search of new land routes to the Roman Empire. After a ten-year journey Zhang Qian returned to China and recommended that a route across northern Burma be opened, linking China to Bactria (the ancient country of Afghanistan). The terrain, however, made it impracticable.

The trail now goes cold, although traders and, more likely, Buddhist pilgrims must have crossed northern and central Burma on their way between China and India. During the seventh and eighth centuries, contemporary Chinese histories record trade between the Pyus, in Lower Burma, and China. There is even a description of Pyu musicians playing at the Tang court. All this came to an abrupt end in CE 832 when the Pyu Kingdom was vanquished by an army from the kingdom of Nanzhao in what is today Yunnan Province in south-western China. In the ninth century Burma's role as a corridor of trade waned as sea routes from Europe, the Middle East and India via Ceylon and the Andaman Islands to China were developed, bypassing the Burmese coastline. The Burmese version of their early history (and indeed their history until 1886) is documented in the *Glass Palace Chronicles*. Compiled in the 19th century, this tome relies heavily on myth and legend.

First Unification

In 1044 an event took place which left an indelible stamp on Burmese history. Anawrahta, himself the son of a deposed king, seized back the Burmese throne of Pagan. Essentially a warrior, King Anawrahta was also something of a statesman. He spent the first few years of his reign consolidating his power, including the defeat and absorption of his neighbouring Shan Kingdom. More crucial still was his conversion, in 1056, to Theravada Buddhism by Shin Arahan, a visiting monk from the court of the Mon Kingdom in the south. Anawrahta had wearied of the Tantric spirit and animal worship by which the original forms of Buddhism had been 'corrupted' and took to the 'pure' Theravada form of the faith with startling zeal.

Thirsting for further knowledge, he appealed to the Mon king for a copy of the Theravada Buddhist scriptures, the Tripitaka. When this was not forthcoming he massed his forces and marched on Thaton. Returning victorious, he brought back with him not only the prized scriptures but also the Mon king Manuha himself, his white elephant (this is the first reference to the sacred Buddhist White Elephant), and his entire court. With the overthrow of the Mon Kingdom, the only other powerful domain in the region, it took only a few mopping-up operations to bring the remaining petty states into line. Thus for the first time, Burma was united into approximately its present-day form under the guidance of a national religion. A period of education ensued with the sophisticated southern Mons passing on their knowledge to the northern warrior Burmese. Not only did they provide a religion but also the liturgical language that went with it, Pali, in which the Theravada texts are recited.

This was the start of one of Burma's short excursions into internationalism under the cloak of Buddhism. Pagan, with its host of pagodas, became the world capital of Theravada Buddhism. Anawrahta conceived the idea of a Buddhist Empire to challenge the doctrinal dominance of both the Indian and Chinese Buddhists. 'The Burmese people,' observes the historian, Dr Htin Aung, 'began to consider themselves as champions of the Indo-Chinese peninsula, whose peoples were tied to them by the silken threads of Buddhism.' Anawrahta made overtures to the rulers of Nanzhao and Ceylon, possessors of the teeth of the Buddha. Not surprisingly, however, both refused to part with their treasures and gave him copies instead.

With Buddhism, Anawrahta had given his subjects a religious identity, but he also built canals and irrigated the lands of dry Upper Burma to ensure the production of food–much of the irrigation used today dates from his time. He died (he was gored by a buffalo) in 1077 after a 30-year reign leaving 'a legend of power, of religion and of authority'.

Burma remained unified for the next 200 years, thanks largely to Anawrahta's statesmanship and forward thinking. Most of her energies were devoted to Buddhism and the building of pagodas. In the middle of the 13th century, Mongol troops were moving across Asia, invading one country after another. In 1253 they invaded Burma's north-eastern neighbour Nanzhao, and assumed that Burma would bow to their superior military power. How wrong they were: Kublai Khan sent several embassies to King Narathihapati of Pagan. The Burmese answer to the first embassy was disinterest, to the second, execution of the envoys. War was inevitable. King Narathihapati, relates Marco Polo, 'gathered together an army of 2,000 large elephants. On each of these was erected a wooden castle of great strength and admirably adapted for warfare. Each of these castles was manned by at least 12 fighting men. In addition he had fully 40,000 men.' Apparently the Khan's soldiers were mesmerized at first by the advancing castle-bearing elephants, but having regained their equilibrium, they showered arrows on the unsuspecting beasts, who bolted for the forest, throwing off their hapless riders. (According to the *Glass Palace Chronicles*, 'the Battle of Ngasaunggyan was a furious battle, and arrows fell so thick that even the *nat* spirits fighting on the Burmese side were wounded.') On the return of his defeated army King Narathihapati, master of 300 concubines and consumer of 300 curries daily, tore down numerous pagodas to fortify his city against the Mongols in China, but they did not invade for a further two years. The Mongols, Marco Polo would have us believe, were an army of jugglers and jesters from the Khan's court, although the Burmese chronicles disagree. Before any confrontation could take place the king fled south, thus gaining the ignominious title of Tarakpyenrin: 'the king who ran away from the Chinese, leaving his capital to the invaders.'

ELEPHANT WARS

From the fall of Pagan until the establishment of full British control some 600 years later, Burma went through successive periods of disintegration and reunification. On the one hand was the persistent centrifugal force which lay behind the tendency to split up into kingdoms based on ethnic identity. On the other, was the perennial Bamar Buddhist dream of an empire essentially comprising the present-day nation.

The religious element of the Burmese dream was the concept of Universal Sovereign. To achieve this status, the monarch had to be in possession of the Seven Gems: The Golden Wheel, probably the Wheel of the Law, an impression of which was on the foot of every Buddha; the Divine Guardian of the Treasury; the Horse; the Jewel Maiden; the Jewels that Wrought Miracles; the General, whom it was impossible to defeat; and the seventh of these gems, a White Elephant. 'Every Burmese king,' attests colonialist Sir George Scott, 'longed for the capture of such a treasure during his reign as a token that his legitimate royalty is recognized by the unseen powers.' This was perhaps because the Buddha's final incarnation before attaining Nirvana had been, it was believed, a white elephant. In any event the 'Lord White Elephant' played a seminal role in the wars that plagued Burma during the next hundred or so years.

The fall of Pagan in 1287 (ending the First Burmese Empire) found the various ethnic groups re-forming their kingdoms. The Mons made a temporary capital at Martaban, on the east coast near their former homeland, though in 1365 they moved to Pegu (in those days a sea port), whence they controlled Lower Burma. To the north, a Shan kingdom centred on Ava was dominant, while sandwiched in between were the vanquished Burmans with their capital at Toungoo. In the west the Arakanese, always slightly removed from the mainstream, continued with their capital at Wethali until 1433, when they moved it to Mrauk-U. Throughout this 200-year period the Mon Kingdom at Pegu was the most powerful. It experienced a period of flourishing commerce and religious fervour. During this time the city played host to throngs of visiting monks and philosophers. During the reign of King Dhammazedi and Queen Shin Saw Pu (1453–1492), the stupa of the Shwedagon Pagoda was raised to a height of 92 metres (303 feet) and gilded, for which the Queen donated her weight—a slender 40 kilograms (88 pounds)—in gold.

In 1541 the Burmese, under King Tabinshweti, managed to oust the Mons from Pegu and found the Second Burmese Empire. From 1550 to 1564 his successor, King Bayin-naung, was consolidating his power and wealth. Merchants, both foreign and Burmese, flocked to the newly powerful kingdom. Cesar Frederick, a Venetian, visited the great city in 1563 and reported that Bayin-naung involved himself extensively in affairs of trade and that in consequence 'the King doeth take it for a most great affront to bee deceived of his Custome;...but rubies, saphyrs and spinals pay no custome in or out, because they are found growing in that countrie.' By 1564 this powerful monarch had conquered the Shan Kingdom to the north and Chiang Mai to the east. His most devastating victory was at Ayutthaya, then the capital of Siam.

By 1559 the Second Burmese Empire, centred at Pegu, was once again in decline (though it continued to exist until 1752). King Razagyri of Arakan noted its waning power, seized his opportunity and sacked the city. He carried away not only his rival king's daughter and the treasures from Ayutthaya, but also the same surviving white elephant, 'which in his eyes,' asserts Father Manrique, a Portuguese Jesuit who visited the Arakan court in 1632, 'was of greater value than all the kingdoms of the world.' This prize enabled him to authenticate his regime by using the title 'Lord of the White Elephant' (Hsin Hpyu Shin), which he had inscribed on his coins.

Arakan and its capital, Mrauk-U now entered a brief golden era. To reach Mrauk-U then (as today) it was necessary to take a long boat trip through a maze of creeks. The houses stood on wooden posts, their roofs thatched with palm leaves with walls made of bamboo matting, but 'the princes and grandees,' continues Father Manrique, 'have wooden walls to their palaces which are ornamented with carvings and gilt mouldings.'

BREAST-FEEDING

The Lord White Elephant, who was still very young, had been led forth from his house, which was decorated with a royal golden spire, and was receiving his breakfast of milk, drawn by himself from the breasts of Burmese women, who daily presented themselves at the Palace, eager for the honour. They were waiting now in a row, some young and slender and pretty, some, though still young, fatter and less comely, but all with their eyes shining with their ardour and their devotion.

The Sacred White Elephant was an ill-conditioned beast, lean in the flank, in spite of the care lavished on him. He was only white in the technical sense; that is to say, when his scented bath-water was splashed over him, his mouse-coloured skin turned a reddish colour instead of black. He had twenty toenails instead of a mere sixteen, and his bad-tempered little eyes were rimmed with red. A hundred soldiers in scarlet and white guarded his Palace, and a row of dancing-girls, in their little white muslin jackets with wired tails, and their pretty silk tameins, were waiting to dance to him after his meal should be finished. Two attendants led him down the line of young mothers. A speckled trunk would come waving out and seize upon the proffered breast, pulling it up and outwards. The women awaiting their turn trembled with eagerness. One woman fell upon the ground in a fit before he reached her, the milk already spurting from her breasts, and her lips foaming; her ecstasy had proved too strong.

F Tennyson Jesse, The Lacquer Lady, 1929

On the march

(following pages) Rice terraces located in one of the beautiful valleys leading up to the highlands of Loimwe. People of the Akha minority farm these terraces

Singuttara Hill, half a day's journey to the north of Mrauk-U, was the site of Arakan's most fabled possession, the Buddha image was supposedly made in about 500 BCE by a 'heavenly sculptor' during a visit of the Gautama Buddha to Singuttara Hill, and is said to be one of five contemporary images (of the rest, legend has it that two are in India and two in paradise). Father Manrique describes the pomp and ceremony involved in a royal pilgrimage to the hills: the king himself travelled on a raft which was a replica of his Mrauk-U palace, and he and his court 'shimmered and glowed as they surged up the slope'. Arakan's other treasures were also shown to Father Manrique. He was led through chambers 'panelled with scented timbers such as sandalwood and eaglewood'. Father Manrique was also presented to the king's ultimate pride and joy, the Lord White Elephant. 'I can say that when he went out, even on an ordinary occasion, as in springtime to take his bath, he was conducted there under a white canopy embroidered with the insignia of royalty, and to the sound of music. Following him were servants with golden water-heaters, ewers, scrapers, and other golden utensils of the bath.'

On the death of King Thiri-thu-dhamma in 1638, followed shortly by that of the White Elephant, the ruin of the kingdom came slowly but surely. A succession of weak kings, rebellions and assassinations meant that they were no match for a strong army. In 1784, the Burmese king Bodawpaya invaded Arakan, succeeded in recovering all the prizes taken by the Arakanese two centuries before, and in addition carried away the Mahamuni Image. Throughout the centuries this image had symbolized Arakan's strength and autonomy, and with its disappearance their kingdom was also to vanish.

THE IMPACT OF THE WEST

The age of exploration and trade began in Europe in the 15th century. The sea routes to the East brought Italian, Portuguese, Dutch and finally British travellers and traders. In the early days when the ships had rounded the southern tip of India they hugged the coastline along the Bay of Bengal to Malay peninsula, stopping en route at Burmese ports. Pegu is often mentioned in contemporary merchants' journals, pointing to the city's importance as a trading post.

By the mid-16th century, Portuguese merchants, now firmly ensconced in Goa on India's western coast, proceeded to gain a foothold on Burma's Tenasserim coast. They even had a hand in helping the Burman king Tabinshweti of Toungoo overthrow the Mon king of Pegu. With their bases in Goa and Tenasserim and later at Malacca, the Portuguese were now in a position to control the sea routes round the southern tip of India across the Bay of Bengal to the Malacca Strait. An irritation with which they had not reckoned, however, was the bizarre behaviour of one of their countrymen, Felipe de Brito. In 1600 his Burmese patron, King Razagyri of Arakan, sent him to become governor of the port of Syriam. He immediately fortified the town and declared Portuguese sovereignty to the satisfaction of his compatriots in Goa. But on return from a trip to Goa he married the Viceroy's daughter and, equipping himself with copious arms and ammunition, declared himself King of Syriam. Such was his strength that he was able to force passing ships to come into Syriam and pay custom dues, whether it was their destination or not. He is also said to have forcibly converted thousands of natives to Christianity. This situation continued for 13 years before he came to a bloody end: in 1613 Burmese laid siege to Syriam and captured the city after 34 days. 'King' de Brito was captured and impaled—it reportedly took him three days to die.

Strangely, this extraordinary episode did not seem to sour the Burmese appetite for foreign trade. In 1617 the British East India Company sent their first representatives, Henry Forest and John Staveley. The king dispatched four galleons with presents to greet them. They returned to India with a letter from the king inviting English ships to Burmese ports and offering free trade as an incentive.

By the mid-18th century there were French, Dutch, Portuguese and British trading posts along the southern Burmese coast. The Burmese now came into contact with the full onslaught of European diplomacy. The Mons and the Burmese were fighting their final battle for supremacy, as the French and the British were themselves fighting for dominance in the area. The French courted the Mon Kingdom. At the time the British were also negotiating with the Mons, in their case for a base at Cape Negrais (on the southern tip of the Irrawaddy delta). But neither side had foreseen the strength of the remarkable Alaungpaya, a village headman whose career began with his refusal to take the oath of allegiance to the Mons when they arrived in his small town of Shwebo. He proceeded to collect an army, march south and, to the amazement of the French and British, succeeded in ousting the Mons and provisionally set up his capital at Dagon which he christened Yangon, or 'end of strife'. Thus it was that the third and last Burmese Empire came into being.

The next 70 years saw the Burmese Empire expand and move its capital again, this time to Amarapura, 'the City of Immortals', on the banks of the Irrawaddy, near present-day Mandalay. The Europeans, ever keen to secure trade agreements and access to the back door of China, sent a succession of envoys and embassies. The Burmese enjoyed playing the game of diplomacy and (like the Chinese with the kowtow) they discovered the European Achilles heel: 'the shoe question'. Burmese court etiquette required those attending an audience with the king to remove their shoes. Captain Michael Symes, who led the British Embassy in 1792, complied with this request but nonetheless found himself 'squatting in the audience hall, suffering from the aches and pains brought by the unnatural posture. The king and queen made a late, brief and entirely silent appearance aloft a preposterously high throne, and the envoys were allowed to watch the king chew betel and the queen smoke a huge cheroot.' Although Captain Symes was prepared to accept such treatment, his successors were less broadminded, especially as trade agreements were not forthcoming.

The traditional Burmese warboats were immense canoes with low sharp bows and high recurving sterns, double-banked with 20–30 rowers a side. The whole exterior of the hull and sometimes the oars were gilt. A short staff rising from the stern of the warboat bore the sacred and royal emblem, the hti *(umbrella)*

Diplomatic overtures degenerated into gunboat diplomacy. King Bodawpaya, in the process of enlarging his kingdom, had captured Arakan (along with the Mahamuni Image) and had thus given Burma a common border with British India. His successor King Bagyidaw continued this expansionist policy, with frequent raids into Assam and Chittagong until, in 1824, the British were provoked into declaring war. A difficult, disease-ridden campaign followed with British troops advancing up the Irrawaddy as far as Prome. But King Bagyidaw dismissed the massive territorial concessions that were extracted from him in the subsequent treaty of Yandabo with superb nonchalance. (The British were enraged by what they considered his arrogance in the 'most grandiose fashion'.) However, there could be no doubt that their use of the Irrawaddy enabled the British forces of the East India Company to gain a decisive victory. Just 30 years later, in 1853, the two adversaries were once more locked in conflict. The outcome was the same—only this time the whole of Lower Burma was annexed by the British.

King Mindon, Burma's penultimate king, built Mandalay, the last of Burma's royal capitals, and transferred the court there in 1857. Mindon's motives in building Mandalay were both religious and secular. There was an ancient prophecy that a religious centre would be built on this site to mark the 2,400th anniversary of Gautama Buddha's birth, and King Mindon was a deeply religious man. He was also a saddened man. By then the British had occupied half his country (the half which contained the greatest religious monument of all, the Shwedagon Pagoda, which he was never allowed to visit). He was constantly reminded of the British presence by hoots from the Irrawaddy Flotilla Company's vessels as they plied up and down the river. So to fulfill the prophecy, and as a gesture to the British of his continued potency as a monarch, he created the City of Gems.

It was for control of the Irrawaddy that a third Anglo-Burmese War was fought in 1885. Growing French influence in the north of Burma was a source of some anxiety to the British in the south. But they were unaware of a comprehensive treaty, which included crucial shipping rights on the river, that the French were secretly negotiating with King Theebaw. In the finest Gallic tradition it was an affair of the heart which actually sparked off the war. Fanny Moroni, a Eurasian favourite at court in Mandalay and lady-in-waiting to Queen Supayalat, was also the mistress (and of course confidante) of the deputy French Consul, Monsieur Bonvilleu. Her lover compounded his indiscretions by returning to Mandalay from a spell of home leave accompanied by a French wife. In revenge, the enraged mistress divulged the details

King Mindon built Mandalay to fulfill an ancient prophecy and to restore the glory of the Kingdom of Ava

of the French secret plans to the British. The subsequent war consisted of a straightforward push up the Irrawaddy to Mandalay and lasted but a few months, with scant resistance from the Burmese army. This period of Burmese history is fascinatingly described in F Tennyson Jesse's historical novel *The Lacquer Lady* (see page 29).

British control of Burma was now complete. The period from 1890 to 1920 can be termed the 'golden era' of British rule. There was little bitterness on the part of the Burmese towards their British conquerors, partly because the British brought

THE AYEYARWADY—MOULDER OF BURMA'S HISTORY

The Ayeyarwady (formerly named the Irrawaddy) made Myanmar. From its source in the Eastern Himalayas the great river sweeps down from the heart of Asia to the Indian Ocean. Over the centuries deposited silt has formed the promontory of Lower Myanmar. For almost 1,600 kilometres (1,000 miles), from Bhamo to Pathein, the Ayeyarwady is easily navigable year round and thus has formed one of the major arteries of Asia's waterborne trade.

Since the time of Buddha there have been political capitals on the river, but it was not until the 14th century that the most strategic area, halfway up the Ayeyarwady's navigable waters (around present-day Mandalay), was settled. Thence it was possible both to control the river highway and to guard 'the smiling fields of rice' from Chinese and Shan invaders. The early 15th century saw the arrival of European traders, some of whom penetrated far up the Ayeyarwady, lured by Ava (then Burma's capital) 'in which grow rubies and many other precious stones'. However, for the next 300 years the Europeans, seeking trade elsewhere, were content merely to flirt with Burma.

Britain's interests in Burma were rekindled in the 1790s. By then firmly established in India, she needed to secure a steady supply of Burmese teak with which to build her ships, and to open up the market for her Lancashire broadcloth. When no trade agreements were reached by conventional methods, there seemed no alternative to gunboat diplomacy. Following a series of Anglo-Burmese Wars resulting in British control of Burma, the Irrawaddy came alive with activity, with vessels of the Irrawaddy Flotilla Company carrying a reported nine million passengers a year, some in luxury paddle steamers. The company advertised that their freight included 'silk, tamarind, marble Buddhas, elephants sometimes'. Burma's riches were now sucked into British colonial trade. Teak logs were lashed together and floated downriver, rice from the Irrawaddy's fertile plains, crude oil, grains, lace, sugar, tea, tobacco and silk were exchanged for manufactured silks and worsteds, condensed milk, corrugated iron, cutlery and eventually, of course, sewing machines and cars.

It was a continual source of amazement to the pre-War colonialists that the Burmese did not 'have more vigour about them' as regards material gain. An exception was Kipling who understood: 'now, if bountiful providence had put you in a pleasant damp country where rice grew of itself and fish came up to be caught, putrified and pickled, would you work?' Despite this, Burma was, prior to the World War II, the world's largest exporter of rice. And the country's 'rice bowl' is the rich alluvial land of the Ayeyarwady delta. This area is some 240 kilometres (150 miles) wide and 290 kilometres (180 miles) long and, it has been calculated, the deposit of silt is causing it to encroach into the Bay of Bengal at a rate of approximately five kilometres (three miles) per century—an astonishing metre (about one yard) each week.

Advanced guard of a movable flying column attacking a village occupied by the enemy (sketch by a military officer). The third Anglo-Burmese War erupted in 1885 over control of the Irrawaddy River, a vital link in British colonial trade. The British consolidated their grip over Burma in just a few months, meeting only scant resistance from the Burmese forces

order and discipline to the country, and also because they did not overly interfere with Burmese society. Though undoubtedly a considerable measure of empathy developed between the Burmese and the British, sadly they never really understood one another. A Burmese minister is recorded to have said to a pre-colonial British envoy: 'your customs are so completely opposite in so many points. You write on white, we on black paper. You stand up, we sit down; you uncover your head, we our feet in token of respect.'

The British made one serious mistake: in the administrative structure of empire, Burma was put under the umbrella of British India and therefore made answerable to Calcutta rather than London. Given the age-old enmity between the Indians and the Burmese this was astonishingly short-sighted. To add insult to injury, in 1920 India was granted a degree of political autonomy. Burma was denied such status, being thought politically too naive. These measures sowed the seeds of the Thakin movement, which in time developed into a strong nationalist push for independence. In 1937 these efforts were rewarded when Burma was accorded separate status within the British Empire.

WORLD WAR II AND INDEPENDENCE

At the outbreak of World War II, Burmese sympathy was with the British, but they wanted to strike a bargain whereby they could aid Britain in return for dominion status after the war. However, such a promise could not be extracted. In desperation, while the older politicians continued to try diplomacy, Aung San, the leader of the Thakins, and 29 other young men slipped out of the country and went to Japan for intensive military training. Following the bombing of Pearl Harbour on 7th December, 1941, the Japanese advanced across Southeast Asia taking Rangoon with the help of Aung San and his '30 Comrades'.

At first the Burmese welcomed the Japanese invasion: they saw it as liberation from colonial rule. Moreover, the Japanese promised them independence and they were fellow Asians. The Japanese propaganda machine assured them 'the Japanese air force will respect your pagodas, but war is war, and if your Shwedagon Pagoda is damaged by us, we will build it anew with bricks of gold'. The honeymoon period was short, however. Independence was not immediately forthcoming, and individual rights basic to the Burmese were being infringed. In May 1942, a disappointed General Aung San sent an envoy overland to India to negotiate an agreement with the British under which his Burma Independence Army would turn and fight against the Japanese in a combined operation. On the advice of Lord Mountbatten, then Supreme Allied Commander in the Far East (and subsequently Earl Mountbatten of Burma), Aung San's army of 10,000 men waited until March 1945 before fighting alongside the Allies. Meanwhile, the Japanese had become suspicious of Aung San and appointed their own officers to oversee the Burmese army.

In Upper Burma a bloody battle raged. General 'Vinegar Joe' Stilwell had been forced to retreat over the Western Hills to India, losing most of his men en route. It was now decided that in order to recapture Burma from the Japanese it was necessary to build a permanent line of communication from India across to Kunming in south-western China, where there were Allied bases, as well as those of Chiang Kai-shek's Chinese Nationalist forces. So construction of the Ledo Road began. Some called it the man-a-mile road, owing to the immense losses from accidents, disease and Japanese snipers. The plan was for the Ledo Road from India to join up with the Burma Road from Mandalay and Lashio and thence cross the mountains to Kunming. The other method of transporting supplies from India to China was over 'the hump'. Transport planes, often badly maintained and overloaded, would weave their way over and around the Himalayan peaks. Some 650,000 tons moved across the hump, but at a staggering cost—around 1,000 lives and 600 aircraft were lost in the process. The other key to the eventual recovery of Burma from the Japanese was the legendary Chindits (commandos dropped behind Japanese lines) under the equally renowned General Wingate (see page 41). The Japanese finally surrendered in Rangoon in May 1945, the same month that Hitler was defeated in Europe.

The Burmese welcomed the British as liberators, not as conquerors, but they wanted independence, and wanted it as quickly as possible. The British colonial machine returned to Burma for three years. In London in January 1947, General Aung San and the British Prime Minister Clement Attlee signed an agreement whereby Burma was given immediate dominion status and, beginning in 1948, total independence. At the same time her application for membership of the newly formed United Nations was approved. Finally she was given the option of remaining within the British Commonwealth. On his return it was, however, decided by Aung San and the Constituent Assembly that Burma should not remain in the Commonwealth. The historians' view on this point seems to be that Burma still held two bitter memories: first, her loss of sovereignty in 1886; and second, her unintentional involvement in the Anglo-French rivalry of the 19th century. It was feared that to remain within the Commonwealth would sooner or later involve Burma in some rivalry or conflict that was not her concern. So at dawn on 4th January, 1948, Burma regained her independence and left the British Commonwealth. Aung San did not live to see his dream fulfilled. On 19th July, 1947, he was assassinated in Rangoon, aged only 32, as he and his team were drafting the new Constitution. Another member of the Thakin party, U Nu, stepped into his shoes and thereby became the first Prime Minister of the Union of Burma.

THE CHINDITS

The successful conclusion of the remarkable Burma campaign in World War II must be largely attributed to the Chindits. By the summer of 1942 the Japanese, after taking Singapore, had advanced up through Malaya and Burma, compelling the Allied forces to retreat in to India. As so often in wartime the hour produced the man. 'After the disasters in Malaya and Burma,' explained John Masters, 'an unusually talented artillery officer, Orde Wingate, had thought out a way to show the Japanese, and our own troops, that we could use the jungle.' A long-range penetration group known as the Chindits was formed under the controversial Wingate. The name was derived from 'Chinthe', the mythical lion which guards a pagoda entrance (a particularly fine pair sits at the foot of the Mandalay Hill). Chinthe is said to be the only 'living thing' in Burmese Buddhism which is allowed to use force.

The idea was for columns of highly trained men to pass through the Allied and Japanese lines to attack and destroy the enemy supply lines. This sort of expedition was dependent on an excellent communications network, connecting the Chindits with their supply bases in India and also with the Allied fighters and bombers. In 1943, General Wingate accompanied the British Prime Minister, Winston Churchill, to the Inter-Allied Conference in Quebec. Here Wingate spoke so eloquently on this revolutionary method of warfare that the much-needed equipment 'descended on us in torrents including the vital air back-up.' This was made up of the No 1 Air Commando, US Army Air Corps, who boasted a number of C-47 aircraft specially adapted to snatch gliders off the ground into the air, as well as troop-carrying gliders and bombers. The ability to retrieve gliders was vital for the repatriation of the wounded.

The build-up of the Chindits to a strength of 24 battalions continued through 1943, with rigorous training at bases in India. All soldiers took a daily dose of mapacrine, which turned their faces an unhealthy yellow, to ward off the dreaded malaria.

In January 1944, with the Japanese still facing the British forces along the general line of the Indian frontier, the Chindit operation began. Some walked, others were airlifted, and in all 10,000 men and 16,000 mules—their vocal chords cut—entered Burma and infiltrated the Japanese lines. It was a bitter campaign which was to last for 20 months, and leave thousands dead on both sides. In July 1945, the 14th Army alone killed some 11,000 Japanese. Scores of Allied soldiers fell into Japanese hands, whereas to the Japanese surrender was unthinkable: just six were taken prisoner in Burma. With the Chindits chiselling away at the Japanese strength from within, the conventional forces were able to make a successful three-pronged advance from India and China, achieving ultimate victory in August 1945.

Note: John Masters was a well-known novelist
(see literary excerpt next pages). During World War II
he was an officer in the Indian Army and fought in Burma.

The other method of transporting supplies from India to China was over 'the hump'

NIGHT FLIGHT

*I*t was dark now. The aircraft, C-47s from the R.A.F. and the U.S.A.F., stood in the centre of Tulihal airfield, in several ranks, back to back. Planes had already begun to take off, two at a time. There were no gliders. I marched my plane load to the check point, and gave my plane number to the guide waiting there, shouting to make myself heard above the roar of engines. The guide led off between the tails of the aircraft. The engines blew up dust in great whirls so that I bowed my head and jammed my hand on top of my head to keep my hat on. Half an hour earlier all mules for this night's flight were reported loaded, so as I climbed the ramp I was expecting to see what I did see, the stern ends of three large mules jammed tight across the forward half of the cabin, their noses close against the forward bulkhead and the door leading to the cockpit. Two mule leaders and our Transport Havildar stood in the narrow space forward of the mules, soothing them as they fidgeted and nervously tossed their heads. A strong bamboo pole, anchored to ring-bolts in the body of the aircraft, stretched across the cabin forward of the mules, and their heads were tied fast to this pole. Thinner poles ran down between them, anchored to an extra-thick breech pole which ran tight under their quarters, pushing them forward and giving them no room to manœuvre or kick. Their saddles and loads lay stacked on the metal floor which now, before take-off on a C-47, was sharply tilted down from front to rear. The mules only kept their footing because of the straw spread under them.

I counted my men and shut the main door of the aircraft. So far everything, including how to close the door of a C-47, had been practised and rehearsed. Now began the unrehearsed, and unrehearsable.

The flight-lieutenant in command of the aircraft stood in the forward doorway, and stared interrogatively at me between the twitching ears of the centre mule. I raised my thumb, he raised his. That door shut with a clang. The lights went out. The engines started up.

The engines changed pitch and the plane throbbed wildly. Airfield lights and the lighted cabins of other aircraft and the blue flare from engine exhausts passed slowly by, shining fitfully through our windows on to a dark, damp face, a rifle barrel, a rolling eye. The mules threw up their heads and tried to kick, long ears back and huge teeth gleaming. The pilot opened his throttles. The plane surged forward and I felt myself being pushed down and back. The mules bucked and fought and I heard one of the bamboo poles break. The havildar readied his carbine. Faster, faster, the tail began to rise and the floor to level off. Five of us jumped up and pushed forward against the mules' sterns. The airfield lights sank and disappeared, and a steady moonlight illuminated the cabin. I was staring down the muzzle of Havildar Shivjang's loaded carbine.

Slowly the mules calmed as we steadied on course and the bellow of the engines cut back to the throb of cruising speed. The pilot poked his head round the door and Shivjang turned, the carbine up. The pilot withdrew his head and the door slammed. It was the breech pole that had cracked and I kept three men there, in turns throughout the flight, pushing forward against the mules. Those orders given, I unfolded the small-scale map tucked into the outer flap of my haversack and looked out of the window. There was the Chindwin. We ought to cross it directly over Thaungdut. If so, out of the right-hand windows, I should see the horseshoe curve near Sittaung, and a smaller river coming in on the left bank.

It was so. I checked the pilot's course all the way. This plane-load, at least, was going to know exactly where it was, in case of a forced landing. It is much worse for Brigade Majors than for ordinary mortals to shoot up their own troops, or ask the Japanese for a cup of tea, both of which had happened among the gliders that never reached Broadway.

After an hour the plane's nose dipped and the mules slid forward. Now they were pressing against the forward bulkhead, and the three unhappy muleteers. But any further displacement would only send them into the pilot's compartment, to look over his shoulder, and perhaps offer him advice in his task. They would not slide back on us, so I withdrew the rearguard and prepared for the landing. We crossed the Irrawaddy five miles north of Tigyaing. The moon shone bright on the silver river, over a mile wide there between dark featureless jungle.

The pilot switched on his landing lights and a moment later I saw Chowringhee. It was very different now from that silent clearing which I had flown over in a bright midday two weeks earlier. Down there, under the port wing, lights glittered in a long rectangle, more brilliant in the surrounding blackness than the great Calcutta street after which it had been named. Two cones of brighter light advanced slowly at the far end, turning. Other cones shone outward into the jungle, or diagonally athwart the strip—C-47s, taxiing to the dispersal points, standing, unloading. A plane passed directly below us, its swept-back wings black against the lights, and pale points of fire shimmering from the exhausts. Another plane circled above us, in silhouette against the sky, and another above that. I saw a bright cone of light rushing towards the strip ... she was down ... now us.

John Masters, The Road Past Mandalay, 1961

SILENT SUFFERING

It was in the party that Thakin Aung San's sterling qualities began to show most prominently. There were many things about him as a student leader which were impressive: he wrote pure and pithy prose, in Burmese or in English; he was precise, and hardworking; he was a thinker. But it was politics which put him to the hard test and brought out his many qualities. As University students we had a dandy time; we wore silk, went to the cinema, swaggered, ate the best food when we pleased; money arrived regularly from home and we had nothing to worry about. At the Dobama Asi-ayone, life was different. People saw us superficially as young Thakin politicians, but the inside story was really hard. We were poor, and we worked hard, subsisting some days on just one bare meal, often on a few cups of tea. Party organization did not interest me, and I was happy to leave that to Thakin Aung San and Thakin Than Tun, while I offered to take on fund-raising, and the speaking tours. Our associates came to me frequently, because I was fund raiser, for money to buy meals with; they came hungry and in pain. But Aung San never came to ask for money for food. When he was hungry, he would concentrate on a book, sit tight in a corner, and bear it bravely without a word of complaint. He cultivated indifference and built his strength.

Thakin Aung San's room at the party headquarters was notorious for untidyness. He slept in a crude bed which was always unmade. The bugs kept people away from his bed and his room; only Aung San with his indifference could live and sleep in his room. Once we had a few visitors from the district, Thakin members, men and women, and the boys at the headquarters gave them Thakin Aung San's room — he was general secretary then — because they did not want the visitors to sleep in the corridor. The visitors were pleased to have the secretary's room, but only before the bugs started to make their presence felt. Around midnight, unable to take the torture any longer, our visitors fled from the room, carrying their sheets and blankets, and sought refuge in the corridor.

'Aung San's Sterling Qualities' by U Nu (first Prime Minister of Burma),
Aung San of Burma, *compiled and edited by Maung Maung, 1962*

BURMA SINCE INDEPENDENCE

Economically and politically Burma now found herself in an unhappy situation. The war had brought her agriculture and industry to a standstill, while the post-war colonial period had not lasted long enough to capture the benefits of the stability it had previously conferred. Furthermore the main minority groups were fighting the new Government for autonomy. In 1948 the defeated Chiang Kai-shek withdrew from the Chinese mainland for Taiwan. Elements of his Kuomintang army remained on Burma's border with Yunnan province and were a constant source of trouble. General Ne Win, one of the early members of the Thakin movement was by now commander of Burma's armed forces and its Minister of Defence. By the mid-1950s he had managed to contain the worst of the rebel fighting. In 1958, ten years after independence, the ruling AFPFL party split, and U Nu's majority in parliament was threatened. Coming on top of economic problems, this induced U Nu to hand over the reigns to Ne Win.

Triumphant Burmese leaders in London outside No 10 Downing Street, after their historic meeting with British Prime Minister Clement Atlee on 25th January, 1947. This meeting saw the signing of an agreement granting Burma independence in 1948, and membership of the newly formed United Nations. Pictured (left to right) are Thakin Mya (Minister of Home Affairs), General Aung San, U Tin Tut (Minister of Finance), and Thakin Ba Sein (Minister of Transport)

MIRACLE ESCAPE

Following the missing of 200 bren guns from the Central Ordinance Depot(COD), there were rumours of the plot against the cabinet ministers. There had been bomb explosions at AFPFL HQ and U Saw (leader of an opposition political party and former Prime Minister) was shot in the face. Luckily, nobody was hurt.

One day before the assassination, Bo Tun Hla (Bogyoke Aung San's personal assistant) got reliable information about the plot and he reported it to Col Tin Tun, one of the commanding officers, and requested him for some security guards. The colonel after conferring with three other COs selected 4 soldiers who were well trained, experienced and loyal. They were sent to Bo Tun Hla for the close security of Bogyoke Aung San. Bogyoke was very angry when he heard about this and he did not allow them except for one sergeant (Hla Mg) but without his sten gun. Bogyoke said 'I am clean and just. Nobody will plot against me'.

The then Home Minister U Kyaw Nyein was abroad (in Europe) and Pyawbwe U Mya (*father of Myo Lwin*) was in charge of the Home Ministry. Bogyoke's assistant Bo Tun Hla came to see Pyawbwe U Mya and asked him if he had taken security measures with regard to the information. The minister replied he had taken security measures but did not mention what they were. Pyawbwe U Mya had assigned some armed police to the gate of the Secretariat (Ministers' Office). But Bogyoke Aung San told the Minister to remove them saying that '*if they hate me they will kill me. If they hate you they will kill you*.' He didn't expect the majority of the cabinet to be killed.

On that fateful morning, Aung San's personal assistant Bo Tun Hla sent Sergeant Hla Mg to buy *kaukswe noodles* for a snack. Sergeant Hla Mg left the office but without closing the inner door of the cabinet meeting room securely.

The people of Myanmar never forget 19th July 1947 the day Bogyoke Aung San and his cabinet ministers were assassinated. However, very few people know about the three cabinet ministers and a secretary who miraculously escaped the assassination. They were Ministers Pyawbwe U Mya, U Ba Gyan and U Aung Zan Wei along with secretary U Shwe Baw.

The seating arrangement in the Cabinet Meeting Room was U-shaped with Aung San sitting in the centre and the ministers all around. The four assassins in uniform carrying tommy guns burst through the door. The gunmen aimed at Aung

(above) Pyawbwe U Mya with Begum Aga Khan and first President Sao Shwe Thaike

San in the centre and sprayed the bullets to the right. Suddenly the room was filled with smoke creating a smoke-screen. The three ministers sitting on the left hand side crouched under the table.

The whole room was shrouded in smoke. My father Pyawbwe U Mya was sitting next to Secretary Shwe Baw who took him by the arm and they crawled to the window under the cover of smoke. They climbed out of the window and along the parapet to the next door clerk's office. Both of them were very shaken and tried to calm down until the shooting stopped. Then my father telephoned the then Governor Sir Hubert Rance to report the assassination. The governor asked them to go across to Government House to discuss the immediate formation of an interim government and other necessary actions that needed to be taken. They looked so shaken the Governor offered them cognac. Unfortunately due to Aung San's command there had been no armed guards at the entrance to the Secretariat.

On that very same morning about 7 am, Col. Tin Tun ordered the Sixth Company of his troops to search for the missing arms in house of the opposition leader U Saw that evening. Hearing of the assassination, the troops didn't wait for the night. They went straight to U Saw's house. The gate was closed and they jumped over the gate and shot a guard in his leg before they entered the house. U Saw's followers tried to draw their guns but U Saw stopped them and they all surrendered. (*U Saw was later tried and executed for his part in the plot.*)

It is highly deplorable and deeply regrettable that the tragedy might have been averted **IF**

1. Bogyoke himself was not so over confident
2. Others including the ministers had more experience in taking security measures
3. What if Bo Tun Hla had not sent Sergeant Hla Mg to buy *kaukswe* and if he had closed the door securely

Every year people from all walks of life mourn and pay tribute to the fallen leaders who died working for independence.

U Myo Lwin (the son of Minister Pyawbwe U Mya)
Deputy Director General (Retired), Ministry of Hotels and Tourism

(top) Pyawbwe U Mya; (below) Independence Day—lowering the Union Jack

Two years later free elections were held as a result of which U Nu once again became Prime Minister. But U Nu was more interested in religion than economics: in 1956 he convened the Sixth Buddhist Synod. Notwithstanding his manifest merits and his having been an original member of the Thakin movement, U Nu was not the strongman needed to put the country back on the road to recovery, nor indeed to deal with Burma's ethnic minorities, who were once again stirring. The 1948 Constitution stated that after ten years of the Union of Burma, the principal minority groups could elect to become autonomous. In 1962, Ne Win took control again, this time permanently by means of an almost bloodless coup; followed by the incarceration of all leading politicans for up to six years. Later that year a manifesto proclaiming 'The Burmese Way to Socialism' was published by the Revolutionary Council. Foreign businesses were closed, the State took control of all banks, horse racing and all other forms of gambling were stopped, many Chinese and Indian business people left, tourist visas were limited to 24 hours and minority demands for autonomy were answered with military repression.

Burma's almost total seclusion continued for more than a decade. In 1974, the veil was lifted gingerly. Some foreign investment was allowed, mainly in the natural resources field, and tourist visas were extended to seven days. In 1975 when an earthquake rocked Pagan, the government accepted funds from the United Nations for the repairs (though all the restoration work was carried out by Burmese experts). In 1979 Ne Win withdrew Burma from the Non-Aligned Movement, citing the increased influence of the Soviet Union through her proxy, Cuba. This was a surprise to the outside world but, in retrospect, seems consistent with Burma's historical determination to avoid getting caught up in the conflicts of others.

Burma's tentative emergence to the outside world during the 1980s was accompanied by a quickening economic pace. In comparison with the stagnant 1950s and 1960s, however, almost any economic development would seem like a boom. Japan, the occupying power of a generation previously, now appeared in a more constructive role, leading the way, as in so many other Southeast Asian economies, as a source of finance and as a trading partner.

The predominance of rice was now less pronounced—Burma ceased to be the world's premier rice exporter in 1962, and teak and other hardwoods overtook rice as her largest export in 1985. Nevertheless Burma remained, as she had always been, an essentially agricultural nation, with an estimated 70 per cent of the working population engaged in agriculture, with a further 10 per cent in light industrial or resource-based activities such as lumber, mining and crude oil production.

THE NE WIN INHERITANCE

By the late 1980s it had become clear that Ne Win's policies of isolationism and socialist economics had not worked. Burma, whose wealth of natural resources should have placed it at the forefront of the region's economies, had declined to the point that it requested and, in 1987, was granted by the United Nations Least Developed Country (LDC) status to help with loan repayments. The hardships of daily life resulted in widespread demoralization.

Sporadic outbreaks of anti-government demonstrations occurred during 1987. Then in the autumn of that year one day, without warning, the citizens of Burma heard at 11am that their government had ordered the demonetization of all currency notes above the value of about US$2, these were replaced with new denominations. Those who had savings in the bank were able to change their old currency for new, with no loss. But people who held amounts of cash elsewhere were given a month's grace to hand in the old notes, in exchange for 40 per cent of the notes' face value.

In spring 1988 a brawl in a Rangoon teashop mushroomed into a confrontation. Coincidentally, in March that year Aung San Suu Kyi, the daughter of Burma's revered hero Aung San, returned from Oxford, England (where she was married to a university lecturer) to Rangoon to look after her ailing mother, who had recently suffered a debilitating stroke. Meanwhile, the rumbles of student protests were moving across the country. On 23rd July came the astonishing announcement from Ne Win that he was stepping down and that a referendum would be held to choose the political system: one-party or multi-party. There ensued a kind of Rangoon spring, with the army standing back and allowing countrywide demonstrations calling for political change for nearly six weeks, but when servicemen in uniform began to join the demonstrators, General Saw Maung, the titular head of the army, cracked down. Thousands of students involved in the demonstrations fled to the Thai border, where refugee camps were set up. The country's universities were closed and remained so for much of the next ten years.

The new 21-man cabinet, claimed to be an intermediary government, one which would stay in place until law and order was restored.

The government allowed the formation of scores of political parties, but one stood out among the rest: the National League for Democracy (NLD). One of its founding members, and future leader, was Aung San Suu Kyi (pronounced 'sue chee'). She had always said that if her country needed her she would be there, perhaps little realizing what rigours that would entail. She chose to give the first major speech of her campaign at the Shwedagon Pagoda one hot August day. A graceful, slight woman with an animated face that breaks easily into a huge smile, she immediately captivated her audience, which swelled to hundreds of thousands. Several former politicians joined the NLD and, with Aung San Suu Kyi at the helm, the party went from strength to strength. After some months of uncertainty the government announced that elections would be held in May 1990. At the end of December 1988, Aung San Suu Kyi's mother, Khin Kyi, who herself had been a successful ambassador for Burma in India, died. As the widow of Aung San and the mother of Suu Kyi, her funeral was attended by thousands. She was buried in Shwedagon Pagoda Road, alongside another of Burma's heroes, U Thant, former Secretary-General of the UN, and Queen Supayalat, the last queen.

In March that year when electioneering Aung San Suu Kyi travelled south to the delta region where an incident heralded things to come. At dawn Aung San Suu Kyi and some of her supporters were returning from a campaign foray. In one of the three cars her party flag was displayed which was objected to by the authorities. A discussion ensued and the tension was dispelled. The government's concept of electioneering was unusual. All party literature had to be submitted for censorship. The government-controlled newspaper carried editorials on the perils of multi-party systems. Open-air political gatherings of more than four people were forbidden. Aung San Suu Kyi simply ignored this last injunction, and whole towns were brought to a halt when she came to speak. In return, the government made every effort to intimidate NLD candidates, forcing many to withdraw—but they were replaced by others. The omens were not good for fair elections on the day. As the founder of independent Burma, Aung San is remembered each year on Martyrs' Day, 19th July. During Aung San Suu Kyi's speech that day in 1989, she not only remembered her father's great achievements but also levelled criticism at Ne Win. Was the government going to allow free elections? Would they allow the transfer of power? Ne Win was furious and the following day Suu Kyi was placed under house arrest, where she was to remain for six years.

As the election approached, rumours persisted that perhaps it was going to be 'free and fair' and that the NLD might win. Could this be true, especially as Aung San Suu Kyi and U Tin U, the party leaders were both under house arrest? But in the event that is exactly what happened; the elections were free and the NLD won a landslide victory, winning 392 out of the 485 seats. However, the government refused to honour the result of the election; instead they announced that they were the only government which could stop the country disintegrating into chaos again. Neither Aung San Suu Kyi nor U Tin U were released from house arrest and instead some 80 senior NLD members were arrested.

NEW IDENTITY
In the aftermath of the election, on 27th May, 1989, the government changed the country's name from Burma to Myanmar, and one month later on 18th June, many towns had their names changed—again the dates on which the changes were made are divisible by nine.

As regards the election result, the cabinet announced that no new government could take over until a new constitution was in place. The original 1949 constitution, promulgated at the time of Independence, had been replaced in 1975 by Ne Win. It took three more years before the government convened a national convention to draft a new constitution. Meanwhile in 1991, Aung San Suu Kyi, still under house arrest, was awarded both the Sakharov Prize and the Nobel Peace Prize.

Just after the election the government announced an 'open door' policy to woo foreign investment. A five-year economic strategy was put in place. New roads were built, parks beautified, Rangoon pavements which had become a steeple-chase to walk along, were re-laid. Deals were done with Thailand to sell vast portions of Burma's teak forests, the same with the prawn fishing rights—all this sustained effort was to persuade the people of Burma and her ASEAN neighbours that the country was on the road to recovery.

Trade boomed across the 'open' Burmese/Chinese border. The government was successful in negotiating deals with the warring minorities, with whom they signed cease-fires. So by 1994, things seemed to be on the move economically and perhaps even politically: 700 delegates were sitting discussing the new constitution. A certain amount of Asian investment was visible, and new hotels were springing up. A natural gas pipeline into Thailand was being laid—a potentially large foreign currency earner. Aung San Suu Kyi, though still under house arrest, had several much-publicized meetings with Secretary One, Khin Nyunt, and some 1,500 political prisoners were released. It seemed a reasonable possibility that she herself might soon be released. But this was not to be until 10th July of the following year, after she had endured almost six years under house arrest.

ASEAN countries continued in their policy of 'constructive engagement'. The SPDC took a swipe at Aung San Suu Kyi by making it known that the new constitution would bar from political office any national who is married to a foreigner and anyone who has lived out of the country for 20 consecutive years. She had married Oxford don Michael Aris in 1972 and had lived abroad since the 1960s, until returning to look after her mother in 1988.

The economic crisis in Asia had meant that many investments in Myanmar had been withdrawn. The trade sanctions imposed on the country by the United States and the European Union at the end of 1996 were beginning to hurt. Tourist numbers fell with the hoped-for increase in tourist numbers not materializing.

Due to a shortage of foreign currency, the SPDC banned 'unessential imports', leaving some of the smart new hotels with no Coca-Cola to sell. Myanmar's full membership of ASEAN took effect in 1997. Meanwhile, Aung San Suu Kyi had become a virtual prisoner in her house again; even if she wanted to go to the market she had to ask permission. (Immediately after her release she would speak at Sunday meetings outside her house—those appearances were forbidden in November 1996.) On several occasions permission to travel up-country has been refused. Visitors to her compound were restricted and by 2000 she was back under house arrest. The SPDC, desperate to try and polish their global image, employed an American PR firm, Bains and Co. A group of visiting Singaporean MPs suggested to the SPDC than an Economic Advisory Board be set up. This would help potential foreign investors through the minefield of bureaucracy and uncertainty that they faced.

NEW CONSTITUTION

May 2002 saw Aung San Suu Kyi released from house arrest and so began a year of feverish political campaigning on the part of Suu Kyi, NLD and the other opposition parties. Rallies—always with government permission—drew large crowds throughout the country and many of the NLD offices were reopened.

In May 2004 the National Convention re-convened but was boycotted by the NLD with Daw Suu and other NLD leading members back under house arrest. So the saga continued with each spring the Convention meeting then taking a break during the monsoon period until 2007 when the 14 years' work was finally finished and a 54-member commission was appointed to draft the constitution. In late 2004, General Khin Nyunt had been removed from office and put under house arrest, the Military Intelligence organisation he headed was abolished and all of its officers were purged.

With international sanctions biting the lack of funds was a constant aggravation for the regime so to alleviate this problem they forged several lucrative deals with neighbours China, Thailand and India. Teak forests were sold, natural gas was to be piped to Thailand and China, a deep sea port would be built on the Bay of Bengal by the Chinese with a highway connecting the new port to Kunming in Western China—these are but a few of the on-going projects agreed to swell the government coffers.

A surprise was sprung in 2005 when the supposedly cash-strapped government suddenly announced that Nay Pyi Taw (*see* pages x-xv), built in secret in central Myanmar, was to replace Yangon as the country's capital.

SAFFRON REVOLUTION

As nearly always in modern Myanmar unrest is caused by the difficulties suffered by people in their everyday lives—the spring of 2007 heralded another breaking point. By February the prices of basic commodities and fuel had risen by 40% and in August that year the President suddenly without notice removed the subsidy on fuel causing an immediate rise of some 60%. Political activists who staged a peaceful walk in Yangon to protest against the sharp rise in the cost of living were arrested.

Tensions escalated sharply after an incident in Pakokku, in central Myanmar, during which some monks were brutally assaulted by the security forces. This triggered the protest movement led by monks, who began marching in Yangon and other cities, often while chanting the Metta (Goodwill) Sutta and holding their alms bowls upside down to symbolise a refusal to accept offerings from the military. The processions of monks grew gradually in size until in Yangon there were tens of thousands marching to the city centre, drawing the admiration and applause of equally large crowds. The marches were eventually dispersed though filmed by the Oslo based independent news agency DVB.

Cyclone Nargis

The government announced that a referendum on the new constitution would be held on 10th May 2008 followed by multi-party elections in October 2010. A few days before the referendum was to be held disaster struck in the form of Cyclone Nargis—the destructive winds sped across the Bay of Bengal hitting land at the Delta region. The number killed by this vicious cyclone is thought to be around 138,000 with another 2.4 million left homeless and destitute. American anthropologist Ingrid Jordt along with many people in Myanmar reckoned this was "a sign that the regime was illegitimate and that the country was being punished as a whole for the rulers' bad action against the monks". Throwing decency and sense to the wind the government refused to postpone the referendum, so it went ahead with according to government records 92% voting in favour of the draft constitution—even though the Ayeyarwady delta region was devastated. NGOs already working in the country along with world's aid agencies desperately tried to help the stricken population. To begin with foreign aid agencies were denied entry but luckily wisdom soon prevailed and overseas help was welcomed.

In 2009 Aung San Suu Kyi's term of house arrest was drawing to a close—the length of time had already violated the UN's stipulation that 5 years was the maximum a person could legally be kept under confinement, she should have been freed in 2008.

Throughout 2010 preparations continued for the multi-party elections, in which about 20 pro-government and opposition parties participated. The NLD did not participate because it believed that to do so it would have to expel Aung San Suu Kyi. It therefore chose not to re-register as a party ahead of the elections.

The election took place on 7th November with the government party USDP winning the majority of the seats Of the 664 new members of parliament 75% were elected with the remaining 25% appointed from among members of the military. On 13th November Aung San Suu Kyi was released from house arrest.

GOVERNMENT OF PRESIDENT U THEIN SEIN

The new government was established the following March. The prime minister of the former military government U Thein Sein became the new civilian President in March 2011. U Thein Sein has now been President for three years and during that time he has achieved some remarkable goals. Ban Ki-moon, Secretary-General of the United Nations praises U Thein Sein for his "vision, leadership and courage to put Myanmar on the path to change".

President U Thein Sein was born on 20th April 1945 in Kyonku village, Ngapudaw Township, Pathein District in the Ayeyarwady Division of Myanmar. The third child of a family of humble farmers; by all accounts his father was a wise man who for the second part of his life was a revered Buddhist monk. Thus the young U Thein Sein learnt the values of honesty and trustworthiness, for which he is well-known, in his early days.

His career began in the military with U Thein Sein graduating from the Defence Services Academy in 1968; already he had the reputation of a thoughtful leader. So followed four decades in the army where the majority of his jobs were administrative posts rather than combat positions. He climbed up the military ranks and in 2007 as a General became the country's Prime Minister.

However under a new constitution a general election was to be held in the autumn of 2010 to put in place a civilian government. So on 29th April that year U Thein Sein resigned his military commission to become the civilian leader of a political party, the Union Solidarity and Development Party (USDP), and to prepare for the up-coming parliamentary elections. His constituency was to be the Zabuthiri Township of the capital Nay Pyi Taw. U Thein Sein won the seat at the

November election, polling some 91% of the vote. The following March the new government was convened at which point U Thein Sein was voted President and sworn into office on 30th March 2011.

With reformist President U Thein Sein in place things began to change in Myanmar. It appears that during the first five months from his inauguration in March, to August that year, the President was contemplating both the domestic and international situation; in August his bold moves began. First he met with Daw Aung San Suu Kyi the opposition leader who had been released from her long stint of house arrest. Secondly he halted work on a huge dam being constructed by the Chinese in the north-

President U Thein Sein with Daw Aung San Suu Kyi

east of the country. He had listened to the local people who were upset that some 90% of the energy generated by the dam would be exported to China and also that the ecology of the Ayeyarwady might be endangered. Both these moves pleased his domestic audience but also alerted international leaders and the media that here was a President who was set to implement changes.

So followed a catalogue of important moves, labour laws were reformed, political prisoners released, press censorship first eased and later abolished, the local currency the kyat was floated thus freeing the domestic economy, just to mention a few things. All this meant that the end of 2011 and 2012 saw a stream of world leaders visiting U Thein Sein including President Barak Obama. The world leaders also visited Daw Aung San Suu Kyi, as one minister put it "U Thein Sein is a reformist icon, Aung San Suu Kyi is a democracy icon".

President U Thein Sein's economic and political reforms meant that the trade sanctions that had been imposed on the country by the US and EU administrations some 16 years previously were now dropped; thus opening the door to international investment. As President U Thein Sein has said "only when we have real economic progress will the democratic process flourish, but we need three things. Capital, technological capacity and human resources development. We also need the support of our people, the international media and the international community".

A remarkable three years of socio-economic and political reforms led by a man not afraid of bold goals and the difficulties of progress.

A massive 19th-century wall hanging (kalaga) of brown/green wool cloth (approx. 3.66 x 2.67 metres or 12 feet x 8 feet 9 inches), with appliqué of woollen and cotton fabrics. It is ornamented with silver sequins and details are painted in Indian ink and watercolours. It was bought for a mere £12 at the Colonial and Indian Exhibition of 1886. The subject matter is unknown but probably illustrates one of the jataka stories or is taken from Burmese legend

THE NAME CHANGE

On 27th May, 1989 the authorities changed the name of Burma to Myanmar (the 'r' at the end is to help English speakers end the word with a rising tone). This was followed on 18th June by a name change of many towns, street names and so on. Below is a list of the name changes the visitor is most likely to encounter, with the old name in the left-hand column.

Akyab	Sittwe	Mandalay	no change	Rangoon	Yangon
Amherst	Kyaikkhami	Martaban	Mottama	Salween	Thanlwin
Arakan	Rakhine	Maymyo	Pyin U Lwin	Sandoway	Thandwe
Ava	Inwa	Mergui	Myeik	Sittang	Sittoung
Bassein	Pathein	Moulmein	Mawlamyine	Syriam	Thanlyin
Burma	Myanmar	Myohaung	Mrauk-U	Taunggyi	no change
Chindwin	no change	Pagan	Bagan	Tavoy	Dawei
Irrawaddy	Ayeyarwady	Pegu	Bago		
Karen	Kayin	Prome	Pyay		

GEOGRAPHY

Geographically, the Myanmar are blessed in all respects. This country of roughly 673,500 square kilometres (260,000 square miles) is enclosed by a horseshoe formation of mountain ranges which give dual protection from invaders and weather. Along her border with India and Bangladesh, the Western Hills—an offshoot of the eastern Himalayas—form a massive wall as they swing southward in an arc through the Naga and Chin Yomas (or hills) to the Rakhine (formerly Arakan) Yoma, which end just short of the Ayeyarwady delta. Myanmar's northern border with China is flanked by a semicircular continuation of the Tibetan range, where even the passes are well over 3,000 metres (10,000 feet) above sea level and which boasts South-east Asia's highest peak, Hkakabo Razi (5,920 metres or 19,296 feet). Her eastern border with China, Laos and Thailand is guarded by the Kachin Yoma which meld into the limestone tableland of the Shan Plateau (a continuation of China's Yunnan Plateau) with an average elevation of 1,000 metres (3,300 feet); at their southern end the Kachin Yoma break into parallel ranges known collectively as the Taninthayi (formerly Tenassarim) Yoma. Down the heart of Myanmar, running along the Ayeyarwady, are the Bago (formerly Pegu) Yoma, and it is on their southernmost spur that the great Shwedagon Pagoda stands. Within this horseshoe frame of mountains, the centre is cut by four river valleys: those of the Ayeyarwady, the Chindwin, the Thanlwin (formerly Salween) and the Sittoung (formerly Sittang). The Bay of Bengal marks the southern limit of the country.

In the delta region, mostly rice is grown. In the rest of the country crops abound: cotton, sesame, tea, jute, sugarcane, maize and tobacco. (Burma, observed Kipling, 'is a delightfully lazy land full of pretty girls and very bad

Some timber is still felled with the aid of elephants, which then drag the trunks down to the banks of the Ayeyarwady River. Here they are lashed together to form a raft on which perches a hut to house the captain, who pilots the craft downstream

cheroots.') This land of plenty also boasts a wealth of mineral and other natural resources: jade, emeralds, sapphires, rubies as well as a variety of semiprecious stones, tungsten, silver, copper, tin, oil and Myanmar's second-largest export by volume after teak, beans and pulses. Its biggest export earner is natural gas, most of which is piped to Thailand. Most of the teak comes from the forests in the north, where the majority of trees are still felled with the help of elephants, which drag them down to the banks of the Ayeyarwady. Here they are lashed together into large log rafts on each of which perches a hut to house the captain, who pilots the craft downstream. Some will make the full journey to the sawmills of Yangon. For others the destination will be Mandalay, where the logs are unlashed and then, trunk by trunk, hauled out of the river by water buffalo. When tracts of the forests were in the hands of the Thai lumber companies during the 1990s, modern machinery was used—which itself scarred much of the terrain. Happily the Nay Pyi Taw government at present seems to be employing a more ecological approach to one of its most precious assets.

The highlands encircle and protect the country. So thick is the jungle, and so poor the soil in most of these areas, that their people (predominately Myanmar's ethnic minorities) are forced to lead a nomadic existence. These hill tribes still practice the *taunggya* (slash-and-burn) method of cultivation. The method of clearing a hilly site provides a pertinent illustration of Burmese economy of labour

(right) Fishermen prepare to put out to sea; at the next morning's market their catch will be on sale

coupled with ingenuity. Starting at the bottom of the slope a line of trees is notched lightly on the upper side; proceeding uphill the incision becomes deeper until at the top a line is cut right through; these then fall on their neighbours below, sending the rest down like a pack of cards.

Fishing is one of Myanmar's contradictions. Buddhist philosophy forbids the taking of life, yet fish is the country's favourite food. So a compromise has been found: it is acceptable to buy fish (and indeed meat and poultry—butchers in Myanmar are predominately Muslim or Chinese) as long as one does not actually order the animal in question to be slaughtered. So where does that leave the fisherman? He is regarded by some as the lowest category of man who will undoubtedly be banished to the 'Bong of Animals' in the next life. To others the fisherman 'is nobly drawing demerit on further reincarnations by providing the nation's favourite food'. And to his own conscience? Why say some as a joke, he is saving the fish from drowning. He plucks the fish from the water, laying them on the bank to recover, and if they die that is not his fault. The result of this somewhat tortuous logic seems to be that every Burmese river is peopled with fishermen. On the bank men stand knee-deep in mud, with a cylindrical basket in which to store their catch strapped on their backs. As one sails past, an object shaped like some prehistoric creature may bob to the surface: this is one of the fish traps used in deeper waters. Meanwhile, varieties of small craft move slowly across the surface of the water, a line dangling over the gunwale, the occupant dozing under his hat.

In 1962, Myanmar lost her place as the world's premier rice exporter. Her population has more than doubled since pre-War days, but lacking the benefits of modern technology her agricultural output has not kept pace. The quality of Myanmar's rice has also suffered. Farmers have to sell a certain percentage of their crop to the government, at a fixed price, for subsequent export. Naturally the free market has been getting the best quality. At present the government is being advised on modern techniques and new grain varieties by overseas specialists.

'The most calm and contented of mortals' was a 19th-century British view of the Burmese, and this seems true of the great majority of her people today. What possible reason could there be, the Burmese seem to ask, to go about harvesting the abundant fruits of this country with a greater sense of urgency? If they do decide to adopt a less relaxed pace there is little doubt that Myanmar, with its immense untapped wealth, could become a significant factor in Asia's resource-based economies.

THE PEOPLES OF MYANMAR

An ethnographic map of Myanmar shows a patchwork of peoples. The main group, the Burmans, live in what the British called 'Burma Proper', the lowland areas along the Ayeyarwady River. Of today's population of some 60 million, the overwhelming majority are Burmans, while the remainder of the population is divided into seven main minority groups and some 60 smaller ones.

There is evidence of man inhabiting the Irrawaddy valley (now called the Ayeyarwady) some 5,000 years ago. Perhaps these settlements were staging posts on the main route from Assam to Indo-China. But the first permanent settlers of whom we can be certain were the Mons, who had come from the east in about 200 BCE. They named the lush country they had discovered Suvannabhumi (Golden Land). Shortly afterwards, first the Pyus and then the Burmans (Mramma) fled their native south-east Tibet in the face of aggression from both the Tibetans and the Chinese. The Pyus formed the spearhead of the migration: they came to rest in the southern reaches of the Irrawaddy, while the Burmans themselves settled in central Burma. In the seventh century the Mons, who had settled in the south-east, fought and defeated the Pyus, pushing them north where they apparently merged with the Burmans and made their joint capital at Pagan (now called Bagan) in CE 849.

The peoples of these early migrations shared the same Mongoloid features. The Karens, however, are of totally different stock. It is thought that they originated near the Gobi Desert, which their ancestors called the River of Sand. The final major group, called the Tai-Shans, came south from present-day Yunnan Province in south-west China. During the eighth and ninth centuries they had made periodic raids into Burma, attacking the Pyu Kingdom. When in the 13th century they in turn were conquered by Kublai Khan and became a suzerain state of his empire, a vast exodus of these Tai-Shan people ensued. Many went to Thailand. Another major group of Tai-Shans settled in Upper Burma, building their capitals first at Sagaing and then in 1364 at Ava, and extending their territory as far south as Prome (now called Pyay).

Karen villagers: they are thought to have migrated to Burma from near the Gobi Desert

Thus the situation remained, until the Burmans unified the country (for the second time) in 1555 and the Tai-Shan people, now called Shans, resettled on the high fertile plateau to the east of Ava (now called Inwa). In 1752 the ever-turbulent Mons, who had been centred on Pegu (now called Bago) since its founding in AD 825, had a final fling against Burman supremacy; but by 1760 the Burmans had firmly reasserted their power.

At the time of their annexation of Burma, the British felt that 'the great want of the country is population'. A supposed four million lived in Lower Burma and two million in Upper Burma. However, the latter figure was largely guess-work, since many of the ethnic groups had disappeared into the hills as a result of constant bullying at the hands of the corrupt regime of King Theebaw.

The minority peoples adopted differing attitudes towards their Burman oppressors. The Shans attributed their loss of position to trickery. The two groups were in conflict over a certain tract of land, for which the robust Shans were prepared to fight, but the Burmans called in a hermit to arbitrate, and declared that the winner of the land would be whoever first built a pagoda on the site. In no time the physically superior Shans were in the lead. During the night the crafty Burmans erected a bamboo shell, covered it with cloth and plastered it white. The next morning the Shans were so shattered to find the pagoda 'completed', and even with offerings to Buddha in place, that they never dreamed of looking inside the structure.

The Karens blamed the divine power for their misfortunes. The creator, they believed, threw three clods of earth on the ground: from one sprang the Burmans, from the second the Karens and the third the Kalas (foreigners). Because the Karens were so talkative, the creator threw another handful to the Burmese, thus making them supreme.

These animosities towards the Burmans, deeply ingrained in the culture of many of the minority peoples, help to show that Myanmar has never been a totally homogeneous nation.

To colonialist Sir George Scott, Burmese dress in its rich variety of forms suggested 'wind-stirred tulip beds, or a stir about of rainbows'. Of all Myanmar's ethnic groups the Burmans themselves are the least frivolous dressers. Both sexes wear cotton sarongs called *longyis* (silk for grand occasions), with neat, often white, blouses (*eingyi*) for women and ordinary cotton shirts for men. On special occasions, however, Burmese men don white collarless shirts under crisp cotton waist-length jackets. Traditionally both men and women wore their hair long, coiled in a variety of styles on top of their heads, sometimes filled out by a hairpiece. The men would encircle their topknot with a scarf—one finds some older men coiffed thus today—whereas women complete the effect with a bone comb and seasonal flowers. The maidens of Yangon popularly believed that to sweep the western stairway of the Shwedagon Pagoda was to bring 'the doer beauty of long and black hair in the next existence'.

A young Palaung girl in her finery on her way to the local pagoda festival. The Palaung womenfolk are birds of paradise against the restful greens of their mountain jungle landscape

One of the largest minority groups are the Shans. When, in 1515, they were pushed out of Central Burma, the majority resettled on a high plateau sandwiched between the Kingdoms of Ava and Siam. Fine agriculturists that they were, the Shans were quick to make the best of its temperate climate and fertile soil. Denied the independence promised in 1947, many Shan feel a close bond to their ethnic cousins across the border in Thailand. Indeed, portraits of the Thai king are displayed in the homes of some Shan. Some of the territory in Shan State is still classified as a 'brown area' (with restricted access for tourists, due to security reasons), as it is controlled by Shan rebels, who have in effect become warlords. Part of Shan State forms the notorious Golden Triangle region straddling the borders of Myanmar, Thailand and Laos. It is the growth of opium and production of methamphetamine in this virtually impenetrable region that largely finances the militant activity of the few remaining Shan rebel groups.

Of all the country's ethnic groups, only Shan men traditionally wear trousers. With more the appearance of divided skirts, these are baggy garments which hang from a wide, loose waist-band folded over and tucked in, and worn with the same crisp jackets as the Burmans. The Shans also originated the rectangular fabric shoulder bag, though today these are carried by men throughout Myanmar. Shan men and women both use *khamouts* (elegant, conical-shaped straw hats similar to those worn in Thailand) as protection against the fierce midday sun.

A Palaung mother and baby epitomize 19th-century colonialist Sir George's Scott remark on the varieties of Burmese dress: A 'sight which is not easily forgotten, wind-stirred tulip beds, or a stir about of rainbows are the only suggestions which can be offered.'

Three other minority groups living in Shan country are of Mon-Khmer rather than Shan stock: the Padaungs, the Palaungs and the Inthas. The Padaung womenfolk traditionally wore gold rings around their necks and ankles. From the age of six or seven a new ring was added each year. The original purpose of this custom was to repel prospective kidnappers—though one might think these gold-encased 'giraffe women' constituted a positive invitation—but the practice is now discouraged for medical reasons. However, Padaung ladies of middle age are still to be seen wearing their bondage: once ringed they cannot in effect be released, for the golden corset has stretched and eventually replaced the neck muscles. It is very difficult to see Padaung ladies in their own villages, as the area where they live is off-limits to tourists. However, for US$3 you can visit some elderly ladies who are being housed in Nyaung Shwe.

The Inthas live around the breathtakingly beautiful Inle Lake, just south of Taunggyi, the capital of Shan State (founded by Sir George Scott). Not far away, around Kalaw (a favourite hill station retreat of the colonials, and still a 'little England' of 'stockbroker Tudor' houses rounded by aster- and snapdragon-filled gardens), are the various Palaung settlements. The Palaung womenfolk are positive birds of paradise against the restful greens of their jungle landscape, and the drab browns of their smoky villages. An unmarried girl might wear a thick, red-striped *longyi* with an embroidered green jacket, a cotton tasselled 'halo' perched on her long shiny black hair. Her *longyi* is not tucked in like a Burman's, but held in place by a wide, white belt. For a working day the velvet jacket is replaced by an embroidered cotton one, slightly faded from constant washing and the sun, and the halo is discarded in favour of a band around her forehead, supporting the weight of a produce-laden basket on her back. When she marries she can substitute the embroidered coat for a blue or purple jacket with red facing; around her waist hangs a collection of thin lacquer bands and her head is encased by cotton strands from which at the back dangle silver beads—a stunning ensemble worn with great panache. The Palaungs' predominant crop is tea, which they sell in the form of hard balls rather larger than cricket balls; they are also famous for their *lapet* (pickled tea). Before roads reached their remote villages, the *lapet* was carried over the hills to the Ayeyarwady where the baskets were strapped to rafts and floated down river semi-submerged.

Another of the biggest ethnic groups in Myanmar is the Karens. The predominately Christian Karens are excellent soldiers, and during colonial times were widely recruited and promoted within the British Army. Like the Shans, the Karens also felt that they had been unfairly treated as a result of the 1947 Constitution. In a welcome development, the main Karen rebel group, the Karen National Union, and the government have made progress in peace negotiations begun in late 2011.

OSS officer John Colling, and Kachin scouts in Burma during World War II. The Office of Strategic Services was a US government intelligence agency operating during World War II

Both the Kachins, who inhabit the mountainous regions in the north of Myanmar, and the Chins, whose home is to the west of the country, provided a plentiful source of soldiery for the British. Many Kachins were trained by the American Office of Strategic Services (OSS) during World War II in the fight against the Japanese. The Kachin national dress in particular is another eye-catcher: red calf-length *longyis* worn over tight trousers and black velvet jackets decorated with silver bangles. The men, in their dark *longyis* and blue jackets, carry silver-decorated shoulder bags and elegantly curved silver swords and scabbards.

Geographically, both the Chins and their southerly neighbours, the Arakanese, have been cut off from Myanmar Proper more than the other minority groups. The Arakanese were able to retain their autonomy over centuries by standing up for themselves—they sacked the Burmese capital on several occasions. The Chins on the other hand were content to keep to their hills. Today, the Burmese remain suspicious of the Arakanese and warn prospective visitors to take care.

Despite the diversity and geographic separation of Myanmar's ethnic groups, these peoples share with each other and with the Burmans themselves a wide variety of social customs—the *longyi*, *thanaka* cosmetics, betel and *lapet* are to be found throughout Myanmar. Pay a visit to a Burmese family, whether as a friend or total stranger, and first you will be offered tea and then betel and *lapet*. These delicacies are stored in boxes of either lacquer or silver. In the betel box the top layer will house orange peel, lime and chopped areca nut with fresh betel leaves underneath. Select your leaf, spread it with nuts, lime and peel and chew it, spitting out the strong red juice. Said to aid digestion, the betel has a pungent taste and leaves the novice a little numb in the mouth and light in the head. *Lapet* is also a mild stimulant but with culinary distinction. Young tea leaves are pressed in bamboo containers and stored in a moist atmosphere which gently ferments them. Before serving, they are mixed with morsels of dried shrimps, roasted peanuts, fried crispy garlic and broad beans.

Another quality which Myanmar's minority groups share is expertise in weaving. Very often the women of the village will form a weaving guild, each area producing its own distinctive fabric. In more primitive villages it is common to hear the clack of the loom coming from under the house, in the cowshed. The craftswoman sits on the earth floor, outstretched legs resting against a bamboo pole, her work suspended from an H-shape frame held taut by a strap around her waist.

The Kachins and Chins, inhabiting the lower-lying and relatively fertile hills in Myanmar's north and west, have been able to develop settled societies based on a self-sustaining system of slash-and-burn agriculture. Every few years, having exhausted the goodness of the land they have cleared from the jungle, the whole

Economy of time and motion—this Palaung woman carries her stylish umbrella on her head and a bundle of pink Shan bananas on her back. The fat pink fruit are some of the tastiest to be found anywhere in the world

village moves on. Choosing a new site is obviously of critical importance: the traditional method of doing this (and who can be sure it is not practised today?) has a specially Burmese other-worldly quality. Each householder would go out to select a favourite site and from it bring home a clod of earth. That night he would place it under his pillow and await an auspicious dream. The following day the village soothsayer would analyse the dreams. If there was no outright dream winner, a large fowl would be cooked and eaten by the householders and the clean bones put in an earthenware pot. The participants, with eyes averted, each picked out a bone

and the one to pick the largest had the honour of leading the village to its new home.

RELIGION AND SOCIETY
THE ARRIVAL OF BUDDHISM

Buddhism is a religious system which acknowledges no supreme deity or god, Sakya Buddha is in fact the fourth Buddha of this 'world cycle' (it is prophesied that the arrival of the fifth Buddha will bring to an end the current world cycle). Many believe Gautama Buddha was born Prince Siddhartha of the Gautama clan in India in around 566 BCE, although the records vary on this date. At the age of 30 he left his home, wife and son to become a holy man and for six years he led a life of austerity (eating, the legend has it, one grain of rice a day). Eventually he realized this was not the way to salvation, so he began to advocate and teach the path of the Middle Way. Put simply, this is the avoidance of extremes, the cultivation of tranquillity, the acceptance of *karma*. The goal of all Buddhists is to

(above) A group of Kachins who have travelled from Myanmar's far north to visit the Shwedagon Pagoda in Yangon, the major Buddhist shrine. All are wearing thanaka *make-up as much-needed protection against the sun*

attain Nirvana, freedom from an otherwise endless cycle of rebirths. The realization of this goal is in the hands of the individual. A higher state in future incarnations can only be achieved by living a pious life, adhering to the Five Precepts (the Buddhist Commandments), and following the Middle Way.

Buddhism came to Myanmar in several stages. Around the beginning of the Christian era, Indian merchants and missionaries travelled to Myanmar, teaching both the Northern and Southern Buddhist scriptures. The great Indian King Ashoka, promoter of Buddhism, is said to have visited the Shwedagon Pagoda in around 260 BCE to pay homage to its relics of the four Buddhas. If this was indeed the case, Ashoka's endorsement would have added considerably to the momentum of Buddhism in Myanmar. But it was not until 1056 that Sri Lankan Theravada Buddhism was fully established in the country by King Anawrahta. The Burmese had always cherished the concept that all men and women are equal. To find these very concepts at the heart of Buddhism, the religion which was being sponsored by their king, made it readily acceptable. The Buddhism adopted in Myanmar was the Southern or Theravada (Hinayana) denomination.

THE NAT SPIRIT GODS

Myanmar's brand of Theravada Buddhism is unique. When King Anawrahta was converted to Theravada Buddhism in late 1056, he realized that he was not going to be able to stamp out entirely the intricate web of animism, alchemy and tantric rites practised by the Ari monks and their followers. So he disbanded the elements he regarded as most irreverent and then showed his tolerance of the *nats* (spirit gods) by allowing them into the pagoda precinct. Anawrahta decreed that Thagyamin, King of the Nat Gods and guardian of Buddhism, was to be added to the original 36 *nats* and considered their leader. Images of the 37, in attitudes of worship, were then placed in the newly-built Shwezigon Pagoda in Bagan (not to be confused with the Shwedagon Pagoda in Yangon), in order that 'the people come to worship their old gods, and then they will discover the truth of the new faith of Buddhism'.

Today there are still 37 'inner' *nats* (those allowed into the pagoda precinct), and hundreds of 'outer' *nats*. The list of 37 has varied somewhat from Anawrahta's time, and is made up of a strange melange of heroes and tragic historical characters, the majority of whom met violent ends. The exception was Kunshaw, 'The Lord of the White Umbrella' and father of Anawrahta. Kunshaw's father was killed before he was born, and the throne usurped. His mother fled the court, bringing up her son in poverty. On the death of the usurper's son, Kunshaw was proclaimed king by popular demand and, out of the goodness of his heart, took into his palace the two pregnant wives of his predecessor and made them his queens. Their sons he brought up as his own. However, on reaching adulthood, his ungrateful stepsons persuaded Kunshaw to enter a monastery and then deposed him. Years later, when Anawrahta regained the throne and offered it to his elderly father, Kunshaw refused: 'I am old to look upon, old in years. Be now king thyself,' he protested. He died shortly afterwards and was elevated to the 'nathood', but as a monk, not a king.

Nats play an important role in the everyday life of the Burmese; if not properly appeased they can prove very troublesome. The beauty of a Burmese maiden is enhanced by adorning her hair with a sprig of blossom; likewise fresh flowers decorate tastefully laid stalls in the market. These are not, as one might imagine, efforts to glamorize the 'shop window' but are in fact signs of homage to the *nats*. You will see the outer *nats* shrines everywhere, perched in trees or housed in little bamboo hutches along the wayside. The most evident of these are the shrines of the 'house' *nat*. On the south side of nearly every house hangs a coconut. The strips of red and yellow fabric with which these are sometimes adorned are offerings to Eing Saung, the protector of the household. In times gone by the four corner posts of the house, which were thought to be his favourite abode, were draped in white cloth.

The traditional home of the *nats* is Mount Popa, which sits in the middle of the arid Myingyan plain, south-east of Bagan.

Nat culture remained deeply ingrained in both secular and religious matters. Included in the court oath of loyalty to the Burmese kings (read before an image of Buddha) was the statement that by serving his royal master with obedience, the candidate 'under the aid of the 5,000 *nats* that guard religion' would be free from all 96 diseases. It was only with the building of Mandalay in 1857 that a particularly barbaric *nat* custom was brought to an end. Previously, during the construction of a new city, someone would be buried alive under each corner of the perimeter wall. These unfortunates were supposed then to be reincarnated as evil *nats* and to keep the city's foes at bay.

Not all *nats* are of such violent disposition. 'The little lady of the flute' acts as guardian and playmate of children (causing them to smile in their sleep). Happily, *nat* worship today manifests this gentler side of its nature, with daily offerings to one's favourite spirit to bring safety and success in one's everyday life.

The Burmese Cosmos

Also apart from the mainstream Theravada Buddhism, is the Burmese concept of the cosmos. In the centre stands mythical Mount Meru, shaped like half a serrated eggshell upside down, half above an ocean and half below. On its slopes are the six seats of Devas, the beings who by good works and incessant meditation 'have risen above man's estate on the path to Nirvana'. Above them are the 16 seats of Brahmas—those who live in sublime contemplation. Below are the eight great hells, and the numerous smaller ones. Around Mount Meru extends the vast Thamohodaya Ocean containing thousands of small islands clustered around four main ones: North, South, East and West. The human race inhabits the southern island; the Burmese, Chinese and the Indians on the main island itself, the rest on its satellites. Whereas life on the southern island is difficult, on the remainder paradise reigns, especially on the northern island, where 'gorgeous clothes hang ready-made from the trees, dainty meals of all kinds grow up and cook themselves'. But the inhabitants are unhappy for they are always reborn on the same island, making it impossible for them to progress towards Nirvana. The 24 Buddhas from the 64 previous worlds and the four Buddhas of the present era of existence all reached Nirvana via the southern island.

QUEST FOR NIRVANA

'How great a favour has the Lord Buddha bestowed on me in manifesting to me his law through the observation of which I may escape hell and secure my salvation.' To the Buddhist Burmese the quest for Nirvana—literally the extinction of all passions and desires, which has also come to mean a state of beatitude—is the pivot of life. Nirvana is the zenith of the Ladder of Existence, the Four States of Punishment being its nadir. An individual's position on the Ladder will depend on how much merit has been accrued during his previous lives. Those unfortunates doomed to the States of Punishment have to endure thousands of years in bubbling furnaces, their ever-renewing flesh being torn to shreds by odious gargoyles and five-headed dogs. The destiny of mortals who did not curb their passions and were abusive on earth is the profoundest state of hell, the 'Bong of Animals'. Some animals, though, such as the hare, white elephant and pigeon, are exempt from the Bong, as they are believed to have been former incarnations of Gautama Buddha. The vulture, too, is above the Bong as it does not take life but rather lives off carrion. Once having fallen into these macabre states of hell it is not clear how the victim climbs out; but avoiding them appears to depend on close adherence to the Five Great Precepts, while one's advance up the Ladder is a question of accruing merit.

A further dimension to this accounting system is *karma*. If one's former life has been meritorious, one is reborn not only higher up the scale but with good *karma*. There is no recognized method of improving one's *karma*, though some employ a *bedin-saya*, a sort of fortune-teller, to prescribe a *khame* or charm to keep evil influences at bay.

The accumulation of merit is therefore all important, as it can save a soul from the bubbling Bong of Animals and store credit for a future life. If one stops in a village, hot and weary from a long motor-car journey, the villagers will provide *lapet* or their local brew (such as toddy wine), hose down the tyres, offer to show one their pagoda and suggest a siesta on the cool floor of one of their houses. These gestures of hospitality are offered with such charm that the traveller is unconscious of the ulterior motive—to gain merit. This search for merit is evident in practically every aspect of Burmese daily life. At one end of the scale is the placing by the roadside of clay pots from which any thirsty traveller may refresh himself. At the other end is pagoda building: 'No work of merit is so richly paid as the building of a pagoda.' (Conversely, and, one is inclined to feel, somewhat unfairly, the repairing of an existing pagoda, unless it happens to be one of the renowned shrines such as the Shwedagon, gains no merit for the repairer, but only for the original donor.) This is surely one of the key factors underlying the astonishing profusion of pagodas with which the Burmese countryside, and in particular the plains of the Ayeyarwady, are so liberally sprinkled. Of course it is only the rich who are able to make this grand gesture. For the majority, the quest for Nirvana consists of attempting to live by the Five Great Precepts, preparing food for the monks and indulgence in premeditated acts of merit such as freeing caged birds. (One might well inquire how the catching of the birds in the first place affected the merit of those concerned.) There is even a festival for the liberation of fish. In the rainy season when the rivers rise to form flood lakes, the trapped fish are caught and kept in huge 'chatties'. They are later released, amid much fun and frolic, into the river.

Even a remote hill village will probably boast a flourishing kyaung *(monastery). With the government schools far away, parents are extra keen for their male children to have their* shinbyu *(initiation ceremony), so as to enter a monastery and ensure a good education. This merry bunch were living in a small monastery in the middle of the fields in Inwa*

BECOMING A MONK

Until the age of 12, when the male child normally has his *shin-pyu* ('to make a monk'), his Buddhistic life cannot commence and he is cast among the animals on the Ladder of Existence. The day he is accepted as an *upathaka*—a believer—it becomes within his power to raise or lower his status in his next life. The *shin-pyu* is an occasion of feasting. An auspicious day is chosen by the astrologer, invitations are dispensed by the female members of the family, not in the form of cards but in packets of *lapet*. As the day draws near, the novice receives instruction in monastic etiquette. In some rural districts the boy is confined to his house for seven days before his initiation for fear that jealous evil spirits will kidnap him. On the appointed day he is dressed in princely garments and jewels, mounted on a white pony and leads a procession around the village. This journey symbolizes Prince Siddhartha's royal life, which he renounced in order to search for enlightenment. The journey ended, the boy disrobes before the head of the monastery, has his head shaved and is washed by rubbing with seeds and saffron. Then, prostrating himself before the head monk, he asks in Pali (the original language of the Buddhist scriptures) for admittance to the monastery so that he may strive towards gaining Nirvana. Once accepted he is given his monastic robes, a offerings bowl is hung around his neck and, while festivities continue in his house, follows the monk to his new home. Buddhism abhors physical suffering and a small boy's life in a monastery is not a hard one. He will learn and observe the ten precepts (the five most important, The Five Great Precepts, forbid taking life, stealing, adultery, lying and drinking intoxicating liquor), learn his lessons, go an offerings round each morning for his food and carry out domestic duties in the monastery. Depending on how pious his family is, his stay could be anything from one week to several months (or even for life).

MONKS AND BURMESE SOCIETY

Supporting Myanmar's substantial monastic population imposes heavy demands on the national economy, but society expects nothing in return save the merit gained through guardianship of the monks. However, the situation was different prior to the country's annexation by Britain, when education was in the hands of the monks. All boys attended the monastic school free of charge, where they learned the Buddhist scriptures and the rudiments of mathematics as well as how to read and write. In those days the Burmese could boast the highest rate of literacy in Asia. The British started to modify this system in the 19th century by introducing lay and missionary schools. But it was not until after Independence that radical changes occurred. When the Ne Win government came to power in the 1960s the Buddhist establishment was considered potential political opposition.

HOLY FISH

John Everingham, 1988

'The fish are incarnated with a holy spirit. They swim right up the river bank, out of the water, while worshippers press gold leaf on their heads and fill their mouths with rice. Then they swim away.'

The holy fish story is one of Burma's innumerable tales of the *nats'* (spirits') latest, mischievous ploys with human fate. The fish even cropped up in an early explorer's eyewitness account.

Hunting holy fish on seven-day visas was no easy task. Sifting the rumours for facts was tougher; everyone in Burma, it seemed, had heard of them. No one had actually seen them. Only when I found myself knee-deep in the swirling, muddy water of a small river in the central Burmese plains, holding out a large compressed rice ball, and shouting politely to the spirits of the fish to rise, was my skepticism overtaken by anxious excitement. And the sight was awesome. From a huge, seemingly lifeless expanse of brown, a huge head responded obediently pushing gaping jaws out at the knees of a small girl. Then there were a dozen of them, and village children stuffed the protruding heads with riceballs.

Village elders called all children back from the water's edge. There was much swirling among the fish. They popped up heads to eye their benefactors, and splashed fins and tails. Suddenly there was a great surge through the water, heading for the bank. A flabby, man-sized beast clumsily thrashed its passage through the shallows and torpedoed itself up the mud flat—right out of the water.

Villagers crowded around. For several minutes the fish lay there, moving only its jaws to accommodate the balls of rice being stuffed inside. Someone pressed gold leaf to its head, though clearly the gold leaf would not hold for long. Another man was pouring water to stop the fish from drying. Then, as the 'holy fish' sensed the need to return to its own world with its bulging mouth full, it turned, gave a few mighty mud-slinging tail thrusts and propelled itself away.

'Should anyone dare eat a holy fish,' I was told by the villagers, 'They will certainly die or fall gravely ill. It has happened before. Everyone in this area can identify this kind of fish, and they always free them.'

To neutralize the support that Ne Win felt was being given to the ethnic rebels, he commanded all monks to be registered, exposed those living openly with women 'under my nose' in Yangon, and removed the education system from monastic control. Today, education is run by the State and only in the remotest areas are monastic schools still to be found.

Although deprived of a practical role in society, the ubiquitous monks continue to exert a profound influence by their example (though the record, like that of all religious orders the world has ever known, is by no means unblemished), and, perhaps more importantly, serve as a constant reminder of the way of the Buddha. This is reflected in the reverence and piety in which they are held by the vast majority of the lay population. So far as the monks themselves are concerned, their life is certainly austere, though by no means unpleasant. the calm of monastic routine, uncluttered by material paraphernalia, provides the ideal environment in which to study and adopt the teachings of the Middle Way—a life of no extremes in which every thought, word and deed should contribute towards reaching Nirvana.

THE STATUS OF BURMESE WOMEN
The culture and social structure of Myanmar are intertwined with Buddhism. Myanmar boasts a natural democracy and liberation for its womenfolk. From the lowliest origins they could rise to the top; the last queen, Supayalat, was the granddaughter of a fisherman. There has never been any caste system or primogeniture (absence of the latter, of course, fuelling innumerable palace intrigues and murders). Burmese women have for centuries enjoyed the freedom and equality only recently hankered after by their Western sisters—free to choose their marriage partner, to remain the owner of any money brought to the union and with freedom of divorce. A Burmese marriage is only a public declaration between the couple involved that they wish to be man and wife. This emphasis on the individual helps to explain why there is no such thing as a family name in Myanmar. Nor, therefore, do women change their names on marriage. During the days of the monarchy the Burmese did not support a middle class; as historian Dr Htin Aung says, 'not because as in Czarist Russia there were only aristocrats and serfs, but simply because there was neither an upper nor a lower class.' As land was considered a gift of nature and could be acquired by clearing it, there was no landed gentry. The village was the basic unit of society and was generally self-sufficient and self-maintained. Within that unit the women played their equal part. It was not (and is not today) uncommon for the women to be the business managers while the men cared for the children.

The initiation ceremony of a small boy into the monkhood at the Shwedagon Pagoda. The day starts with the boy clothed in royal dress being carried on the shoulders of his proud father, under the shade of the 'royal' gold umbrella. Later the family party repairs to the monastery which is accepting their son. They donate food to the monks, the little boy swaps his royal garments for those of a monk and his head is shaven

NAT FESTIVAL

Anastasia Edwards

On every street corner in Mandalay, men were defying the August heat with energetic waves and cries of 'Taungbyon! Taungbyon!', rallying people to pile into and on top of the dilapidated buses and trucks which, throughout the night and day, were making their way to the site of one of Myanmar's greatest *nat* (spirit) festivals. Their fervour was contagious, and I soon found myself joining the convoy of vehicles making their way to Taungbyon, an hour to the north of Mandalay.

A dusty rural village for most of the year, Taungbyon had been transformed into a vast fairground to which thousands of pilgrims had flocked from all over the country. A complex labyrinth of thoroughfares, lined with stalls, had been rigged and connected the various temples to the stages on which spirit mediums danced. Among the most intriguing stalls were the tattoo parlours, offering the devout myriad motifs with which to grace their bodies. One young man, who had obviously devoted his whole afternoon to the enterprise, sat with his *longyi* hitched up to his thighs, while another painstakingly tattooed his left leg, from the knee down, with an abstract lotus design similar to those ubiquitous in Burmese temples.

Some of the stalls were bare platforms, in the corners of which stood painted *nat* figures. These I learnt were rented to pilgrims from far away as sleeping quarters—2,000 kyat gave the lessee about 30 square metres (100 square feet) of platform for the two weeks of the festival, and an additional 500 kyat purchased the use of a single light bulb rigged to a car battery.

Turning into one thoroughfare, I was swept up in the flow of people squeezing their way to prime positions around one of the platforms upon which a spirit medium was dancing to the frantic strains of an ensemble of a dozen musicians. Dressed in a shiny, white, woman's *longyi*, he sported long, fake eyelashes and sticky, red lipstick. A can of beer in one hand and a fistful of crisp, one-kyat notes in the other, his arms were poised over his head as his hips swung wildly to the beat of the music. Suddenly, he threw the handful of notes towards the group in which I was standing and, with excited screams, everyone around me dived to grab the auspicious money.

As the stage cleared the beat of the music accelerated. The spirit medium started to dance faster and more frantically, and to beckon wildly for something. A cluster of wealthy donors—the patrons whose sponsorship of the mediums curries them favour in the afterlife— produced a bottle of Johnny Walker which the dancer, covered in a sheen of perspiration, swigged with relish.

It was precisely because I did not understand a word of the proceedings that I was able to understand the popular appeal which *nats* have commanded for more than a millennium. This physical and sensual dimension of Myanmar's indigenous religion, flaunted so openly by the spirit medium and received with such enthusiasm by the crowd, explains why King Anawrahta's attempts to suppress it failed. Buddhist doctrine was no match for the *nats*, and Anawrahta had no choice but to incorporate them into the Buddhist pantheon. I later found out, in a dusty facsimile of a book entitled *Folk Elements in Burmese Buddhism*, bought in a Yangon bookshop, said that the festival at Taungbyon was in fact founded by Anawrahta to rival the indigenous festival on Mount Popa. It was a graceful, if ironic, concession, symbolic of so much of the contradictions within Myanmar's heritage still so palpable today.

Among the most intriguing stalls at the nat festival are the parlours of tattooists, who painstakingly decorate the bodies of the devout with a myriad of motifs

FESTIVALS AND THEATRE

'It is the nature of the Burmese to make festivals'—an assertion amply borne out by the Burmese addiction to festivals and theatre. Like practically every important aspect of Burmese society, and in particular those involving entertainment, they take place under the auspices of the pagoda.

Myanmar's rainy season (during which merrymaking is impractical) coincides with the Buddhist Lent, which marks the period of the Buddha's meditation prior to his enlightenment. They both end in October. From then until the following July, every town and village will periodically buzz with one or another festival of some description. There are national festivals for celebrating the New Year (the Water Festival), the harvest, the end of Buddhist Lent (the Festival of Light), the presentation of new robes to the monks (the Weaving Festival), and many more. Also each pagoda will have its own birthday festival and each community its favourite *nat* to honour. In addition, special events such as the raising of a new *hti* (umbrella) for a pagoda, will require an individual celebration.

Days before a festival, a village of bamboo stalls mushrooms around the pagoda. Men, women and children dash about arranging their wares; sideshows of old-fashioned roundabouts with brightly coloured papier-mâché animals materialize. A carefree carnival spirit permeates the air. If the festival is at one of the more renowned pagodas, pilgrims—including whole families with goods and chattels stuffed into bullock and pony carts—converge from far and wide.

Beneath its easy-going appearance, this comic dance is a routine which requires extreme skill and vast resources of energy, hence its popularity among male dancers

These frenzied preparations give way to the commencement of the festival itself. As the dawn mist hovers over the festival ground the pagoda wakes. The swish of brooms can be heard as devotees sweep away the remnants of yesterday's offerings. The arrival at the flower stall of the day's fresh produce brings a heady aroma of jasmine and rosebuds and awakens the men and women whose job it is to wire the blooms into nosegays. Fires are kindled; some people prepare their own breakfast, others hunt out the *mohingha* stalls which have sprung up as if by magic. (*Mohingha* is the traditional breakfast fare of noodles in soup.) The vendor sits behind a low table covered with a multitude of bowls. These contain an eccentric-seeming variety of delicacies: chopped coriander, fried garlic, bean

crackers, hard-boiled eggs, fish cake and sesame seeds. On one side is a large basin of rice noodles, covered with a muslin cloth to keep the heat in and the flies out; on the other a large cauldron of fish soup steams over a charcoal fire. Hands flickering, the vendor combines in an empty bowl a handful of noodles, a sprinkling of each of the chopped ingredients (deftly cutting the eggs and fish sausages with scissors), a ladleful of fish broth, a pinch of chili powder and finally a squeeze of fresh lime: delicious! A popular and expert *mohingha* cook can single-handedly serve 250 bowls at one breakfast session.

A festival may last for up to a week. During the daytime there will be bands, processions to the pagoda, dancing—an extravaganza of colours, movement and especially noise—generally incorporating the particular activity which symbolizes the purpose of the festival. However, the peak of many festivals occurs at night. At the end of Buddhist Lent, for example, the return of Buddha to earth is marked by lights on every building, while during the Weaving Festival, young girls compete by the light of the full moon in making new robes for the monks.

Festival evenings and nights are frequently devoted to the *pwe*, or evening entertainment. According to Sir George Scott, 'There is no nation on the face of the earth so fond of theatrical representations as the Burmese.' As light begins to fade, activity centres on the large stage. The auditorium is a fenced-in area with rush matting on the ground and is free to all, so it is first come, first served. The whole family settles down for the night's entertainment with bedrolls for the

This is an instrument now rarely seen. A Burmese orchestra is made up of a fascinating mixture of instruments, to foreigners both strange to the eye and the ear

A WINDOW ON THE PAST

*I went with Pe Maung to my first pwe. Pwes, or public stage performances,
are the most Burmese of occasions. There are four main types of
performance: the historical drama (zat pwe), the marionette version of the
former (yok thay pwe), the song-and-dance show with solo dancers and
comedians (anyein pwe), and the dancing ensemble (yein pwe). All are
held in the open air and are free to the public, the expenses being met as
an act of charity by some local rich man. They start in the cool of the
evening and continue to sunrise.*

*My first pwe was of even then a rare type, a puppet show. A bamboo
and matting stage was set up in the fields, with various attendants
pumping up pressure lamps as darkness fell. Families from far and wide
arrived in their bullock-carts, set down their mats, huddled the children in
blankets and set out their picnics. The play was set in the days of the
Burmese kings, with princes and princesses, courtiers, wizards, dragons
and ogres (beeloos). The speeches were long and involved, covering some
complicated medieval story, but the puppets took on an almost human life
of their own. Members of the audience watched raptly for a bit, got up and
strolled about, had a cheroot and a snack to eat, and often rolled up in
their blankets and had a bit of a snooze. As a huge yellow moon rose above
(full-moon time was pwe time), and as the puppets, lit by the petrol lamps,
bowed and gesticulated in their ancient and tinselly finery, I caught a
glimpse of what life must have been like in the court of the Burmese kings,
who had ruled in Mandalay such a comparatively short time ago—fifty-
one years, to be exact. The British took Mandalay in 1886. Until then the
Upper Burma kings had lived in seclusion in their teak palaces,
surrounded by shimmering silks, proud to be 'Guardians of the White
Elephant'. At his accession in 1878, the last king, Theebaw, goaded on by
his young queen, had not less than seventy-nine of his close relatives—
men, women and children—put to death in 'The Massacre of the Kinsmen',*

allowed by custom to a new king uncertain of his throne. One story has it that, in order to conceal from onlookers the sight of royal blood being spilt, the victims were trampled to death under carpets by palace elephants. This world, and indeed the world of spirits and demons, was still vividly alive in the minds of the simple Upper Burma villagers.

Leslie Glass, The Changing of Kings—
Memories of Burma 1934–1949, 1985

A cart becomes the dressing room for a minthani or female dancer at an evening pwe (performance). This lively form of entertainment often continues from dusk until dawn, so the cart may well become her temporary bedroom. As the 19th-century Superintendent of the Shan States, Sir George Scott, said, 'There is no nation on the face of the earth so fond of theatrical representations as the Burmese'

children and tiffin boxes. For the less provident, hawkers weave in and out selling nuts, snacks, cigars and cigarettes. The Burmese are a nation of smokers, from nearly the smallest child ('Burmese children never smoke before they can walk.') to the oldest grandmother who sits, intent on the *pwe*, an enormous cigar clenched between her gums and holding a small basin to catch the ash and sparks—for Burmese cigars sometimes behave akin to fireworks. If more substantial sustenance is required, a galaxy of food stalls with such delights as 'husband and wife' onion cakes (cooked in separate moulds and then joined) is stationed around the fence. A Burmese theatre audience resembles nothing so much as a restless, constantly murmuring sea.

There are two distinct groups of *pwe*: light and serious drama. The first is of the variety-show genre. Burmese, like Chinese, is a monosyllabic language and affords ample opportunity for puns. However, the highly developed Burmese art of clowning with all the facial subtleties of mime, lets even the non-Burmese speaker in on most of the humour. The second group consists of the more serious Wethandaya Wutha (the Ten Great Birth Stories), which illustrate the last ten incarnations of Buddha before he attained enlightenment.

Both types of theatre involve song, dance and dramatic music, and the cast is supported by an eight- to ten-man orchestra. The most spectacular instruments are the *saing-waing* and the *kyi-waing*. Both are made of elaborately carved (and often gilded) panels standing 60 to 90 centimetres (two to three feet) high and forming a circle some 1.5 metres (five feet) in diameter. Suspended from the inside of the panels are either drums or gongs with the player sitting in the middle. He constantly tunes his drums by applying and kneading a sticky paste of burnt rice husk. There are no written scores, so all the music must be learned by ear. Each group has an apprentice who plays the *wa le kot* (bamboo cymbals): the apprenticeship system ensures the music's passage from one generation to the next. This strange orchestra can produce effects ranging from the ponderous and

The chief instrument of the traditional Burmese orchestra is a saing-waing, It is a circular tub-like frame, round the interior of which are suspended vertically some 18 or 20 drums, graduate in tone. The performer squats in the middle and plays it with his hands

lovelorn to the warlike and triumphant, playing for hours on end with unflagging zeal. The Western ear takes time to adjust to its discordant crashes and rhythmic eccentricities, but in time they cast a mesmeric spell.

The dancers also display tremendous stamina. Of the 120 basic steps most are executed with bent knees. Lissom bodies, clad in court dress from the Ava period, perform a series of sinuous, tentacular movements. The skirt is a narrow, sequined tube with the added hazard of a 60-centimetre (two-foot) train which the dancer, with consummate skill and elegance, flicks out of the way with a supple foot, without disturbing the smooth glide of the dance. The steps for men and women are the same and to see a man dancing the role of a princess is by no means unusual.

In early April, the Burmese seemingly go mad: battalions of young people line the streets armed with vats of water, from which they fill all available receptacles in order to throw the contents at hapless passers-by. Only the elderly and the monks are exempt. Sir George Scott recounts the following experience of a newly arrived Englishman: 'The victim reached Rangoon on the second day of the water-feast, and having no Indian outfit got himself up in a tall hat, frock coat, and the rest...On the verandah he found three or four Burmese girls, who forthwith asked permission to throw water on him. He naturally supposed they were asking whether he wanted to see the master of the house, and nodded violently. Whereupon they capsized their bowls of water over him, including the hat in the libation. The astonished man took it to be the custom of the country to cool down over-heated foreigners, but thought the inclusion of his hat an unnecessary detail.'

This three-day orgy of water throwing marks the beginning of the new year and the visit to earth of Thagyamin, King of the Nats. The festivities start with an *a-kyo-nay* (preparing to greet day), when sacred water pots are filled and made fragrant by the addition of aromatic leaves. Food is prepared both for the monasteries and the neighbours, and bamboo stands are erected for communal hair-washing. The noblest part of the body must be clean to honour the celestial guest. In the days of the monarchy there was a ceremonial washing (*tha-gyan daw gyi*) of the king's hair. The water for this ceremony was carried from the springs of the beautiful Gaung Se Kyun (Shampoo Island). This islet, near Mawlamyine (formerly Moulmein), seemingly hangs above the water, inspiring the idea that it was suspended from the heavens by an invisible thread. The hair-washing takes place at dusk in readiness for the god's arrival at midnight. A special shampoo is used, made by soaking the dried bark of the *tha-yaw* tree, then boiling and pounding acacia seeds, and then mixing the acacia powder with *tha-yaw* water.

The god's arrival is heralded by a gunfire salute. The large pots are filled with water, and sacred *tha-byay* leaves are ceremoniously emptied, after which the water-throwing revel begins. Children armed with water pistols ambush the unsuspecting, young maidens exchange their thin muslin blouses for ones of thicker fabric to avoid any immodesty when their garments become wet and clinging. During the next three days everyone tries to live according to the Five Great Precepts (the Buddhist code of behaviour) and children are especially well-behaved. Thagyamin, they are warned, brings with him two books, one bound in dog-skin to record the names of those who are sinful, the other bound in gold for those who have gained merit. The *atetnay* (rising day) marks Thagyamin's return to the heavens and ends the festivities, though some enthusiastic revellers squeeze in another day, declaring that he has returned to earth to collect his forgotten pipe or umbrella.

The prelude to the Buddhist New Year is Thingyan or the Water Festival. Special platforms called pandal are erected along the streets of Yangon. As the festival begins, groups of young people on the pandals operate hoses, dousing anything or anyone who comes by. The serious side of the festival is, as Aung San Suu Kyi explains, 'a time for taking stock of the past year and using the last few days before the new year comes in to balance our "merit book"'

FACTS FOR THE TRAVELLER

GETTING TO MYANMAR

The majority of international arrivals are still via Yangon International Airport but the number of international carriers into Mandalay is growing and it is now possible to fly direct from Bangkok to Nay Pyi Taw, very helpful for the international business community.

At present at least 15 Asian carriers make stops at Yangon. As yet there are no direct flights from North America but the situation changes day by day with direct flights from the Gulf and Germany as the latest additions. Most flight arrivals are still from Bangkok, there are numerous direct flights from other Asian cities, including Singapore, Seoul, Hong Kong, Kunming, Chiang Mai, Kuala Lumpur, Hanoi, Ho Chi Minh City, Phnom Penh, Guangzhou, Calcutta and Taipei. Bangkok Airways and Thai Airways International fly three times a day between Yangon and Bangkok and Myanmar Airways International and Air Asia twice daily. Silk Air and MAI have twice daily flights between Yangon and Singapore.

At the time of going to press four overland crossings operate between Thailand and Myanmar and one between Myanmar and China, but be sure to have your valid Myanmar visa, visa on arrival is not possible. It is currently possible to enter from northern Thailand via Tachilek (Mae Sai) and to travel to Kyaing Tong (formerly Kengtung) but from there you must fly to Heho, north of Inle Lake. Travelling from Bangkok, the Mae Sot crossing to Myawady is currently open to foreigners as well as locals. Tour operators are already offering packages out of Bangkok using this route.

For years dive tour groups travelling only to the Myeik Archipelago entered Myanmar via the far southern port of Kawthaung (opposite Ranong in Thailand). Now it seems it is possible to travel onward towards Myeik but a flight from Kawthaung may be neccessary as we cannot yet ascertain if the Kawthaung Myeik highway is open.

Another uncharted road allowing crossing into Thailand between Htee and Ban Phu Nam Ron (about 200 kms from Bangkok) has been announced open to foreigners, but we are still trying to locate the relevant highway, which eventually reaches the coast at Dawei, sight of major infrastructural work related to the energy sector.

Provided you have valid visas, entry from Ruili in Yunnan (opposite Muse in Myanmar) is possible, again please note, at the time of going to press. Travel by road in Kachin State between Myitkyina and Bhamo is not encouraged due to the fragility of cease-fire status. For those planning to take a cruise down the Ayeyarwady river from Bhamo, it is advisable to fly there from Myitkyina.

GETTING AROUND

BY AIR

Domestic air routes are now served by six carriers. Myanma Airways (www.maiair. com) the national carrier, which offers the cheapest tickets, flies to many of the country's 60 airstrips. The 1990s saw two newcomers, Air Mandalay (www. airmandalay.com) and Yangon Airways (www.yangonair.com). These airlines are both joint ventures with overseas investors. They fly modern planes, with well-trained crews and, unlike their competitor, adhere to their published schedules. Even newer on the block are three privately owned airlines, Air Bagan (www. airbagan.com), Asian Wings (www.asianwingsair.com) and Air KBZ (www.airkbz. com)—all three fly to the main destinations as well a few lesser known airfields. None of these airlines own very many planes so one of the problems of the huge influx of visitors to Myanmar is the difficulty of securing a seat on a domestic plane.

BY TRAIN

Travelling by train is an excellent and enjoyable way to see the country, if speed and luxury are not an issue. The Yangon to Mandalay Express is supposed to take 15 hours but often runs late. The majority of the rolling stock is old though new Korean coaches have recently joined the stable—a few steam engines still function. Some of the coaches' shock-absorbers are so bad that when going over a particularly bumpy section of track you can find yourself on your neighbour's lap. However, this is all part of the adventure. Several of the overnight trains have a few sleepers as well as quite comfortable reclining seats. During the day, at each of the many stations stops, hawkers board the train. They balance huge trays piled high with myriad hot and cold goodies, always decorated with a flower to appease the business *nat* (spirit). Delicious nuts, fresh bananas—some fat and pink-skinned—and of course the popular cheroots and cigars can be bought. The hawkers walk along the train, loud shouts advertising their wares.

The early section of the journey on the 'up' train from Yangon to Mandalay, as it is still charmingly called, (the return, Mandalay to Yangon is of course, the 'down' train) travels through the beautiful and lush central plateau. From the train window, mile upon mile of rice paddies, peppered with pagodas large and small, as well as copses of mature trees, pass by. Perhaps the most beautiful month to make this journey is September. By then the rains have more or less finished, much of the paddy is flooded, the pagodas' reflections shimmer in the water and groups of farmers work the enclosures. The air is clear and fresh so the colour quality is excellent. For a photographer the conditions are perfect. April, on the other hand, during the Water Festival, is not the time for a photographer to be on the train. Travel Ordinary Class and the majority of carriages have no glass in the windows. Even the glass in the windows of the Upper Class carriages is no protection—whenever someone opens a window, even a fraction, in comes the water. It does not seem to matter which window it comes through, everyone in the carriage gets wet.

It is possible to get to most areas of Myanmar by train, but away from the main lines, service is erratic and very Spartan. Foreign visitors need to buy their tickets from the railway stations in the main towns. In Yangon go to the Foreigner Ticket Centre just inside the entrance of the fine station building. With its grand old-style Burmese roofs, reminiscent of the Mandalay Palaces, it is situated in the heart of the city. For the traveller who wants something different it is possible to hire a special coach dating from pre-war days, which is then hitched to a train running either the Yangon/Mandalay line or even Thazi to the old hill station of Kalaw and down to Shwenyaung, around ten kilometres from Inle Lake. This is a stunning journey as the train steadily climbs up from Thazi through the teak-clad hills on to the high plateau of the Shan States. The coach, with its salon and dining room, comes with its own private cook. During the evening it parks in a siding so dinner can be served without the accompanying bumps of the track.

BY ROAD

In recent years several coach companies have sprung up. They offer comfortable, air-conditioned buses to the main destinations. The journey to Mandalay certainly will be faster than taking the train—one firm advertises 'First-aid service and travel rugs provided'. Ask a travel agent to book a seat on a coach run by a reliable company.

For individual travellers it is possible to hire a car or a van with a driver. Be sure to establish the price with the driver before you begin the trip, including whether it includes the cost of fuel. Your hotel or travel agency should be able to direct you to a reputable car rental company. Many of the taxi drivers who base themselves outside hotels are also available for day trips. As the roads are so bumpy check the state of the tyres—not forgetting the spare—before you start your journey. Foreigners can drive in Myanmar on an international licence but it is not advisable because traffic laws put the onus of blame on the person in charge of the vehicle in the event of an accident. There is no longer petrol rationing in Myanmar and in recent years chains of service stations run by private companies have opened throughout the country.

Fairly good quality bicycles are now available in the main tourist towns. An especially good place to cycle around is Bagan—early-morning or mid-afternoon onwards thus avoiding the heat of day—a perfect way to visit the stunning pagodas.

A pair of half-lion, half-griffin chinthes stand guard at the Mingun jetty on the banks of the Ayeyarwady River. Legend has it that these mythical beasts rescued a princess from the nats (spirit gods), who had stolen her and hidden her in the forest. Her distraught father, the king, tried to find her, without success. Years later, the princess was returned home by a lioness. Since then the lioness, (which during the course of centuries metamorphosed into the chinthe), has become the emblem of 'protecting watchfulness'

Age is highly respected in Myanmar. This elderly couple continue to live in the family unit, contributing their wisdom and guiding the family's path along the Middle Way—the avoidance of extremes, the cultivation of tranquillity, the acceptance of karma

The river cruiser The Road to Mandalay is an extremely luxurious craft which mainly sails between Bagan and Mandalay. A perfect, if pricey, way to enjoy the river as described by the painter, R Talbot Kelly, in 1909. 'In general the scene is one of placid beauty... between its banks the Irrawaddy sweeps in splendid curves, producing an ever-growing sense of bigness and dignity. Some of its reaches are very wide, and have more the appearance of an inland lake than a river.'

A group waits on the banks of the Ayeyarwady River for a boat to arrive. As the vessel lies alongside, goods will be hastily piled on to the carts

RIVER TRANSPORT

Another calm and pleasurable way to travel within Myanmar is on the various rivers and canals. A variety of passenger boats sail on Myanmar's major river, the Ayeyarwady, (formerly known as the Irrawaddy) which is navigable for much of the length of the country. This great river has played a crucial role in Myanmar's development (see page 36). Adventurous and hardy travellers should board the local ferry in Mandalay (at the Mingun Pier) and sail downstream to Bagan. When you arrive at the required boarding time of 4am—the boat will sail at 5am—there is already much activity going on. Huge sacks of grain or cement are being carried up the slippery gangplank by porters, their *longyis* hitched up and tucked in at the waist. Once on board, secure an area of floor on the upper deck, or, for a little more comfort book the cabin in the prow of the boat. A clanging bell announces the boat's departure as it sets sail downstream. As dawn breaks the vessel gently glides by Sagaing where a vast number of pagodas, still blurry silhouettes, begin to take form. The long day's gentle sail is punctuated by stops. A group of people stand on the river bank and suddenly the engine groans and the boat veers towards the shore. Ropes are thrown and caught, wooden gang planks are thrown down. People nimbly negotiate the gangplank, slippery in a second, some with babies strapped to their backs, some balancing baskets full of produce on their heads. If the journey is made during the dry season, a sailor with a long bamboo pole will stand on the prow of the ship watching out for sandbanks. The sand constantly shifts throughout the year, so the captains cannot rely on charts. Occasionally the sandbank spotter will stick his pole in the water to help the boat around a bank. This desultory journey should take 12 hours but can take many more. There is plenty of food on hand. On the upper deck you can buy freshly cooked curry—the chickens walk on at one stop and are in the pot soon after. Also a steady stream of hawkers selling titbits get on and off the boat. It is possible for the enthusiastic traveller to continue the journey further downstream for two days to Pyay (formerly Prome) or even for four days as far as Yangon.

Nowadays there are several speedier and much more luxurious ways to make the same and many other river journeys. At the bottom of this scale on the Mandalay to Bagan run are several local 'tourist' boats. The upper deck of a newish local boat is reserved for tourists, and is either furnished with comfortable rattan chairs or airline-style seating. Whichever the seating, the most pleasurable way to spend the early and late part of the journey is out in the open-air on the spacious top deck. Chairs are provided and when the midday sun beats down retreat back down below. The boats make fewer stops along the way, so the journey is faster than on the regular ferry and, unless the sandbanks intervene, the schedule is more reliable—however much of the local colour is missing. Then there are the luxury cruisers (see page 246). Without doubt the most stunning of these is *The Road to Mandalay*. Run by the Orient-Express Hotels group, this river steamer was built in 1964 to sail on the Rhine. Bought by the present owners in 1994 and transported to Myanmar, she has been totally refitted and is a delight to behold. Great care has been taken in the decoration to incorporate the best of Burmese handicrafts: table lamps and wall brackets made of lacquer, glass screens engraved with the *pitakatia* design of an entrance to a Bagan temple. The walls are hung with old prints of Myanmar, architectural drawings of the Bagan monuments and so on, and the overall result is extremely stylish. The cabins are grand deluxe, and include satellite television and in-house video channels. Trips on this cruiser are sold as three-day packages, incorporating a day's sightseeing either end of the river journey—a trip for those prepared to dig deep into their pockets. The other cruisers, the *Irrawaddy Princess* and the *M/V Pandaw* (a new vessel operated by the Irrawaddy Flotilla Company), operate a two-day Bagan to Mandalay service, a luxurious alternative to the standard ferry boats. Done in the style of the First Class deck of a 1920s flotilla vessel, the accommodations are finished in teak and brass. With only 16 cabins, the *M/V Pandaw* offers an intimate travel experience. It has an impressive private collection of art and antiques, as well as a number of artefacts and photographs telling the 140-year history of the Irrawaddy Flotilla Company. Its traditional riverboat design means the *M/V Pandaw* is capable of reaching remote parts of the river inaccessible to other boats. The Irrawaddy Flotilla Company also offers a selection of Expedition Cruises going as far downstream as Pyay and as far upstream as Bhamo, near the Burmese-Chinese border. Cruises along Myanmar's other great river, the Chindwin, are also on offer. The *M/V Pandaw* is available at certain weeks in the year for special charters.

VISAS

Most visitors to Myanmar must obtain a visa prior to departure for Yangon. There are three types of visa available: Tourist, Business and the Religious/Meditation visa all three are valid for a single entry, four-week visit. These are obtained at any Myanmar embassy or consulate. In mid-2012 it became possible to obtain a Business visa on arrival at Yangon Airport with the validity of 70 days.

Visa on arrival for tourists: At the time of going to press tourists may enter the country at Yangon Airport provided they meet the required criteria, please see www.mip.gov.mm and also www.mofa.mm.

CUSTOMS AND FOREIGN EXCHANGE

Myanmar's customs regulations and procedures are no longer as stringent as they once were. But you still need to declare valuables and money over the value of US$2,000 on arrival at the airport. A simple customs declaration form is handed out on the incoming plane and the customs section of the arrival is a matter of a stamp on the form. You also need to present your customs form on departure if valuables have been declared, also make sure you have your departure card signed ready for inspection. Twelve major currencies are accepted but to date credit cards can only be used to settle bills in some major hotels and they need four or five day's notice. However, Visa said in August 2012 it was taking steps to entering the Myanmar market and MasterCard signed an agreement with a Myanmar bank the following month.

The business of changing money in Myanmar which has always been complicated and a little furtive is now easy. In April 2012 the Myanmar Central Bank announced a 'managed' flotation of the local currency the kyat, thus getting rid of the previous system of two exchange rates one official and one black-market. So all hotels and most guesthouses will change US dollars for the local kyats at the current rate. There are counters at most private banks (and in the arrivals lounge at Yangon Airport) where US$, euros and some other currencies can be changed into kyats. Be warned that if your dollars are not crisp, new and unfolded they will not be accepted. All very strange when you see the scruffy state

April is the month that the fragrant magnolia flowers are in abundance. As one approaches the row of flower stalls, a wall of heady perfume greets the prospective buyer. These exquisite little flowers, also much loved by the Chinese, are a favourite hair decoration, as well as being taken to the pagodas and bottled as a perfume

of the kyats that are given in exchange for the crisp dollars—but it is essential to travel with a good **amount** of fresh clean US dollars. This necessity will cease of course once credit cards are in use again and that is dependent on more USA sanctions being dropped. The export of Buddha images, or any large antiques such as lacquered screens and chests, generally requires a special licence; lacking this, such items are usually confiscated at the airport, without compensation. Foreign SIM cards do not work in Myanmar but at Yangon Airport on exiting the Customs Hall there is desk where it is possible to hire a local SIM card—these work all over the country. Or it is possible to buy a local SIM card downtown outside the Telegraph Office a grand colonial building on Phayre Street.

A passenger negotiates the slippery gangplank after Cloud Vessel *has moored on a mud bank at one of its numerous ports of call along the Ayeyarwady. The river is navigable from Pathein on the coast to Bhamo 1,610 kilometres (1,000 miles) to the north*

HEALTH

Yellow fever is the only required vaccination, and only if you are coming from an infected area. However, world health authorities recommend that travellers have the following vaccinations: typhoid, tetanus-diptheria, hepatitis A, measles, mumps, rubella and a polio booster. Malaria can be a problem anywhere in Southeast Asia, and Myanmar is no exception. The deadly strain of malaria is present and taking anti-malarial precautions is advisable. The recommended drug is constantly changing, so check with a tropical diseases specialist for the latest anti-malarial drug suitable for Myanmar. Avoid getting bitten by mosquitoes by using mosquito repellents and covering up at times when the insects are biting. As in all health matters pertaining to your trip, consult a doctor. The dry, dusty conditions of winter and the early spring months can cause eye irritation. Eye drops are a must during this time of year. Aspirin, antibiotics, mosquito repellent and other first-aid items should also be packed, as they may not be readily available locally.

The one thing to be very careful about, especially up country, is water. Never drink from the wayside clay water pots which are everywhere for thirsty travellers—visitors' antibodies will not be able to cope. Always drink bottled water, making sure the cap is still sealed, or of course boiled water. Many of the soft drinks are good—go for the carbonated ones, which are safer. Avoid ice in drinks unless you are in one of the big hotels, where it should be fine. Do not be tempted by succulent-looking portions of cut fruit in the market. Just buy a whole melon, or orange. On the food question, stir-fried dishes that are cooked to order are safer than curries, which could have been sitting around for some time. Sometimes the eating utensils look a little grubby, so travel with some tissues and give the bowls and spoon and fork a wipe—the locals do, so no one will be offended.

CLIMATE AND CLOTHING

Myanmar's climate can be divided roughly into three seasons: the cool and dry season, from November to March (the best time to visit); the hot and dry season, from March to May (called 'summer'); and the rainy season, from May to October. These seasons overlay three climatic zones. The country lies mainly within the tropics; the Tropic of Cancer runs between Bhamo and Lashio some 160 kilometres (100 miles) north of Mandalay. The delta area supports a typical hot, humid, tropical climate, with an average rainfall of 254 centimetres (100 inches) per year and temperatures reaching around 33°C (90°F) all year round. On the Shan Plateau to the north-east, temperatures drop during the cool season (November to February) to around or below freezing at night. Generally temperatures during the cool and dry season rarely exceed 29°C (85°F) during the day, and average a pleasant 16°C (61°F) at night. The higher elevations of Pyin Oo Lwin (formerly Maymyo) and Taunggyi keep these areas considerably cooler, and hill nights can be freezing: warm clothing should be packed if visiting around December. Otherwise, light cotton or linen clothing is recommended. Some modern synthetic fabrics are also excellent: they breathe well, drip dry more quickly than cotton and do not wrinkle. When visiting religious sites a certain dress code must be adhered to, and skirts must not be too short or tops too skimpy. In some pagodas, such as the Shwedagon in Yangon, a visitor who is thought to be improperly dressed will be lent a *longyi*—and given a lesson on how to tie it.

During the rainy season, an umbrella will come in handy; it is too hot for any other rainwear. Formal attire will merely take up room in your suitcase—leave it at home (or in Bangkok). During the hot and dry season, temperatures in Yangon reach 41°C (105°F), and in Bagan daytime highs may soar to a dangerous 49°C (120°F). Light clothing, sunglasses, a hat, sunscreen, and a water flask are recommended. Last but not least, pack a pair of comfortable walking shoes which you can slip on and off easily—in Myanmar one should always remove one's shoes before entering a temple or private home.

The popular belief is that the best time to visit Myanmar is from November through to February in the cool season. But all the seasons have their charm— least of all perhaps the rainy season. The months following the rainy season, September to November, are magical. Everywhere is fresh and green, the colours have not yet been burned off and the dramatic cloud formations on the horizon continually disperse and reform. At the other end of the spectrum, in March to May, the landscape is parched and dominated by browns and oranges. In Yangon and Bagan it is stiflingly hot in the middle of the day, and the red brick pagodas radiate incredible heat, even at sunset. A fun time to visit is during the Water Festival (around mid-April). Just as the heat becomes too much, some obliging soul is bound to empty a bucket of water over you. Water is never thrown at a photographer when taking a picture, they just line up behind, buckets to the ready—the moment the camera is down, over goes the water.

MONTHLY TEMPERATURES AT MANDALAY

| | Temperature °F | | | Temperature °C | | | Precipitation | |
| | Highest recorded | Average daily | Lowest recorded | Highest recorded | Average daily | Lowest recorded | Average monthly | |
		max.	min.			max.	min.	in	mm
J	91	82	55	45	33	28	13	7	0.1	3
F	99	88	59	47	37	31	15	8	0.1	3
M	108	97	66	54	42	36	19	12	0.2	5
A	110	101	77	64	43	38	25	18	1.2	31
M	111	98	79	69	44	37	26	21	5.8	147
J	107	93	78	68	42	34	26	20	6.3	160
J	106	93	78	72	41	34	26	22	2.7	69
A	101	92	77	71	38	33	25	22	4.1	104
S	103	91	76	69	39	33	24	21	5.4	137
O	102	89	73	62	39	32	23	17	4.3	109
N	98	85	66	56	37	29	19	13	2.0	51
D	90	80	57	44	32	27	14	7	0.4	10

A MEETING IN RANGOON

Josceline Dimbleby

" *T*he day after we arrived was my birthday. It started with a cup of green tea made with large leaves from high up in the mountains of the Shan States, far better than any I had tasted before, with no trace of bitterness. For breakfast we

were offered Burma's most famous dish, Mohingar—a fish broth with fat rice noodles, which have a mildly fermented taste. Almost everyone eats Mohingar for breakfast and it is also served in homes, restaurants and from street stalls throughout the day and evening, with variations. River, lake or seawater fish— all of which are excellent in Burma—are added to the noodles and broth, with lemon grass, garlic, ginger, shrimp paste, fried onions, hard-boiled eggs, gourd fritters, lentil powder, coriander leaves and other leafy herbs. It is a comforting dish at any time.

I had an introduction to a Burmese authoress, Daw Mi Mi Khaing, who had published a book on cooking and entertaining 'In the Burmese Way'. Mi Mi Khaing was now old and almost blind but nevertheless invited us to dinner at her house in Rangoon. During the summer she lived in the cooler Shan States with her husband Sao Sai Mong, a Shan prince said to be charming and elegant. It was winter now,

though to us Rangoon felt hot and humid, Daw Mi Mi welcomed us into her small colonial house. She was petite and still had black hair, a sharp intelligence and real panache. She talked about Burmese food and family customs, and explained that rice is the fundamental part of every meal; other dishes are to make it palatable and varied.

The rice Daw Mi Mi served that evening was cooked in coconut milk with fried onions. A tender duck curry made in the Burmese way with fish sauce and lots of garlic and onions was served with it. We also had our first taste of butterfish; smeared with coconut cream, chopped ginger and spices, then steamed in banana leaves, it was real winner. There were some excellent Burmese salads too: intensely sweet little tomatoes with a chopped roasted peanut dressing: smoky grilled aubergine mashed with chopped raw onion and green peppers; grated green papaya with lime; and a delicious white seaweed salad. Pickled tea leaves featured in a famous salad, and a pressed catfish and tamarind relish was intriguing too. Somehow we still had room for a rich semolina pudding made with creamy coconut milk and topped with crunchy poppy seeds. Finally, as at most Burmese meals, we ended by eating lumps of palm sugar, like strong-flavoured fudge, which is said to help the digestion.

Excerpt from "Orchards in the Oasis, Recipes, Travels & Memories"
Quadrille Publishing 2010

MONTHLY TEMPERATURES AT YANGON

	Temperature °F			Temperature °C			Precipitation	
	Highest recorded	Average daily	Lowest recorded	Highest recorded	Average daily	Lowest recorded	Average monthly	
		max.	min.		max.	min.		in	mm
J	100	89	65	55	38	32	18	13	0.1	3
F	101	92	67	56	38	33	19	13	0.2	5
M	103	96	71	61	39	36	22	16	0.3	8
A	106	97	76	68	41	36	24	20	2.0	51
M	105	92	77	69	41	33	25	21	12.1	307
J	98	86	76	71	37	30	24	22	18.9	480
J	93	85	76	70	34	29	24	21	22.9	582
A	93	85	76	68	34	29	24	20	20.8	528
S	94	86	76	72	34	30	24	22	15.5	394
O	95	88	76	71	35	31	24	22	7.1	180
N	95	88	73	61	35	31	23	16	2.7	69
D	96	88	67	55	36	31	19	13	0.4	10

FOOD

Burmese cuisine can be delicious: *mohingha*, the traditional breakfast, *ohn no khaukswe* and *lapet* rate with some of Asia's best dishes. For a short-term visitor to Myanmar, it used to be difficult to sample the real thing with most restaurants serving Chinese food and the hotels British Raj-style curries. However nowadays the five-star hotels in the major tourist destinations have sensibly included some local dishes on their menus. The Traders Hotel in Yangon, for example, serves first-rate *mohingha* along with other Asian fare for breakfast. All over the country now there are many restaurants to choose from and many of those serve delicious local food.

The Burmese take their food seriously. Authoress Mi Mi Khaing explains, 'Burmese food is for eating mainly just before morning's pleasantness is lost to the heat of noon, and again as the cool of evening falls. Ideally, you should, minutes before eating, have a quick pouring bath, put on clean clothes, and go straight to table.'

A breakfast of *mohingha* is a pleasure indeed; a gentle aroma of banana stem and lemon grass rises from a bowl of steaming fish soup and rice noodles, topped by coriander leaf, fried garlic, chilli powder, fried corn crackers and a squeeze of lime, washed down with Burmese tea. *Ohn no khaukswe*, the other 'national' dish, is again a noodle and soup affair—in Western terminology it might be termed a casserole, for there are chicken chunks in the soup. This time the noodles are of wheat, and the soup is strongly flavoured with coconut.

The pickled tea leaf the Burmese call *lapet* is eaten at all times of day, perhaps as the finale to a rich dinner or when visitors arrive unexpectedly. On such occasions a drink of tea and the lacquer box containing *lapet* will be produced. Inside the box are different compartments filled with *lapet*, fried garlic, toasted sesame seeds, fried broad bean seeds and salt. *Lapet* is bought ready-prepared in the market, then kneaded with a little sesame oil at home. It should be eaten thus: 'Take a pinch of each of two or three things together with *lapet*, between tips of three fingers only. In between, wipe fingers and sip tea. Wash fingers only at the end. This is the connoisseur's way.' The taste is refreshing and good, though quite sharp. Those who like spinach salad will be immediate converts.

With Myanmar's abundant supply of fruit and vegetables, salad is served with each meal. Seasonal ingredients are tossed in sesame oil, with crispy nuts and coriander added. In spring it is *marian* (*mayan thi*) season. This is a small green and mauve fruit which resembles an unripe walnut. Its piquant flavour in a salad is a winner.

Of all the dishes the Western palate will sample, the Burmese speciality least likely to appeal is *ngapi*. 'The smell of *ngapi*,' remarked the by no means over-sensitive Sir George Scott, 'is certainly not charming to an uneducated nose.' *Ngapi* is a relish which can accompany any dish. There are three distinct types: *ngapi gaung*, consisting of a whole fish pressed, dried and later eaten baked; *ngapi seinsa*, made from the squeezed and fermented juices of shrimp, which is stored in earthenware pots, not dissimilar to anchovy paste; and third and most pungent, *ngapi yecho* (*taungtha*). This is made from small fish which are left uncleaned in the sun for a day or two ('by which time their condition is better imagined than closely investigated'), then salted, pounded and stored in clay pots.

If you are interested in sampling Burmese fare, ask your hotel or guesthouse for local specialities or, even better, try some of the street restaurants. Festivals always provide good hunting for *mohingha*. A few sensible precautions are necessary: make sure the food is cooked freshly or is steaming hot; wash the spoon, fork and cup with the hot tea provided (you will see the locals do it); never drink tap water and never have a drink with ice in it or eat a piece of already cut fruit or vegetable. Follow these tips and adventurous eating in Myanmar can be a source of true serendipity.

SHOPPING

Shopping in Myanmar offers many rewards and objects appealing to the taste of foreign visitors have become more plentiful. It is now much easier to go home laden with some lovely old lacquer pieces, such as a collection of beautifully carved wooden panels. Perhaps the advent of the new hotels has helped this development. The interior designers employed by the hoteliers were quick to see the potential of adapting Burmese handicrafts to modern tastes. They employed local lacquer factories to make lacquer bowls, which they could fill with massive flower arrangements, and lacquer vases, which were turned into lamps. As a result some lacquer stores now carry these products. A forerunner in this new taste was Elephant House, now in a lovely old colonial house at 6, Inya Road, Yangon. Tel (95-1) 524 430. This shop offers a feast of delights and is not to be missed. Not only have they adapted designs, many of which are exclusive to them, but they have also introduced new colours to the lacquer—a brilliant blue or green for instance. Their furniture, both lacquer and bamboo, is elegant and well made. A few of the beautiful antique pieces carry a tantalizing 'not for sale' sticker—beware, a little like a menu with no prices, that means the object will be very expensive but can be bought. They will also arrange for shipping to any destination. Once finished with the agony of decision making, the exhausted shopper can flop into a cab and drive the short distance to the sister restaurant

LACQUERWARE

Bagan, formerly Pagan, is the centre of Myanmar's lacquer industry and has been producing fine lacquerware since the time of King Anawrahta. It is not clear whether the king imported the craft from Nanzhao, which he visited in an attempt to acquire a tooth of the Buddha, or whether it was brought north from Pegu (now known as Bago) by the conquered Mon artisans whom he re-settled in Bagan. The majority of these lacquer articles are for domestic use, such as betel boxes, cosmetics boxes, and drinking cups. Raw black lacquer is tapped from the *thitsi* tree, a variety of *sumac*, which comes in the main from northern Myanmar. Traditionally the frame is woven in bamboo wickerwork or a horsehair mix, though today wooden bases are used for many articles such as trays and cigarette boxes, as this makes them cheaper to produce and more

durable. On the wicker base a coat of lacquer is applied and left to dry in a cool, airy place—the sun produces blisters—for several days. After a couple of days, when the lacquer is quite hard, it is evenly covered with a paste called *thayo*. *Thayo* is made either from finely ground bone ash and paddy husk, burned and strained through a cloth, or, for articles for everyday use, clay and peanut husk. When this coating has dried, the lacquer item is put on a hand lathe and polished, using ash or a bamboo strip. This whole process is repeated several times. Then the foreground colour is added. On the cheaper pieces the decorations (traditional designs predominate) are simply painted on. The more expensive ones are engraved with a tool called a *kauk*. Normally, three colours are used, each representing several layers and a great deal of time and effort.

Raw lacquer has a variety of other uses. When spread over marble or clay it enables gold leaf to stick (part of the early morning ablutions of the Mahamuni Image in Mandalay is to coat the Buddha with a thin film of lacquer—see page 157). It is also used to waterproof boats and sometimes umbrellas. There are several lacquer trade schools in Bagan and the main street is filled with lacquer shops. One can just go in to the backs of shops to watch master craftsmen and their apprentices busily applying these time-honoured methods.

A young lacquer apprentice learns her trade in the artisan guilds.
A group of young men and women will sit together, under the watchful eye of
the master, as they attempt the simple patterns on lacquer bowls

Green Elephant Restaurant at 33 Thrimingalar (Attia Road). Tel 537 706, another lovely old house with airey terraces to sit and enjoy the stylist décor and the excellent Burmese food (see page 273). To complement the delicious food they serve a Myanmar grown wine, Aythaya which is grown on the slopes of the Taunggyi Mountains in the Shan State. They produce a selection of white, red and rosé wines all very palatable.

The same company operates the boutiques in the Governor's Residence and New World Hotels as well as the Elephant House Rattan Factory (Minnander Road/Sein Kyaw Road, Thaketa, Yangon, tel (95-1) 579 709 (office) and 579 697 (factory), fax (95-1) 533 706. A visit to this factory, around 30 minutes from central Yangon on the road to Thanlyin is well worth while. In a 90-metre- (300-foot-) long hangar the visitor sees the raw rattan being stripped and made ready to weave at one end, with the finished products, which range from lacquer trays to large wicker sofas, being loaded into a container at the other. Wander around the factory and watch groups of girls as they nimbly plait the rattan into the required shape. Two ladies sit back to back on a sofa while they weave the arms of that sofa. Others apply and polish the lacquer objects, or pile finished woven trays into a tower so the varnish can dry. For those who want to take away a souvenir there is an 'export shop' on the premises.

An irresistible shop is J's Irrawaddy Dream now moved from its original showroom in a charming wooden annex beside a colonial house set in the middle of the embassy district, the most desirable residential quarter in Yangon. The shop is now to be found in the annex of the Strand Hotel (see page 123)—though rumour has it that all the shops in the Strand annexe are soon to move as the hotel expands. The store's enterprising owners have persuaded several Karen and Chin ladies to come to Yangon, where they weave exclusive fabrics for the shop. The result is a collection of beautiful silk scarves, bedspreads and shawls in breathtaking colours. The Karen weaver uses traditional methods and sits on the floor to operate the wooden loom. A large leather band around her back acts as a sort of harness and is attached to the loom.

The shop sells a wide range of garments. Some of the ethnic clothes, such as the wrap-around Shan trousers, have been modified so that they fit the Western figure. There are also a host of knick-knacks including fun silver jewellery and pretty woven bags.

A fun new handicraft shop Loft is in a large wonderful space above the Monsoon Restaurant (see page 273), a loft indeed in downtown Yangon on 85–87 Theinbyu Road. Their different and chic collection of life-style objects and jewellery are all made by people suffering from AIDS with the profits being donated to Helping Hands www.helpinghandsyangon.wordpress.com. Your purchases will be wrapped in hand-made paper, your package decorated with little Burmese papier mâché owls for good luck.

For the shopper in search of antiques there are many shops around the country, so ask your guide or hotel for advice. In Yangon visit the well established, slightly eccentric Madame Thair (649 Myakan Tha Lane, 5 1/2 Mile, Pyay Road, Yangon, tel (95-1) 526 140). Her original shop was in the centre of town, up a steep flight of stairs. The room was overflowing with lovely things, every surface covered. Lacquer baskets hung from the ceiling like sides of Parma ham, beautiful Buddha images occupied prominent places among the jumble. Her present shop in her home still has a lot of the charm and many desirable objects. For those looking for antique silver and fabrics, Daw Mya Mya Sein's store (11 Thirizeyar Street, Bauk Taw, Yankin Township, Yangon, tel (95-1) 542 505) is the place to shop. Another long established outlet is Augustine's Antique Shop (33, Thirimingalar Street, Kamayut, Yangon. Tel (95-1) 504 290, e-mail: nbawga@ myanmar.com.mm, a large garage alongside a house is crammed with objects. Patience is needed to sift through and find the good things. For shoppers hunting for Karen rice drums, Augustine's often has a good selection and at competitive prices—shipping can be arranged. This is a very popular place with Yangon foreign residents as well as dealers. Opening hours are strange: Monday to Friday, 5.30pm–8pm; Saturday and Sunday, 2pm–8pm.

Often a tourist's first foray in search of souvenirs, objêts d'art, antiques or other more substantial items will lead them to Yangon's Bogyoke Aung San Market (also known as **Scott's** market) located on Bogyoke Aung San Road, within walking distance of several of the big hotels in the middle of the city. There they will find an amazing collection of fascinating items: finely crafted mother-of-pearl; beautiful silks, lacquerware products of every description; bizarre knick-knacks dating from colonial times (some of which may be of considerable value to collectors back home); cigars; gold and silver jewellery; jade bracelets and many other interesting items. However, when one calculates a desired purchase price (always calculated in Myanmar kyats), one will probably discover that costs can vary from very cheap to outrageously high. Furthermore, many of the most desirable items like antiques or large lacquerware pieces, such as chests and screens, may not be taken or shipped out of the country (contrary, of course, to the merchant's assurances) without obtaining proper documentation—a complex and time-consuming process when dealing with small shops. Thorough searches at the airport upon departure are not unknown. Nevertheless, there are plenty of interesting products that make lovely (and legal) souvenirs.

In Yangon, some of the best-value items are tailor-made shirts and dresses. Buy the material at one of the many fabric stores in Bogyoke Aung San Market. The stall holder will direct you to a tailor in the market. Upon your return from up-country you will find a well-tailored garment and a bill that is almost embarrassingly cheap. If a woman buys a *longyi* length of fabric, it will be sewn up while you wait. (Both men's and women's *longyis* are a tube of fabric). Other exceptional bargains to be found include mother-of-pearl products and silver jewellery.

Do not miss the second-hand book shops in Yangon. The most famous perhaps is the Bagan Book House (100, 37th Street, Yangon, tel (95-1) 277 227) A tiny shop within walking distance of the Strand Hotel, it carries a very good selection of facsimile copies of 19th- and 20th-century books on Myanmar, and a wide range of old paperbacks catering to older tastes and those who forgot to pack some easy holiday reading. Also on offer is a selection of new coffee table tomes and architectural guides to the sites of Myanmar. For the book lover Monument Books at 150 Dhamazedi Road is a must. This two-storey shop is really well stocked with new and old English language books of all sorts, very well displayed and easy to find your way around. Upstairs along with a toy section and architectural books is an inviting café, an area to sit and browse through your purchases. They also have a branch in Mandalay on 26th Street, the road which runs along the south side of the Palace wall. Yangon also boasts another good book shop Myanmar Book Centre at 55 Baho Road, corner of Baho and Ahlone roads (95-1) 221 271. It is a family affair started by a well-known historian and now run by his son; they carry a particularly good selection of historical books on Myanmar.

Elsewhere in the country, Bagan is the best place to buy lacquerware products. The fun thing about buying lacquer in Bagan, as opposed to Yangon, is that you can watch the pieces being made. The showroom and workshop of U Ba Nyein is one of the best to patronize, both in terms of quality and prices. Found in New Bagan (Main Road, Bagan Myothit, tel Bagan 061 65056 ubnyein@gmail.com) this family-run business welcomes visitors with a cup of green tea. The workshop is behind a well-stocked showroom. Watch the men and women inscribing the intricate patterns on to the lacquered piece—this is where many of the pieces for the Elephant House in Yangon are made—their 'exclusive' range is not for sale. Golden Cuckoo (Myinkaba Village, Bagan, tel 061 65156 goldencuckoo.bagan@ hotmail.com) is another good shop to visit as they have a large collection of antique lacquer pieces, as well as the new ones.

Mandalay is where the intricately woven and lavishly adorned tapestries known as *kalagas* are produced. To see them being created visit Aung Nan's Myanmar Handicrafts Workshop (97–99, Sagaing By-Pass Road, Pyitawthar Quarter, Mandalay, tel (95-2) 70 145). The enormous mat shed with a nice brick floor is a veritable Aladdin's cave. Suspended from the ceiling are elaborately carved wooden puppets dressed in a variety of costumes; others are piled into huge baskets on the floor. A collection of antique *kalagas* are placed beside some old lacquerware, or perhaps a Burmese musical instrument. At one side of the mat shed, in the good light, groups of girls sit hunched over a piece of embroidery stretched over a frame. They use old sequins and thread to create the intricately embroidered *kalagas*; it will take six girls some 20 days to finish a medium-sized piece.

To get an idea of the diversity of handicrafts produced in Myanmar, it is worth visiting the official exports showroom known as the Myanma Export-Import Co-operative Syndicate, located in Yangon at 185–7 Pansodan Street. Myanmar produces some of the world's most valuable precious stones and each year holds an International Gem Emporium attracting gem dealers from all over the world, this is now held in the new capital Nay Pyi Taw. So for those interested in precious stones, a visit should be made to the Museum Gem Mart at 12a Kaba Aye Pagoda Road, this a collection of licensed jewellery shops, Myanma Gem Centre is a good one to visit. Two other reliable and well-regarded shops are Elegant Gems at 48 New University Avenue Road. Tel (95-1) 556 009 and MK Gems, 50 Pyay Road 6.5 miles, Hlaing Township. Tel (95-1) 538 643.

Unfortunately the possibility of a different kind of shopping is no longer available as the Na-Gar Glass factory (152, Yawgi Kyaung Street, Hlaing Township, Yangon, tel (95-1) 526 053) has been closed though worth visiting the site. At the end of the lane is a small building which is the showroom and shop, the main room dominated by a 1943 Vauxhall piled high inside with old pieces of glass. The path from the showroom to the workshop leads through what the manager calls a 'glass garden'. All the glass is made from recycled glass and this garden is the open-air storage place. The way that the baskets bursting with discarded coloured glass have sunk and arranged themselves does indeed resemble an eccentric, architectural garden. Under a mat shed stands a group of vast vats which contain molten glass. The artisan collects a blob of boiling glass and blows and shapes it into the required shape, cutting here and there. It is a very nimble and fascinating process to watch.

Many art galleries have sprung up in recent years showing both contemporary and old paintings by local artists. Atmospheric water colours of rural scenes are fine mementos of this beautiful country. Worth visiting are Trish Gallery in Excellent Condominium, Min Kyaung Street, also Pansodan Gallery, 286 Pansodan Street (opp Traders Hotel) and the River Gallery in the Strand Hotel.

Shopping in Myanmar is a diverse and exciting pastime, far removed from the shopping malls of much of the rest of Asia. Pleasant rewards are in store for the determined treasure hunter, who is more likely to find an extraordinary object tucked away in the corner of a shop in Myanmar than anywhere else in the region. Added to this is the fascinating spectacle of watching many of the objects being crafted.

For the moment 'volume' shopping is difficult as there are no credit card facilities. The sooner that credit cards are accepted and overseas transfers are allowed the better because not being able to use or arrange them is a huge inconvenience for both shop owners and visitors.

For visiting business people a very comprehensive service, including translation services and residential search is offered by recently-opened Hintha Business Centres, located very close to the new Hilton Yangon, at 608 Merchant Street. www.hinthabusinesscentres.com

And don't be put-off by the lively bustle on Merchant Street, this is an area where numerous short-haul buses pick up and deposit commuters.

MAJOR FESTIVALS

March/April (Tagu) Tagu is the month when Thingyan, the Water Festival, is celebrated. It marks the visit to earth of Thagyamin, King of the Nats, and the start of the Burmese New Year. The Shwedagon Temple festival also takes place at this time.

April/May (Kason) At the full moon the birth, enlightenment and attainment of Nirvana of Gautama Buddha is celebrated.

June/July (Waso) The full moon heralds the start of the three-month Buddhist Lent.

August/September (Tawthalin) This is the month of boat races, including the lavish festival on Inle Lake.

September/October (Thadingyut) The full moon of Thadingyut marks the end of Buddhist Lent and Gautama Buddha's return to earth. His return is celebrated by the Festival of Lights. For three days Myanmar is illuminated by millions of candles and lamps and a festive air prevails.

October/November (Tazaungmon) During Tazaungmon the Weaving Festival is held. Throughout the night of the full moon the 'clack-clack' of the looms of unmarried girls reverberates around pagoda precincts. They are competing to weave new robes for the monks. If in Myanmar during this festival, try and visit the Shwedagon Pagoda where the beauty and romance of this scene is paramount.

November/December (Nadaw) Nadaw is the month of *nat* festivals.

December/January (Pyatho) During Pyatho the majority of local pagoda festivals are celebrated.

January/February (Tabodwe) Tabodwe is the time of the Harvest Festival (Htamane).

YANGON (RANGOON)

Myanmar's former capital, home to some five million people, is a city of style and dilapidated grandeur. For as long as they survive, the broad, leafy boulevards and slightly pompous architecture will recall the serene confidence of the British Raj of the mid-19th century.

Strolling through Yangon is both agreeable and safe—the main hazard being yawning holes in the pavements—although the worst of these have now been re-laid. However, unlike Noel Coward's mad dogs and Englishmen, you should avoid wandering around during the noon hours as it can be extremely hot.

Yangon bustles—if bustle is the word—gently. One rarely sees anyone pick up their *longyi* and run for a bus: there is always another not far behind. In recent years Yangon's traffic has taken on a different look. No longer do the majority of vehicles date from the 1950s. A recent lifting of restrictions on vehicle imports has resulted in an influx of second-hand cars, almost all of which are Japanese-made sedans, though the occasional late-model Mercedes glides by. Most of the buses and trucks also originated from Japan, though some are from China.

Little markets and food stalls are everywhere. At a busy intersection a man with a bird cage squats under a large tree. People stop to buy a bird and, instead of taking it home, let it free in order to gain some merit. Around another corner sits the proprietor of a thriving typing business, tapping away at an ancient machine. There are marvellous book shops, a daily open-air book market (in southern Pansodan Street), and antique and curio shops to browse.

Yangon is built on a spit of land surrounded on three sides by water. To the west and south the city is bounded by the Hlaing and Yangon rivers, which flow out of the Ayeyarwady and, 32 kilometres (20 miles) south of the city, into the Gulf of Mottama (formerly Gulf of Martaban) to the east of the main Ayeyarwady delta. On the east side of the city is the Pazundaung Creek.

In November 2005 Yangon ceased to be the country's capital and the government transferred all their offices north to the newly built capital of Nay Pyi Taw, thus leaving empty many of the fine colonial buildings. Yangon is the only important city in Asia which boasts such a stock of 19th century buildings. Understandably the present government realizes that to retain and maintain these buildings could be a big tourist draw and therefore money-earner, but they also wish to retain the city as a living breathing entity. To that end the Yangon Heritage Trust (see page 131) has been set up with 187 buildings listed for protection. Once a survey has been produced, discussed and approved by the government it will be decided how and which buildings are to be renovated.

Of course the city has changed over the past several decades; some modest high rises have sprung up, but safely away from the Shwedagon Pagoda. There are traffic jams, supermarkets and mobile phones have become a common sight.

HISTORY

Yangon's history is firmly linked to that of the Shwedagon Pagoda, one of Asia's pre-eminent religious monuments. For more than 2,000 years a community has been in existence around Singuttara Hill, upon which the pagoda stands, both to accommodate visiting pilgrims and to attend to the maintenance and other needs of the great building. For most of the city's history it was part of one or other of the Mon Kingdoms, and at one time served as the residence of the Regent of Pegu (present-day Bago). It also acted as the guard station to the entrance of the Ayeyarwady, most of the rest of the delta being virtually unnavigable. However, without doubt, its primary *raison d'être* has always been religious. A merchant by the name of Gaspar Balbi visited Dagon, as it was then called, in 1586 and was much impressed by the profusion of monasteries: 'Wooden houses gilded and adorned with delicate gardens after their custome wherein their talapoing, which are their friars, dwell and look to the pagoda or varella of Dagon.'

The Burmans, led by King Alaungpaya, finally conquered the city in 1753. It was he who founded the Third Burmese Empire and gave Yangon its modern name, which means 'End of Strife' or 'City of Peace'. At the end of the second Anglo-Burmese War in 1852, Yangon came into the hands of the British and was renamed Rangoon. By this time it was 'no better than a village with the Governor's house and stockade in the middle of it.' The stockade was taken down, the surrounding marshes drained, and a fine city, laid out on a grid system, complete with all the colonial trappings, was constructed. During World War II, Yangon was occupied by the Japanese, but luckily escaped serious bomb damage.

SIGHTS
THE CIRCLE LINE

Perhaps the best way to see Yangon for the first time is to go to the Central Railway Station and take the Circle Line train which chugs slowly around the city. The station is in the fine tradition of British Raj railway architecture, a vast building with its roofs layered and ornate like those of the royal palaces in Mandalay. The ticket booth stands at the entrance to the main hall, an area bustling with humanity. With a ticket in hand, cross the main lines to a siding and to a waiting small train. The seats are wooden, the windows open spaces. Throughout the two-hour journey the traveller can observe the daily life of the city dwellers. The scenery is both urban and rural—rows of vegetables grow in the tidy allotments by the side of the track, and further on there might be a man dangling a long bamboo fishing line into a canal. Other common sights are monks brushing their teeth and children being washed and brushed in preparation for school. Then 'clunk, clunk' go the points and the train is back crossing busy streets. Half the pleasure of this journey is watching the other passengers. A commuter climbs on with his bicycle and perhaps a rolled umbrella under his arm; tucking his *longyi* around his feet and folding himself on to the wooden seat, he settles down to read the newspaper, while children run up and down the corridor. Vendors, trays piled high with cheroots, nuts and fruit get on and off at different stops.

THE SHWEDAGON PAGODA

The Shwedagon shimmers above the city of Yangon—pure beauty, magically blended with an aura of legend and history. The story goes that at the end of the previous world, five lotus buds sprang up on Singuttara Hill (where the pagoda stands today). From each of these plants rose a sacred bird carrying a sacred yellow robe. These robes symbolized the coming of the five Buddhas who would guide the next world towards Nirvana. As foretold, four of the Buddhas have appeared in the present world. (The fifth, Maitreya, is still awaited; his coming is expected to mark the end of the current world cycle.) Each of the four has left a relic to be enshrined on Singuttara Hill: Kakusandha, his staff; Konagamana, his water filter; Kassapa, a piece of his robe; and Gautama, eight hairs. On the seventh day following the enlightenment of Gautama Buddha, two Burmese merchant brothers, Taphussa and Bhallika, were travelling with a caravan of 500 carts when, for no apparent reason, the oxen stopped 'as if chained to the earth'. Thereupon a *nat*, who had seen the merchants' mother in a previous existence, appeared before them with the news of the Buddha's enlightenment. The brothers arrived to pay homage to the Buddha, bearing 'rice cakes and honey food'. In return for their allegiance, the Buddha plucked eight hairs from his head and bade the brothers return to their country and enshrine them on Singuttara Hill along with the previous Buddhas' relics. After a long and arduous journey they arrived in Myanmar and enlisted the help of Thagyamin, King of the Nats, to locate Singuttara Hill. Eventually, the hill and the other relics were found and all the treasures enshrined together.

Much of what is believed about the early history of the Shwedagon has emerged from the mists of time and is clouded in myth. According to legend the first notable pilgrim to the hill was Ashoka, the great Indian emperor, purveyor of Theravada Buddhism and convener of the Third Buddhist Synod. He came to pay homage to the relics in about 260 BCE. By then the jungle had enveloped the pagoda, so Ashoka ordered it to be cleared and restored. Successive kings continued to maintain and enlarge the pagoda. The most extensive alterations were carried out during the 15th century, when Queen Shin Saw Pu had the stupa raised to the height of 95 metres (302 feet) and, for the first time, gilded. Over the years the Shwedagon's development continued and more and more accessories were added (and occasionally removed). In 1612 Felipe de Brito, the Portuguese adventurer who governed the port of Syriam (present-day Thanlyin) for 13 years, made off with a bronze and brass bell weighing 18,000 viss (almost 32 tons), intending to re-cast it into cannon. But 'in the power of the Buddha' the boat bearing it to Syriam sank in the Rangoon River. (The following year Syriam was sacked by the Burmese king, and de Brito taken prisoner and impaled.)

This pagoda has suffered both the ravages of war and natural disasters. In 1768, when an earthquake devastated the top portion, restoration was started and not completed until six years later. The present form of the pagoda is the result of this work. King Hsinbyusin had his craftsmen encase the exquisite architectural features known as the lotus leaves and banana bud at the stupa's summit in solid gold—3,538 gold and silver tiles, ten million bricks and 100,000 brass screws were used.

Fifty years later, on 11th May, 1824, British troops sailed up the river to land, unchallenged, in Rangoon and immediately made the 'Great Pagoda' their key position. 'Considered as military posts,' noted T A Trant, a British staff officer, 'the Dagon was of utmost importance, its elevated brick terraces, which obviated the necessity of additional fortifications, and its commanding situation, rendering it the key of our whole position.' This occupation was short-lived, but a little less than 30 years later, the British returned in force. In April 1852, a flotilla of 15 warships and 15 steamers (under the command of Rear Admiral Charles Austen, brother of the novelist Jane Austen) sailed into Rangoon with 6,000 men and 35 pieces of artillery. This time the British troops had to fight to gain control of the strategic pagoda. They were to remain in occupation for the next 77 years.

The temptation of their surroundings proved shamefully impossible to resist. 'There is a sailor busy with his pickaxes,' observed W F B Laurie, a historian of the second Burmese war, 'excavating a huge golden image with as much coolness as if he were digging a trench. He is looking for treasure.' One officer ordered a passage to be dug into the bowels of the Shwedagon. Under questioning, he claimed that the purpose was to ascertain whether it could be used as a gunpowder magazine. Perhaps the most serious act of vandalism against the Great Pagoda was the attempted removal of the Singu Min Bell. However, this project met a similar fate to that of de Brito's earlier plundering, The raft on which it was being transported to a waiting ship capsized and the attempt was abandoned. Later, the people of Rangoon salvaged the bell and reinstated it in the pagoda.

The Shwedagon is 'calm and sublime, with the smiling look as is seen on the face of Buddha, not smiling in the eyes or mouth, but in the serene expression of inward calm.' Considering the Great Pagoda's haphazard evolution, this totality of

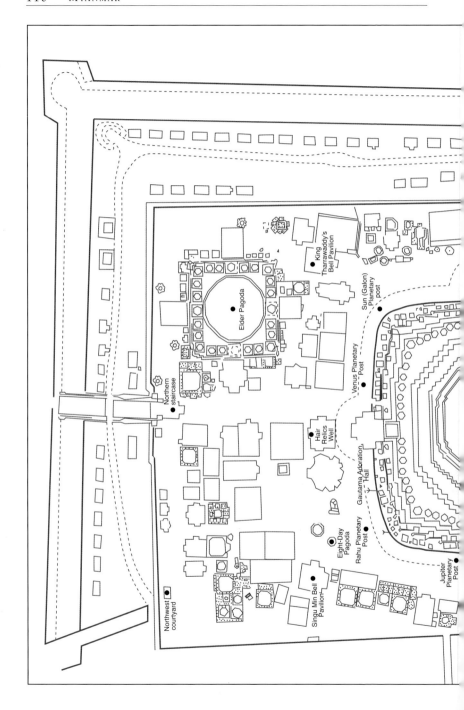

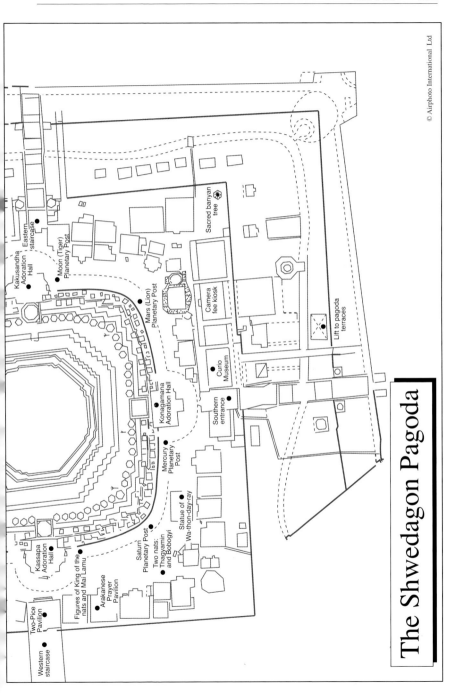

© Airphoto International Ltd

The Shwedagon Pagoda

Western staircase

Two-Pice Pavilion

Kassapa Adoration Hall

Figures of King of the nats and Mai Lamu

Arakanese Prayer Pavilion

Saturn Planetary Post

Two nats: Thagyamin and Bobogyi

Statue of Wa-thon-day-ray

Mercury Planetary Post

Konagamana Adoration Hall

Southern entrance

Curio Museum

Lift to pagoda terraces

Camera fee kiosk

Sacred banyan tree

Mars (Lion) Planetary Post

Moon (Tiger) Planetary Post

Kakusandha Adoration Hall

Eastern staircase

impact on the spirit as well as on the eye is all the more remarkable. We know that the original was of modest dimensions and that it has been cased and recased at least seven times. Yet surely the fluid line of the stupa's main curve and the perfect proportions in relation to its moulding and lotus petals reflect a single conception.

THE APPROACH TO THE SHWEDAGON PAGODA

You will not have been in Yangon long before you catch a glimpse of the Shwedagon. Thereafter from far and near it keeps floating into view, so that before you actually get there you are likely to have experienced several facets of its personality. The most dramatic approach to the pagoda is via the southern, tree-lined Shwedagon Pagoda Road. From the far end the stupa beckons, illuminated by the tropical sun. To the left one passes the memorial to U Thant, former Secretary-General of the United Nations, and a memorial to Queen Supayalat, the country's last queen. Further on to the right is a small pagoda which marks the original southern entrance to the Shwedagon. The energetic pilgrim should alight here at the foot of the southern staircase. The majority, however, will perhaps follow the road to the right and alight from their transport halfway up. Another possibility is to enter the pagoda via the western staircase. Here a new annexe has been built to welcome foreign visitors. Shoes can be safely left and if a visitor is deemed to be too scantily dressed a *longyi* is produced to hide the offending legs—the wearer will be instructed on how to tie the borrowed *longyi*. The annexe also houses a souvenir shop. Once correctly dressed the visitor proceeds into the stairway and up to the pagoda platform via a series of escalators—a little painful with no shoes.

A VISIT TO THE SHWEDAGON

If, however, the point of entry chosen is the southern staircase and you decide not to walk the whole way up, proceed along the road up to the half-way drop off point. At this stage it is possible to enter a lift which will transport you to the pagoda's terraces. Just beside the lift exit is a kiosk where foreign visitors must pay a US$5 entrance fee, this includes the use of still and video cameras. But how much more exciting it is for the visitor to allow the pagoda to reveal its secrets at its own pace. One should enter the southern staircase here. After a moment the eyes become accustomed to the sudden darkness, the nose to the heady scent of *thanaka*, jasmine and sandalwood, and one finds oneself in an Aladdin's cave of 'Nirvana goods'—stalls with fantastic headdresses, Buddha images, religious stones, gold leaf, monks' paraphernalia, lacquerware, *thanaka* wood cosmetics and, near the head of the stairs, layer upon layer of fragrant flowers waiting to be bought as offerings. The stairway crosses the pagoda's former fortifications, a now dried-up moat (until 1928 a wooden drawbridge was hoisted every night). On reaching the top, one encounters a glittering shrine hall dedicated to Konagamana, the second Buddha. Turning to the left (pilgrims must always go clockwise,

Ladies born on a Saturday make offerings at one of the eight planetary posts located round the base of the Shwedagon Pagoda. In Burmese astrology the week has eight days—the equivalent of Wednesday being split into morning and evening—with each day represented both by a planet and an animal. They correspond to eight cardinal points around the pagoda. Thus, these devotees take flowers, light a candle and pour water over the image in the 'Saturday corner'

keeping the pagoda to the right) the full splendour of the pagoda is revealed. First, the golden mass of the bell-shaped lower stupa representing Buddha's inverted offerings bowl commands attention. Then the eyes are drawn towards the banana bud, past the delicate tracery of the *hti* (umbrella), its myriad jewels twinkling in the sun, and bells gently stirring in the breeze.

All around the Shwedagon one finds the calm activity of a religious village, for a great pagoda is the focus of secular as well as religious life, and none more than the Shwedagon. Businessmen come to worship and then settle down to negotiate a deal, students to read, families to picnic—all gaining inspiration from their surroundings. It was here on 26th August, 1988, that Aung San Suu Kyi gave her first political speech; by all accounts a rousing affair.

The pagoda platform occupies an area of 5.6 hectares (14 acres), and is covered with buildings of all shapes and sizes. Some hug the base of the stupa, others the outer rim. Immediately on the right after the shrine hall sits the elephant of the Mercury Planetary Post, guardian to those born on a Wednesday morning. Many visit the pagoda to pay respects to their planetary post. In Burmese astrology the week has eight days—Wednesday being split into morning and evening—with each day represented both by a planet and an animal. 'The planet of a man's birthday will be the main guardian of his fate but at each particular period of a man's life a particular planet throws upon him its painful or its beneficial influence.' The *thin-bon-gyi* (the Great Basket of Learning, ie the Burmese alphabet) is divided between the eight days of the week, and it is customary to incorporate into a person's name the letters corresponding to his birthday. At the eight cardinal points round the base of the pagoda are the planetary posts. Thus, if born on a Sunday, one takes flowers, lights a candle and pours water over the image in the 'Sunday corner'.

Near the Mercury Planetary Post, looking up at the Great Stupa, is a stone statue of Wa-thon-day-ray, the guardian angel of the earth. When Mara, 'the evil one', engulfed the world in a great fire, it is said that the guardian angel first soaked her long tresses of hair (which can be seen wound round her body) and then wrung them out to extinguish the blaze, thus saving the Buddha, who was meditating under the *bo* (banyan) tree. On the south-west corner is the planetary post of Saturn. This is for the Saturday-born and is represented by a *naga* (serpent). Continue a few steps and on the opposite side of some trees are two *nat* (spirit) figures in a glass case. On the left is Thagyamin, King of the Nats, and on the right Bobogyi, Guardian Nat of the Pagoda. In front of them stands a row of gongs; when a pilgrim's prayers are said he will strike the deep-throated gong, then the ground, 'to call upon all living things in the 31 worlds to share in the merit of the good deed.'

The next pavilion—known as the Arakanese Prayer Pavilion—contains some of the finest wood carving in the pagoda. Opposite this hall under the white umbrellas of royalty stand the figures of Mai Lamu and the King of the Nats. Legend tells us that they were the parents of King Ukkalapa, who enshrined Buddha's hair in the pagoda.

The western staircase and Kassapa Adoration Hall were both gutted by fire in 1931 and re-built four years later. The Two-Pice Tazaung (pavilion) which heads the staircase is so-named as the merchants in the city's main market each donated two pice (a halfpenny in contemporary British money) a day for the reconstruction of the staircase and hall. The main image in the Adoration Hall is that of Kassapa, the Third Buddha. Just north of the hall is the Jupiter Planetary Post, for the Thursday-born, whose symbol is a rat. The Tuskless Elephant representing the planetary post of Rahu (the mythical planet for Wednesday afternoon) is on the north-west corner. Standing alone just north of the planetary post is the small Eight-day Pagoda. Around its base are eight niches, each containing a Buddha. Sitting astride each niche is the figure of the relevant animal or bird, each one representing a planet, a day of the week and a direction of the compass. The last explains the apparently haphazard sequence in which the planetary posts are arranged around the pagoda. (For example, Wednesday is followed by Saturday then Thursday.) The Singu Min Bell hangs in a pavilion to the west of the Eight-day Pagoda. This splendid bell was cast between 1775 and 1779 and weighs 23 tons (21 tonnes). In 1825 the British attempted to steal the bell, hauling it down and onto the Yangon River, where it sank. Years later the Burmese managed to recover it using bamboo rafts. From a small, charming courtyard behind the Singu Min Bell, in the north-west corner of the terrace, you get not only a wonderful panorama of Yangon city, but also a superb view of the Great Stupa itself. From here, walk along the northern wall to the northern staircase. This staircase leads to Heroes' Hill, where General Aung San, the architect of Myanmar's independence and father of Aung San Suu Kyi, is buried along with other national martyrs.

Turning back towards the main stupa, immediately to the left is a golden pagoda, the Elder or Naungdawgyi Pagoda. This marks the spot where the Sacred Hair Relics were first placed prior to being washed and then enshrined in the main pagoda. Continue walking towards the main stupa, and just in front of the northern adoration hall dedicated to Gautama the Fourth Buddha stands the Hair Relics Well (Sandawdwin Tazaung). This well is supposed to be fed by the Ayeyarwady and so rises and falls with the tide. Tucked in on the east side of the Gautama Adoration Hall is the planetary post of Venus, for the Friday-born, symbolized by the mole or guinea pig. In the north-east corner of the terrace is a second bell pavilion, which houses the massive Maha Titthadaganda bell, cast by

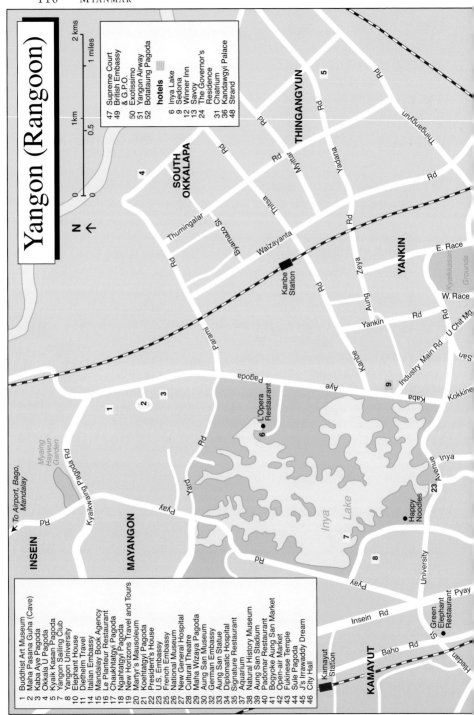

Yangon (Rangoon)

N ←

To Airport, Bago, Mandalay

INSEIN

MAYANGON

SOUTH OKKALAPA

THINGANGYUN

YANKIN

KAMAYUT

Inya Lake

Myaing Haywun Garden

Kyaikkasan Grounds

1   Buddhist Art Museum
2   Maha Pasana Guha (Cave)
3   Kaba Aye Pagoda
4   Okkala U Pagoda
5   Kyaik Kasan Pagoda
6   Yangon Sailing Club
7   Yangon University
8   Yangon University
9   Elephant House
10 Elephant House
11 Diethelm Travel
14 Italian Embassy
15 Mandalay Book Agency
16 Le Planteur Restaurant
17 Chaukhtatgyi Pagoda
18 Ngahtatgyi Pagoda
19 New Horizons Travel and Tours
20 Martyr's Mausoleum
21 Koehtatgyi Pagoda
22 President's House
23 U.S. Embassy
25 French Embassy
26 National Museum
27 New General Hospital
28 Cultural Theatre
29 Maha Wizaya Pagoda
30 Aung San Museum
32 German Embassy
33 Aung San Statue
34 Diplomatic Hospital
35 Signature Restaurant
37 Aquarium
38 Natural History Museum
39 Aung San Stadium
40 Padomar Restaurant
41 Bogyoke Aung San Market
42 Open-air Market
43 Fukinese Temple
44 Sule Pagoda
45 J's Irrawaddy Dream
46 City Hall

47 Supreme Court
49 British Embassy & G.P.O.
50 Exotissimo
51 Yangon Airway
52 Botataung Pagoda

hotels

6   Inya Lake
9   Sedona
12 Winner Inn
13 Savoy
24 The Governor's Residence
31 Chatrium
36 Kandawgyi Palace
48 Strand

L'Opera Restaurant

Happy Noodles

S. Green Elephant Restaurant

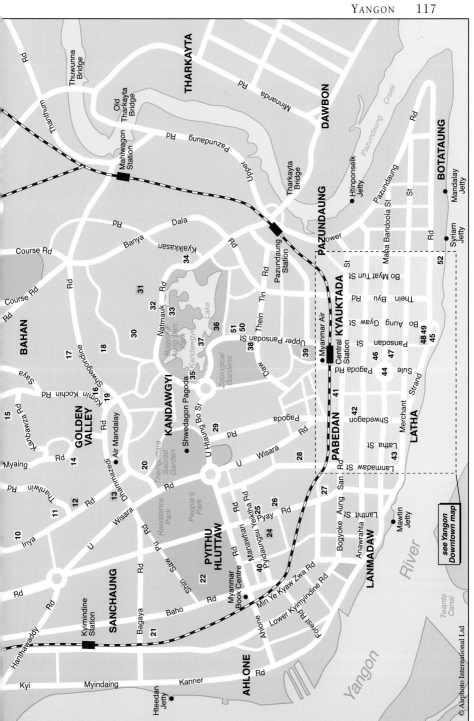

see Yangon Downtown map

© Airphoto International Ltd

SHWEDAGON STUPA TREASURE

The gold of the Shwedagon's stupa is indeed real. From the base up to the mouldings it is gilded. About every ten years it is re-gilded using 28,000 packets of gold leaf. From the top of the mouldings to the top of the banana bud, the stupa is sheathed by 13,153 pure gold plates, each a foot square (one can calculate their total weight at about 60 tons, with a theoretical value at today's prices of some US$3.194 billion.). The *hti*, or umbrella, at the top of the stupa is an iron-tiered structure plated with 215 kilograms (470 pounds) of pure gold, hung with gold and silver bells and diverse items of jewellery, all of which creates the gentle jingle one hears from below. The weather vane at its very top is decorated with 1,000 diamonds weighing in total 278 carats and 1,383 other precious and semi-precious stones. This splendour is in turn topped by a diamond orb, some 25 centimetres (ten inches) in diameter and studded with 4,351 diamonds weighing 1,800 carats, the summit of the orb being crowned with a single 76-carat diamond. This astonishing accumulation of treasure has been built up over the centuries, much of it predating historical records. The major gold plating was carried out from 1768 to 1774 during the reign of King Hsinbyushin. The present *hti* was given by King Mindon in 1871, although he was never permitted by the British to see the Shwedagon. The pagoda is also the recipient of frequent private donations as well as endowments to provide for its upkeep.

Other than the removal of the Dhammazedi Bell by Portuguese adventurer Felipe de Brito in 1612, the attempted removal of the Singu Min Bell by the British in 1825, and later the vandalism by the British invaders during the second Anglo-Burmese War (1852), there does not seem to be any record of significant thefts from this storehouse of Buddhist merit.

King Tharrawaddy in 1841. At the base of the pagoda on the north-east side stands a *galon* (bird), the planetary post of the sun and therefore for the Sunday-born. The shrine hall facing the eastern stairway has been rebuilt several times and was last renovated in 1968. This hall is dedicated to Kakusandha, the First Buddha. Beside the hall is the planetary post of the moon, for those born on a Monday, with the tiger being their mascot. The last planetary post, that of Mars, stands on the south-east base of the stupa: it is represented by a lion and is for the Tuesday-born.

From the south-east planetary post, weave through the various pavilions to the south-east corner of the terrace, where there is a sacred *bo* tree (*ficus religiosa*, or banyan), supposedly a descendant of a cutting from the original tree under which Gautama Buddha attained enlightenment. It is ceremonially washed every May at the full moon. There is a fine view from this corner and on a clear day it is possible to see the Kyaik-Khauk Pagoda at Thanlyin. Just before you arrive once more at the head of the southern stairway, there is a small museum to the left of the main promenade, which contains an assortment of artefacts donated by devotees.

Dawn and dusk are the best times to visit the Shwedagon, the misty glow of the sun softening the timeless lines of the golden spire. Pilgrims, lost in prayer and acts of devotion, are engulfed in a dreamlike haze. Wandering the marble terraces, warm to the feet following the day's fierce sun, and marvelling at the splendour, Ralph Fitch, a 16th-century merchant adventurer, came to a simple conclusion: 'It is the fairest place, as I suppose, that is in the world.'

Maha Wizaya Pagoda

Across the road from the Shwedagon's southern entrance stands the golden Maha Wizaya (literally, 'Great Conqueror') pagoda built by General Ne Win—the bigger and grander the pagoda you build the more merit you gain. Said to have cost some 300 million kyats the building is now sanctified and nearly complete. It was built to commemorate the first convention of Buddhist sects—from orthodox to liberal, held in the Kaba Aye Pagoda in the 1990s. Under discussion was the purification, perpetuation and propagation of the Buddhist religion.

The golden pagoda has beautiful, simple lines. The hollow pagoda is entered on the south side. A short passage lined with Nepalese carvings depicting scenes from the Buddha's life leads into an enormous central cavern. The space has a definite Disney feeling; vast artificial trees stand either side of the four entrances with tremblant flowers hanging from their branches—they represent the species under which the most recent eight Buddhas (four from the present world cycle and four from the previous cycle) reached enlightenment. The dome of the pagoda is the star-studded sky in which the constellations occasionally flash. In the centre of the cavern is a huge platform shaped as a lotus flower and here under the white

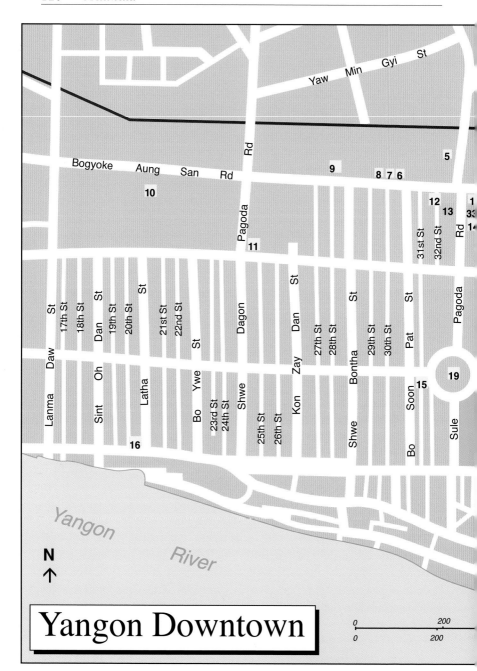

Yangon Downtown

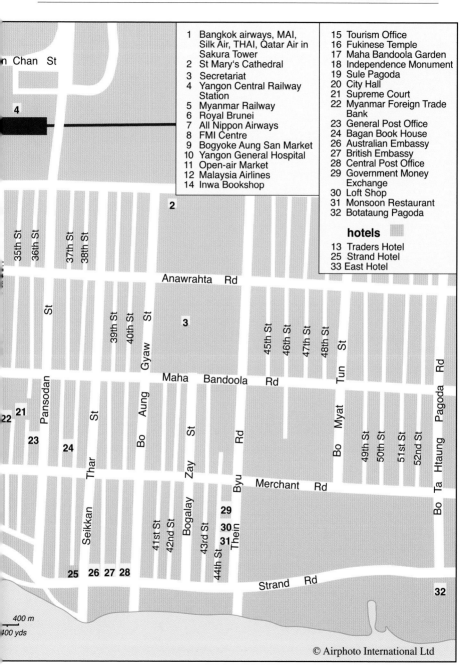

Chan   St

4

1 Bangkok airways, MAI,
  Silk Air, THAI, Qatar Air in
  Sakura Tower
2 St Mary's Cathedral
3 Secretariat
4 Yangon Central Railway
  Station
5 Myanmar Railway
6 Royal Brunei
7 All Nippon Airways
8 FMI Centre
9 Bogyoke Aung San Market
10 Yangon General Hospital
11 Open-air Market
12 Malaysia Airlines
14 Inwa Bookshop

15 Tourism Office
16 Fukinese Temple
17 Maha Bandoola Garden
18 Independence Monument
19 Sule Pagoda
20 City Hall
21 Supreme Court
22 Myanmar Foreign Trade
   Bank
23 General Post Office
24 Bagan Book House
26 Australian Embassy
27 British Embassy
28 Central Post Office
29 Government Money
   Exchange
30 Loft Shop
31 Monsoon Restaurant
32 Botataung Pagoda

hotels

13 Traders Hotel
25 Strand Hotel
33 East Hotel

2

35th St
36th St
37th St
38th St

Anawrahta   Rd

St

39th St
40th St
Gyaw   St

3

45th St
46th St
47th St
48th St

Maha   Bandoola   Rd

Tun   St

Bo   Aung   St

Pansodan
22 21
23
24

Bo   Myat
Bo   Myat

49th St
50th St
51st St
52nd St

Bo   Ta   Htaung

Pagoda   Rd

Thar

Zay   St

Rd

Byu

Merchant   Rd

Bo

Seikkan

Bogalay

41st St
42nd St
43rd St
44th St

Thein

29
30
31

25 26 27 28

Strand   Rd

32

400 m
400 yds

© Airphoto International Ltd

umbrellas of royalty stand the eight Buddhas; with the Four Buddhas of this world (Kakusandha, Konagamana, Kassapra and Gautama) placed opposite the cardinal points and their own tree of enlightenment.

THE ROYAL LAKE

An excellent place from which to view the Shwedagon, is the Royal or Kandawgyi Lake. On the east side of the lake is the Karaweik stone boat. This is a relatively recent copy of a royal barge, and is used as a restaurant where rather good Burmese variety shows are performed every evening. Stand on the 'bow' of the Karaweik and all around is Bogyoke Aung San Park, a well-planted pleasure ground with small paths leading over bridges and a large statue of Aung San standing among some trees. On the western end of the lake (Shwedagon end) there is an excellent spot to stop for supper after an evening stroll through the park Signature (95 1-546488) a restaurant/café which serves good Burmese and Western food.

ZOOLOGICAL GARDENS

On the south-western side of the Royal Lake are the Zoological Gardens. The animals, mostly indigenous species, are well looked after. The elephants are often to be seen taking an afternoon stroll around the lake. When the capital moved up to Nay Pyi Taw many of the animals were moved there as well. Several years ago the Natural History Museum building, also on the lake, was converted into the Kandawgyi Palace hotel and the exhibits moved here to the Zoological Gardens.

SULE PAGODA

In the heart of Yangon stands the Sule Pagoda, a beautiful octagonal golden stupa with a legend dating back 2,000 years. In what must be one of Myanmar's strangest contradictions, this statement of Buddhist calm acts as a traffic island at one of the city's busy intersections. Two missionary monks are said to have travelled to Thaton in south-east Myanmar carrying a hair relic of the Buddha. The King of Thaton gave them permission to build a pagoda, on the site of the present Sule Pagoda (near to the sacred Singuttara Hill), in which to enshrine the hair. The pagoda was long known as Kyaik Athok, literally meaning 'pagoda containing hair relic' in the Mon language. The name Sule probably refers to the Sule *nat*, the guardian spirit of Singuttara Hill. It was to the Sule *nat* that the two merchant brothers, Taphussa and Bhallika appealed to show them the sacred Singuttara Hill on their quest to found the Shwedagon Pagoda.

AROUND THE SULE PAGODA

From the Sule Pagoda it is a pleasant stroll to the Strand Hotel. Walk south along Sule Pagoda Road, and on the left is a small park named after Maha Bandoola, the commander-in-chief of the Burmese army who led the raid into Assam which resulted in the first Anglo-Burmese War. He later (in 1826) unsuccessfully defended the Shwedagon Pagoda against the British forces and died in the attempt—by all accounts, from both Burmese and British sources, he was a remarkable and brave soldier. The north and east sides of the square are dominated by fine colonial buildings, and the City Hall has a distinct Burmese flavour. Walk another block down to the Yangon River, turn left along Strand Road, then left again up Pansodan (formerly Phayre) Street, and enjoy the open-air book market. All sorts of long-forgotten favourites hide among the huge piles of books, a pure delight for the bargain-minded book lover. At the far side of this block stands the Strand Hotel. Either retrace your steps back down to Strand Road and turn left—the hotel is on the next corner—or walk around the block to the right, turning right down Seikkan Thar Street and the hotel will be on the right.

STRAND HOTEL

Fifteen minutes' walk from the Sule Pagoda is the Strand Hotel—a perfect spot for the tired traveller to regain lost energy over a glass of cool, fresh lime juice and to muse on what colonial life must have been like. 'Leading Hotel in the East... patronized by royalty, nobility and distinguished personages,' reads the advertisement in Murray's 1911 handbook. It then goes on to list some of the hotel's distinguished guests, including HIH the Grand Duke Cyril of Russia and the Hon Mr William H. Taft, President of the United States. The Strand, a handsome, white stucco turn-of-the-century building, originally belonged to the Sarkies brothers, also proprietors of the Raffles ('the Savoy of the East') in Singapore.

The hotel was built in 1901 but by the 1980s had acquired the persona of a gentle maiden aunt in reduced circumstances. Everything had become a little shabby. The fine lofty reception rooms were somewhat devoid of furniture. In 1991 that was all changed when a massive renovation programme was launched by a joint venture between the Government of Myanmar and a prestigious group of international investors and hoteliers. In November 1993, the Strand proudly re-opened her doors. To a large extent the colonial air and trappings have been preserved, although sadly the exquisite wrought-iron lift has gone. As one sits, drink in hand, while an overhead fan gently disturbs the air, it is easy to imagine groups of elegant ladies of yesteryear seated in rattan chairs and the accompanying 'men in white drill or pongee silk, a great deal of laughter and pleasant conversation'. The clever use of local crafts is in evidence, such as huge flower arrangements tumbling out of lacquer bowls and vast lacquer panels decorating the dining room where specially made glasses (see page 103) adorn the tables.

As yet the annexe has not been refurbished, so the charm of the former Strand can still be sampled, although it is no longer possible to stay in this section of the hotel building. The rooms have all been converted into, shops or offices with a good art gallery on the ground floor. It is rumoured however that this will all change again soon, with the annexe being brought back into the hotel thus giving them more rooms. A swimming pool will be added along with other extras such as a spa and business centre which are now deemed necessary in a grand hotel. A stay at the Strand, with its Somerset Maugham charm, is hard to resist for collectors of the 'period piece' (for whom its central location is an added bonus). Even for less committed nostalgia seekers, a visit at least is highly recommended.

(top) A fine old car, a bygone era. Until very recently, the streets of Yangon were full of magnificent pre- and post-war cars—the dream of a vintage car enthusiast. The taxi stand outside the Strand Hotel would offer a choice of a Buick or perhaps an old Ford

NATIONAL MUSEUM

A few years ago the National Museum was moved from its old colonial home in Pansodan Street (Phayre on old maps) to a newly constructed building at 66/74 Pyay Road, Dagon Township. Open every day except Monday, Tuesday and gazetted holidays, from 10am to 4.00pm (entrance fee US$5) this rather austere museum is organized on five floors. The feeling of the place is encapsulated in the politically motivated introduction by the Minister of Culture in the museum guide book. '...the National Museum, on its part,' says the Minister, 'is performing the duty of helping to implement the two objectives of "Uplift of National prestige and integrity and preservation and safeguarding of cultural heritage and national character" and "Uplift of dynamism of patriotic spirit" '. This fierce approach has meant the faded charm of the old museum has been lost but unfortunately not replaced by the flare in presentation that has become expected of modern museums—a missed opportunity, especially as the purpose-built building is said to have cost some 4,491 lakh kyats (about US$1.3 million). This museum is now

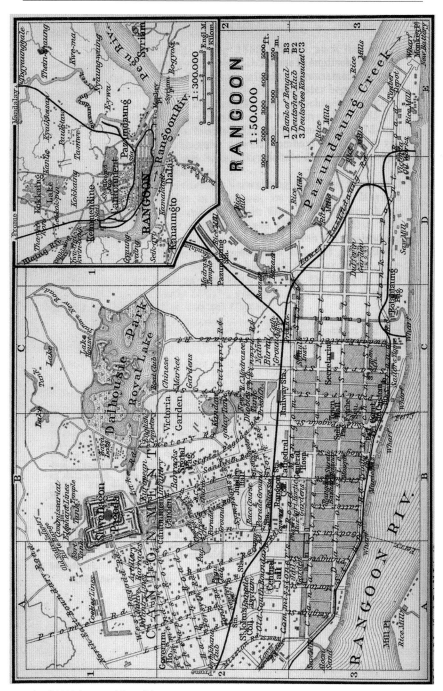

Map dated 1912 from Baedeker of that year

BURMESE ROYALTY

Anastasia Edwards

It was perhaps inevitable the Burmese royalty would not survive the British conquest of Burma in 1885. Britain, a rapidly modernizing society whose monarch had long ceased to wield any real political power, was unlikely to tolerate a feudal royal system in which the king was divine ruler. However, the departure of the last king, Theebaw, and his queen, Supayalat, in 1886 not only ended the royalty. It also saw the complex philosophies and world views that had shaped Burmese royal protocol over the centuries relegated to dusty records and to the scholarship of a handful of researchers.

Nowadays, it is largely in foreign writings that the long-vanished institutions of the royal family come to life. 'The Burmese Emperor is considered by himself and others absolute lord of the lives, properties, and personal services of his subjects; he exalts and depresses, confers and takes away honor and rank,' observed the Italian priest Father Sangermano, who lived in Rangoon between 1783 and 1806 and was able to observe the workings of the royal family at close quarters. 'Every subject is the Emperor's born slave; and when he calls anyone his slave he thinks to do him honour.... The possessions of all who die without heirs belong to the King. To the King it belongs to declare war or to conclude peace; and he may at any moment call upon the whole population of his empire to enlist themselves in his army, and can impose upon them at his pleasure any labour or service.'

Scholars generally agree that Burmese notions of divine kingship had their roots in ancient Indian cosmology. This heritage included a number of codes governing the magical nature of the court regalia and the importance of having Brahman priests in residence to minister to the court and its functions.

Hindu cosmology pertaining to kingship stated that the monarch had a divine status, and by extension that his precincts were the symbolic centre of the universe. This notion resulted in many dramatic moves of palaces from one place to another in the country's history, dictated by the powerful predictions of bevies of soothsayers, numerologists, and astrologers.

Also of Hindu origin were such institutions as the White Umbrella, for use only by the king and his chief queen, and the veneration of the king's elephants, especially the sacred albino elephants. One of the most vivid accounts of Burmese royal rituals can be enjoyed in the loosely biographical novel *The Lacquer Lady*, a section of which is excerpted on page 29.

Unlike royalty in other parts of Asia, there was no hereditary nobility in Burma, which further empowered the king in his divinely sanctioned role as head of state. All royal orders were issued through the Hlutdaw ('palace of release'), the supreme council which met daily to register royal edicts, issue letters, and act as the supreme court of appeal. The King was the theoretical head of the Hlutdaw, which met in a special building within the palace precincts. The Shwedaik ('gold building' or treasury) held far less importance than European treasuries and than the Hlutdaw, as most of the revenue was paid in kind. Unlike the rest of Burma's court, the Shwedaik's officials tended to be hereditary.

For those who wish to read more about Burmese royal life, perhaps the best accounts come from foreigners such as Father Vincentius Sangermano (*Description of the Burmese Empire*, England, 1893) and the British respresentative Michael Symes, whose formal account and journals of two visits he made to the court in 1795 and 1802 are well worth reading (*An Account of an Embassy to the Kingdom of Ava*, London, 1800 and *Journal of his second embassy to the court of Ava in 1855*, George and Unwin, 1955). The only other accounts of note are translations of Burmese chronicles written about the country's kings.

In 1930 when Somerset Maugham visited Burma, few foreigners visited pagodas, as they found irksome the rule of going 'bare-footed'. However, following a dinner with some Burmese friends Mr Maugham threw caution to the wind. '...we went up a long stairway on each side of which were booths... At last we reached the great terrace. All about shrines and pagodas were jumbled pell-mell with the confusion with which trees grow in a jungle... And then, emerging from among them like a great ship surrounded by lighters, rose dim, severe and splendid, the Shwe Dagon.'

due for a major make-over as it feels very neglected—indeed the visitor numbers are said to be a mere 200 per month.

The first exhibition rooms on the ground floor contain some calligraphy and stone carvings. A large room beyond, dominated by four massive gold and red pillars, has become the home of the Lion Throne. When King Theebaw was exiled to Calcutta in 1886 the throne was housed in the Calcutta Museum. It was returned once more in 1948, when Burma was granted her independence from the British. Around the edge of the room are other smaller thrones. For instance the Elephant Throne, made of sago wood, was used to announce the elevation—or demotion—of the palace officials. Upstairs on the first floor is a room of prehistoric relics and another showing pieces from Bagan. The regalia from the last two kings of Myanmar and some of the royal jewellery, which is quite beautiful, is also on this first floor. A large model of the Mandalay Palace (see page 146) and some of the court clothes from the reign of King Theebaw and Queen Supayalat also are on that floor. Many of the exhibits are fascinating, but the ambiance of the building is such that it does not invite a lengthy browse—which the objects do deserve.

BOTATAUNG PAGODA

Close to the Yangon River stands the Botataung Pagoda. The original building, which was bombed by the Allies in 1943, had yet another legendary '2,000-year history'. Hairs of the Buddha are said to have been escorted from India by 1,000 military officers ('Botataung'). When the pagoda was rebuilt after the war it was constructed with a hollow inside so visitors can walk into the stupa; it is entirely lined with glass mosaics, a sort of oriental Hall of Mirrors. Many of the ancient relics have been put into glass cases—though not, of course, the sacred hair relics, which remain enshrined within the pagoda.

BOGYOKE AUNG SAN MARKET

For market lovers this one is a pure delight. It lies just south-west of the Railway Station (itself a fine building), and so is within easy reach of the hotels in downtown Yangon. The market is crowded with stalls selling *longyis*, mother-of-pearl, lacquerware, hats packaged in exquisite turquoise boxes, antique baskets, and with hawkers selling coconut with jelly. At the north end of the market is the food section, and flanking the southern end are some regular shops. Several good lacquerware shops can be found in this section. Screen Stars Store (Nos 9, 10, 95 and 96) and then at 1 and 2 Bogyoke Aung San Market is a particularly agreeable lacquer shop. Its designs are slightly different from those elsewhere (simpler and more attuned to Western

A carved teak figure of the Buddha dressed in the insignia of a Burmese king. It is overlaid and decorated with gesso-like (a white ground of plaster) ornament, lacquer, gilt and jewelled with artificial rubies and emeralds. The costume shows an influence from the 18th-century court dress of Ayuttya

tastes) and so, of course, proportionately more expensive. The original sign, long and Victorian, with beautiful script, now hangs inside, as signs longer than 69 centimetres (two feet, two inches) are liable to government tax. (Incidentally, green shop signs denote government-owned shops.) Since Burmese embroidery has become so popular with foreigners, many stalls now sell both antique wall hangings as well as a collection of fun caps and waistcoats in the same style embroidery. Of course there is always a tailor at the ready to knock up a specially designed creation. If hunting for the traditional velvet flip-flops go to Gold Fish (Nos 206 and 208), again on the south side, where they cater to larger foreign feet. The market, like many things in Yangon, is closed on Mondays and public holidays.

CHAUK HTAT GYI PAGODA
On Kaba Aye Pagoda Road north of the Shwedagon in Shwegondaing Road is a 72-metre (230-foot) reclining Buddha. Sculpted some fifty years ago at a cost of some 500,000 kyats from public donations, it provides a perfect example of how much money Burmese society continues to pour into Buddhism. This particular image holds no special charm, but is remarkable for its size.

MAHA PASANA GUHA
North of Yangon University and the Inya Lake is the Maha Pasana Guha, an extraordinary artificial cave constructed in 1954 to hold the Sixth Buddhist Synod, convened by U Nu, first Prime Minister of the Union of Burma. The cave was built by volunteer labour in the space of just 14 months, and can hold up to 10,000 people. The Sixth Buddhist Synod brought the Institute for Advanced Buddhistic Studies in to being with aid from the Ford Foundation. This institute is tackling the first-ever translation into English of the entire Buddhist canon. U Nu, was closely involved with this project up until his death in February 1995.

KABA AYE PAGODA
Kaba Aye literally means 'world peace' and this pagoda, which stands in the same compound as the Great Cave (as the Maha Pasana Guha is sometimes known), was built to commemorate the Sixth Buddhist Synod in 1954.

BUDDHIST MUSEUM OF ART
Also within the grounds and worth visiting is this museum. A collection of religious paraphernalia, Buddhist texts, some architectural drawings of pagoda shapes and pleasing Buddha images are on show.

Innwa Bank, formerly premises of Oppenheim and Company, Merchant Road

(above) City Hall, built 1936, formerly the site of Ripon Hall; (right) Central Post Office Built 1908, formerly the office of Bulloch and Brothers one of the oldest and most powerful trading firms in Myanmar

YANGON'S COLONIAL HERITAGE

The many colonial-era buildings that survive in Yangon have, inevitably, weathered over the years. Some state their origins proudly with brass wall plaques or marble foundation stones. Others retain only fleeting hints of their former occupants—a set of initials inscribed on a wall or the shadow of a name beneath peeling layers of paint. Many have been repurposed over the years; what was once the headquarters of a pioneering 19th-century Scottish trading firm is now an embassy, an ostentatious private mansion has become an art school, and a former department store later used as a government ministry currently stands empty. Whatever their current-day use, these buildings represent a unique and valuable legacy. Indeed, the sheer density of colonial-era structures in Yangon—from rows of humble shop houses to grand edifices of Empire—is unparalleled in Southeast Asia.

The city's downtown area is considered to be one of the finest remaining examples of a 'colonial core' in the region. This colonial core is comprised of grandiose administrative buildings of state (such as the Secretariat, the Custom House, and the High Court) and the former powerhouses of the central business district (Chartered Bank, the Reserve Bank of India, and Rowe & Co. Department Store). A walk through the heart of downtown Yangon along the lower block of Pansodan Street and Strand Road, between Bo Aung Kyaw Road

and Sule Pagoda Road, provides an uninterrupted vista of colonial structures. To stroll these streets is, quite literally, to step back in time.

While Yangon's colonial core is today a legacy set in stone, its construction was fraught with logistical challenges and the unfinished search for an appropriate colonial aesthetic. Yangon was not much more than a riverside village when the British took over in 1852; within a few short decades it had been transformed into one of the busiest ports in the British Empire. The city's first colonial buildings were designed by military engineers and members of the government's Public Works Department. These early structures tended to be Victorian or eclectic in style and display only very limited attempts to adapt to the climate or cultural setting. Design elements often appear to have been picked in a mix-and-match manner from pattern books such as Owen Jones' *The Grammar of Ornament*, 1856.

A new era of colonial architecture began in 1901 with the appointment a professionally trained architect (John Begg) as Consulting Architect to the Government of Bombay. The following year another architect (James Ransome) was appointed Consulting Architect to the Government of India. As Myanmar was then ruled by the British as part of India, architects based in Calcutta became responsible for state buildings in Myanmar. The first Consulting Architect to the Government of Burma (Henry Seton-Morris) was appointed in 1911. Consulting Architects were expected to design key government buildings and inspect plans prepared for all public buildings. In emphasizing the importance of architecture, the British had begun to realize their vision for a grander and more cohesive aesthetic across India and Myanmar; buildings became a way of imposing their rule visually as well as symbolically.

Consulting Architects and those working in private practices met with numerous challenges in Yangon. Obtaining quality building material was a perennial problem. During the 1910s,

(above) Former Mercantile Bank of India Building, Merchant Road

(top) Yangon Division Court, Built Circa 1900, Formerly the Currency Department; (bottom) 1930s Shop houses on Sule Pagoda Road

the price of timber rose so high as to be almost prohibitive; rumours circulated that all available teakwood in Myanmar was being shipped to New Delhi for the construction of the new British capital of India. Local bricks lacked uniformity; without standard measurements, architects were unable to calculate an accurate gauge and had to repeatedly readjust the half-inch details of their designs. Often, they found it easier to ship materials from England. These included cement, steel frames, decorative elements such as the Ionic capitols for the

British Embassy, Built 1900, Formerly J. and F. Graham Shipping Company

colonnade of the New Law Courts (still standing at the western corner of Strand Road and Sule Pagoda Road), and finishings like the locks and keys for doors and strong rooms in the Chartered Bank (located at the corner of Pansodan Street and Bank Street).

Another, more serious, challenge was the waterlogged land upon which the architects had to build. As many of the building sites were located on reclaimed land, they had to conjure up innovative ways of ensuring that the buildings would be structurally sound. The Secretariat was constructed upon a veritable forest of sunken *pyinkado* logs, while the Custom House sits on a reinforced cement raft embedded six feet into the ground.

The most intransigent problem faced by the Consulting Architects were the demands made on them by the government. In a talk John Begg gave in London in 1920, he provided an example of the many "crass ideas" he was forced to deal with: "I remember once when the design of an important town-hall was entrusted to me, that a message was sent me from a high quarter to this effect: 'Do ask Mr. Begg, whatever he does, to make it castellated'!"

High Court Building, Constructed 1905–1911

Since the days of their construction Yangon's colonial-era buildings have survived war and natural disasters, as well as numerous changes of ownership and systems of government. They have withstood the bombs of World War Two that were dropped on the city first by the invading Japanese army and later by Allied forces reclaiming the city in 1945. Most recently, in 2008, the buildings survived the devastating winds of Cyclone Nargis, which tore down trees and stripped off much of the city's roofing.

Yet one of the biggest threats these buildings have faced is neglect. When the government shifted the capital of Myanmar to Naypyitaw at the end of 2005, it left behind a huge array of state-owned buildings that were once occupied by ministries and government departments. Many of these now stand empty, are only partially occupied, or will be shifted in the near future. Without daily occupancy and regular maintenance, the buildings are falling prey to damp, rust, weeds, and termites—all of which will accelerate their eventual decay. Architects estimate that, without immediate attention, the buildings now have a limited lifespan of between 10-to-30 years.

Today, another threat looms. As many of the buildings occupy prime property in the city centre property, developers are keen to demolish the old structures and replace them with modern tower blocks that will yield more floor space.

In early 2012, the Yangon Heritage Trust was established by historian and author Thant Myint-U to begin working with the government on a conservation plan for Yangon. With the support of donations from governments, NGOs, and individuals, the Trust aims to protect Yangon's 19th and early 20th century buildings as part of a broader urban plan.

As a link between the past and the future, the options for Yangon's colonial era-buildings are plentiful. With a rising middle class and the growth of international tourism, there will be an increased demand for access to leisure activities and tourism services in the city. These buildings can potentially serve as offices, hotels, institutions, museums, restaurants, bars, shopping complexes, department stores, residential units, art galleries, and theatres or cinemas.

Local architects and urban planners involved in heritage preservation point to the need for authentic reinterpretations of old buildings that will take into account the existing social fabric; successfully repurposing can boost a building's economic potential to create new jobs and improve the surrounding urban environment. They hope to offer a new lease of life to Yangon's historic buildings and ensure that these relics of the city's past can also play a sustainable and vibrant role in its future.

(Adapted from the Association of Myanmar Architect's *30 Heritage Buildings of Yangon*, Serindia, 2012.)

For more information, please contact, or visit the **Yangon Heritage Trust**, 22–24 Pansodan Street, 1/F, Kyauktada Township, Yangon.

Tel (95-1) 240544, www.yangonheritagetrust.org.

Inland Waterways Department, Former home of the Irrawaddy Flotilla Company, Built 1933

AROUND YANGON (RANGOON)
BAGO (PEGU)

Once the capital of the powerful Mon kingdom but now a charming backwater, Bago still has many interesting things to see. Situated 80 kilometres (50 miles) north-east of Yangon, it makes an ideal day trip or an overnight stop on the way to Kyaiktiyo. Sections of the road have recently been widened which greatly reduces the journey time.

The Mons are thought to have first settled in the Bago area around the end of the sixth century. Bago was then on the coast and soon developed into a prosperous port. After 1287 and the collapse of the First Burmese Empire, a Mon kingdom was again formed, this time with its capital at Martaban (now called Mottama). But King Byinnya-U, the second Mon king, realized the strategic importance of Bago and transferred his capital there in 1365. So began the city's golden era. The 'great city called Pegu', as it was known then, was frequented by Western travellers and merchants. In 1541 the Burmese again overthrew the Mon kingdom and formed the Second Burmese Empire. This time Bago was made the capital of the whole of Myanmar. The city retained this status for the next 91 years, after which Ava, on the banks of the Ayeyarwady, was thought to be a more central vantage point with better communications. Also, Bago's harbour was silting up, and so the capital was moved north.

Apart from the years 1740 to 1757, when another Mon kingdom briefly came into existence around Bago, the city receded into obscurity. Indeed, it was destroyed by King Alaungpaya in 1757. In 1852 it came into the hands of the British as a result of the second Anglo-Burmese war.

HSIN PHYU DAW

The departure times of internal flights in Myanmar are still a little unreliable. So if when arriving at Yangon airport you discover your morning flight has been rescheduled to the afternoon, visit nearby Min Dahmma Kone (Kyauk Daw Gyi) Pagoda and Hsin Phyu Daw the home of the White Elephants—a ten minute cab drive from the airport. A long staircase leads up to a colossal 37 foot white marble Buddha image. The seated image in the 'earth touching mudra' weighs some 500 tons and is encased in a climatically controlled glass case. The view from the top terrace is stunning over looking beautiful un-spoilt countryside and on a clear day it is possible to see the Shwedagon Pagoda. The main Buddha image is accompanied by other smaller ones. Look down the covered staircase where the murals are of the Generals who commissioned the site in the year 2000. They are depicted laying the foundation stones welcoming the Buddha image and so on—interesting historical documents.

Just at the bottom of the hill is the home of 3 white elephants—not a very happy spot as although they look well they are chained up and pace back and forth. The White Elephant ever important in the history of the country, are supposed to bring 'peace, stability and prosperity' to the country.

THE ROAD TO BAGO

Some 40 minutes' drive from the centre of Yangon is the Htaukkyan War Cemetery. A vast circular colonnade bearing the names of those whose remains were never found forms the centre of the cemetery. One of the names inscribed here is that of The Marquis of Dufferin and Ava (the great-grandson of the Viceroy who annexed Burma in 1856), who ironically was killed at Ava. In all, some 27,000 Allied soldiers are buried here. The cemetery is a calm, peaceful place and is beautifully tended by the Commonwealth War Graves Commission. Each grave has a plaque atop engraved with the regiment's crest. Then comes the name, Private West Yorkshire C Sadler 15 January Aged 23. A message from his loving family, 'He died with England's heroes in the watchful care of God'. In between each plaque is some little shrub, perhaps a box (*buxus*) ball, or lantana covered in pink and yellow flowers. During the years of the war in Myanmar, a team from the War Graves Commission was always with the troops. When someone was killed he would be buried by his colleagues and the spot marked on a map by the War Graves team. At the end of the war, their remains were recovered and re-interred in one of the war cemeteries. Families from all over the world continue to visit the cemeteries (there are three in Myanmar alone). Remembrance Day in November sees the arrival of wreaths of poppies. Close to the cemetery is a curious shrine, a glass mosaic *naga* (serpent) wrapped around a Buddha image.

SIGHTS

SHWEMAWDAW PAGODA

The fine Shwemawdaw Pagoda stands 117 metres (374 feet) tall—taller than the Shwedagon, and overlooks Bago. Its history, the usual mixture of legend and fact, tells of two brothers who returned from India with two sacred hairs given to them by Gautama Buddha, which they enshrined in a pagoda. Later this pagoda was enlarged several times: in CE 825 to a height of 24 metres (81 feet); in 1385 to 86 metres (277 feet) by King Dhammazedi (who also added a tooth of the Buddha to the relics); and in 1796 King Bodawpaya raised it slightly, to 87 metres (279 feet), and donated a new *hti* (umbrella). Earthquakes have dealt savagely with the Shwemawdaw. The most devastating was in 1930, when the pagoda was flattened. It was not rebuilt until the 1950s, when, at the instigation of the then Prime Minister U Nu, it reached its present height and the marble path on the terrace was added. In design the 'Great Golden Pagoda' is not dissimilar to the

A touching inscription on a tombstone of a World War II soldier from Wales. The Commonwealth War Cemeteries in Myanmar are beautifully looked after and are a fitting memorial to all those who lost their lives. Especially comforting is the fact that men of many nationalities and ranks are buried together

Shwedagon. One ascends the covered western stairway and emerges onto a spacious terrace, with the stupa towering above. Beautiful umbrella-shaped trees shade parts of the terrace and a row of terracotta water pots is strategically placed at each trunk, so devotees can quench their thirst with a cup of cool water. Recently the stupa was being re-gilded, this time with gold plates. The pagoda trustees publish a little leaflet on the pagoda's history in both Burmese and English.

HINTHAGON
East of the Shwemawdaw Pagoda is Hinthagon Hill and Pagoda. This site is originally supposed to have been an island (which later became joined to the mainland) large enough for a pair of *hinthas* (mythical birds) to perch one on top of the other, marking the place of Bago's original settlement.

SHWETHALYAUNG
This magnificent reclining Buddha, 56 metres (180 feet) long and 18 metres (56 feet) high, dates from the reign of King Miga Depa. It was completed in CE 994. Resting on glass mosaic pillows, the face achieves serenity despite rather florid painted lines and the ugly shed in which it lies. The Shwethalyaung Buddha was

discovered abandoned in 1881, when the British were constructing the Yangon-Bago railway. It was restored, and then some time later the unfortunate shed was erected. The wide covered area leading up to the Buddha is filled with little stalls—an excellent place to buy carved wooden boxes or spoons, well-crafted from cherry, box and some sandalwood.

KALYANI SIMA

The original Kalyani Sima was a monks' ordination hall constructed by King Dhammazedi in 1476. It was destroyed by King Alaungpaya in 1757, but was rebuilt in the 1950s.

MAHAZEDI PAGODA

This is another pagoda which suffered the ravages of both King Alaungpaya and the 1930 earthquakes. King Bayinnaung built this 'Great Pagoda' in 1560 to house the Kandy Tooth (of the Buddha) which he thought he had acquired, only to discover that it was a fake. The original was still in Ceylon. The tooth was later removed by the victorious Burmese and temporarily installed in a pagoda in Toungoo. It was finally enshrined along with the offerings bowl in which it sits, in the Kaunghmundaw Pagoda in Sagaing.

BAGO PALACE SITE AND MUSEUM

The old palace site of the Mon dynasty is in the process of being excavated. The Hanthawady site is still not officially open to visitors and permission to visit is supposed to be sought in the Yangon office of the Archaeological Department. However, the janitor on the site gate is most likely to allow any foreigners access. Visitors will be directed to speak to the archaeologist in charge, who can be found in the offices next to the Museum. As the visitor walks or drives into the compound, a portion of the red brick wall which used to surround the palace stands on the left and it is possible to make out some foundations of the former palaces. Until recently, much of this area was a military compound. One of the palaces, the Sleeping Hall of the Burmese King Bayinnaung who made his capital at Bago from 1553–1599, has been rebuilt and the Great Audience Hall is presently under construction. Much as at the Mandalay Palace complex, these new buildings, although authentic replicas of the original, have little atmosphere.

During a previous visit, all the artefacts unearthed were stored in a collection of mat sheds at one end of the dig—to see a group of fine stone Buddha images laid out side by side on an old wooden table, some still covered in earth, was a true thrill. Now a proportion of these pieces are on show in the adjacent Museum, while the rest have been sent to the National Museum in Yangon (see page 128). The small site museum is a single-storey octagonal building topped with a Burmese-style roof and has a certain charm. An interesting selection of stone sculptures is displayed around the edge of the one-room building. Each exhibit is well labelled and often accompanied by a quotation from a merchant traveller—such as Samuel Purchas—who had visited the city in the 16th century, at the height of its importance as a trading centre. The core of the exhibition space is taken up with glass cabinets displaying old coins, opium weights and a fine sandstone Buddha image.

To date the earlier Mon site of Okthar to the east, has not been excavated.

KYAIKPUN

As you leave Bago on the Yangon Road there is a most extraordinary sight—four enormous Buddhas sitting back-to-back against a central square pediment. This statue of the Four Buddhas of the present world cycle is again part of King Dhammazedi's immense building programme. Dhammazedi was a deeply religious man and only left the monkhood when appointed king by Queen Shin Saw Pu, who donated her weight in gold to the Shwedagon Pagoda. King Dhammazedi built the 28-metre- (90-foot-) high Buddhas in 1476, but the 1930 earthquake badly damaged the Buddha on the west side. For many years this magnificent edifice was forgotten, and allowed to decay with vegetation sprouting here and there which gave it a mysterious quality. Recently it has been restored. All the surrounding undergrowth has been cleared, the approach was widened and a walkway—with the inevitable hawkers in situ—erected. At the base of the images is a paved terrace from which to admire the Buddhas, which have been newly painted and their robes inlaid with mosaic. Some of the old magic is lost.

KYAIKTIYO PAGODA

Kyaiktiyo Pagoda, atop a huge golden rock precariously balanced on the edge of a crag, is about 65 kilometres (40 miles) east of Bago on the railway line to Mawlamyine (Moulmein). It is one of Myanmar's most spectacular sights. A special permit was required for foreigners to visit the golden rock but not anymore. Once arrived in Kinpun, the village at the bottom of the hill, it is necessary to negotiate a price for a seat in a four-wheel-drive truck which will drive halfway up to the pagoda. The bumpy road twists and turns through tree-clad hills with high mountains in the distance. A 35-minute journey takes the traveller to the end of the road. After a quick drink in one of the little cafés, the climb on foot begins. For those not so fit, or for the elderly, there are bamboo sedan chairs, which are carried by four young men. As the path is both narrow and steep in places the bearers have to possess the agility of a goat. At intervals along the way are little stalls selling *thanaka*, Nirvana goods, odd medicinal concoctions, snakes in bottles, a variety of herbal potions plus some local crafts such as rather charming bamboo spectacles, as well as much-needed drinks. The pilgrim's trek is made more pleasant by children sprinkling the dusty path with water, an act which also helps them with their acquisition of merit.

Three-quarters of the way up, the Kyaiktiyo Pagoda becomes visible across on the next ridge, looking rather small. Sir George Scott set the scene well: 'The boulder stands on the extreme verge of the bare rock and hangs over it as if a gust of wind or a few extra pounds added would make it topple over and crash down the dizzy height far away into the green valley below.' It is on this huge boulder that the tiny gold pagoda is perched.

The last part of the 45-minute ascent is through a little village where the surroundings become more domestic. A brick pathway lined with flowers in pots leads towards the pagoda. But before visiting the pagoda, stop and admire the view from the guesthouse, a one-storey building retaining an 'old world' charm. Walk through the main reception area and out on to the balcony. Built on the edge of the ridge, the guesthouse has a magnificent view over the surrounding tree-clad mountains, with the pagoda to the right. The guesthouse has some 18 double rooms which are nice and clean, and the food is good, so it makes an excellent overnight stop. Nowadays there is a second guesthouse also with a stunning view of the rock and the valley below.

As a result of the increase in visitors recently—Kyaiktiyo is one of the country's most revered Buddhist shrines—a collection of rest-houses, bathhouses, restaurants and shops has sprung up around the pagoda precinct. The area is reminiscent of a French village square. The general babble of noise is occasionally overridden by prayers intoned over a loudspeaker. A sign requesting 'Foreign visitors please report here' greets the overseas traveller. This is the collection point for camera charges.

The pagoda sits slightly below the square. Men are allowed to enter the pagoda enclosure, to pray and paste gold leaf on the boulder, which is by all accounts soft to the touch. Women have to follow the steps down on to the 'ladies terrace'. Sadly, an ugly lower terrace has been added to allow space for the pilgrims to lay down their mats on the marble and pray; some even spend the night there. Although there is now an air of commercialism about Kyaiktiyo, it is still a moving experience to watch the light fade and the swifts swoop over the boulder while a few monks meditate, unaware of the material world around them.

According to legend, the boulder is held safe by the strength of yet another strand of the Buddha's hair which is enshrined in the pagoda. The legend tells that on one of the Buddha's visits to earth, 'on the occasion of teaching the law to his mother', he had given a hair to the hermit Taik Tha, who had kept it in his own top-knot. When the hermit was dying, his adopted son King Tissa (whose mother was a beautiful *naga)* came to pay his last respects. The dying hermit's last request was that the Buddha's hair should be enshrined in a pagoda built on a rock resembling the shape of his head. Thagyamin, King of the Nats, then helped Tissa with his search and found the perfect place for the pagoda.

THANLYIN (SYRIAM)

For those who find they have an extra day in Yangon, either at the beginning or at the end of their trip, a trip to Thanlyin and its surroundings offers a microcosm of Burmese charm—the river, a sleepy former European settlement, the countryside, golden pagodas and distant views of the Shwedagon. Since the 270-metre- (9,000-foot-) long bridge spanning the Bago River was finished in 1993, it is now possible to

drive to Thanlyin. The journey from the centre of Yangon to Kyauktan Pagoda (also called Ye Le Paya) will take about one hour. When travelling over the bridge look back towards Yangon for the fine view of the Shwedagon Pagoda on the horizon. For the more time-consuming old-fashioned route, go to the Thanlyin jetty on Pazundaung Creek. There board a shabby ferry. There are two passenger decks, the sides open to the breeze, the floors crowded with people while hawkers nimbly move about the boat, a brilliant exercise in agility. The journey takes roughly 45 minutes. On arrival at Thanlyin either hire a jeep or a pony trap. (If you want to visit Kyauktan Pagaoda or the Kyaik-Khauk Pagoda, take a jeep as it is too far for a pony trap.)

A golden spire of the Kyauktan Pagoda, near Thanlyin, glistens against the dappled midday sky.
Also called Ye Le Paya ('in the middle of the water'), this pagoda is only accessible by boat

From 1600 to 1613 Thanlyin (then called Syriam) was the stronghold of the Portuguese adventurer, Felipe de Brito. In 1617, The East India Company sent Messrs Forrest and Stavely to Thanlyin, marking the beginning of Burmese-British trade. By 1647 The East India Company had built a dock and house at Thanlyin and the settlement developed into a highly successful trading post with Portuguese, Dutch, French and British bases. The Burmese bought cotton goods and in return sold *ganza* (a fabric similar to organdie), rice and large Martaban jars (used to transport fresh water and grain to sea-going ships). The town flourished until it was destroyed by King Alaungpaya in 1756. When the British annexed Lower Myanmar 96 years later it was Yangon rather than Thanlyin that became the main trading post.

One or two European-style buildings are the only evidence of Thanlyin's days as host to European traders. Today's inhabitants are mostly involved with the oil industry or the local brewery, but there are plans to turn the town into a business and industrial area.

Sights

KYAIK-KHAUK AND PAIDAHGYI PAGODAS

A few miles south of the town up on a hill stands the Kyaik-Khauk Pagoda, a golden pagoda with lines reminiscent of the Shwedagon. The graves of two Burmese writers, Natshingaung and Padethayaza, are to be found just beside the pagoda. Nearby is the Paidahgyi Pagoda which contains a large Buddha. The building's glass mosaic pillars sparkle jauntily in the sunlight while the bells on top of the *hti* provide a gentle, comforting jingle. From the pagoda's platform there is fine view of Yangon, the Shwedagon standing tall beside the city's few highrises.

KYAUKTAN PAGODA (YE LE PAYA)

If one continues on this road going south, some 21 kilometres (13 miles) from Thanlyin one enters the village of Kyauktan. Walk through the market—a particularly attractive and thriving one—take a right turn, and there in front of you in the middle of the river is a golden pagoda. Beside the little jetty are stalls piled high with flowers and eugenia sprigs for pilgrims to take across to the pagoda. Also on sale are strings of rice cracker balls, with which to feed the large and greedy catfish which swim around the island. A small boat will cross to Kyauktan Pagoda or Ye Le Paya (literally: 'pagoda in the middle of the water'). The picture as a whole is magnificent—the glistening gold of the stupa contrasted by the brown water and the dark green of the palm trees.

A SECOND HOMECOMING

*F*lory had never been home to England. Why, he could not have explained, though he knew well enough. In the beginning accidents had prevented him. First there was the War, and after the War his firm were so short of trained assistants that they would not let him go for two years more. Then at last he had set out. He was pining for England, though he dreaded facing it, as one dreads facing a pretty girl when one is collarless and unshaven. When he left home he had been a boy, a promising boy and handsome in spite of his birthmark; now, only ten years later, he was yellow, thin, drunken, almost middle-aged in habits and appearance. Still, he was pining for England. The ship rolled westward over wastes of sea like rough-beaten silver, with the winter trade wind behind her. Flory's thin blood quickened with the good food and the smell of the sea. And it occurred to him—a thing he had actually forgotten in the stagnant air of Burma—that he was still young enough to begin over again. He would live a year in civilised society, he would find some girl who did not mind his birthmark—a civilised girl, not a pukka memsahib— and he would marry her and endure ten, fifteen more years of Burma. Then they would retire—he would be worth twelve or fifteen thousand pounds on retirement, perhaps. They would buy a cottage in the country, surround themselves with friends, books, their children, animals. They would be free for ever of the smell of pukka sahibdom. He would forget Burma, the horrible country that had come near ruining him.

When he reached Colombo he found a cable waiting for him. Three men in his firm had died suddenly of blackwater fever. The firm were sorry, but would he please return to Rangoon at once? He should have his leave at the earliest possible opportunity.

Flory boarded the next boat for Rangoon, cursing his luck, and took the train back to his headquarters. He was not at Kyauktada then, but at another Upper Burma town. All the servants were waiting for him on the platform. He had handed them over en bloc to his successor, who had died. It was so queer to see their familiar faces again! Only ten days ago he had been speeding for England, almost thinking himself in England already; and now back in the old stale scene, with the naked black coolies squabbling over the luggage and a Burman shouting at his bullocks down the road.

The servants came crowding round him, a ring of kindly brown faces, offering presents. Ko S'la had brought a sambhur skin, the Indians some sweetmeats and a garland of marigolds, Be Pe, a young boy then, a squirrel in a wicker cage. There were bullock carts waiting for the luggage. Flory walked up to the house, looking ridiculous with the big garland dangling from his neck. The light of the cold-weather evening was yellow and kind. At the gate an old Indian, the colour of earth, was cropping grass with a tiny sickle. The wives of the cook and the mali were kneeling in front of the servants' quarters, grinding curry paste on the stone slab.

Something turned over in Flory's heart. It was one of those moments when one becomes conscious of a vast change and deterioration in one's life. For he had realised, suddenly, that in his heart he was glad to be coming back. This country which he hated was now his native country, his home. He had lived here for ten years, and every particle of his body was compounded of Burmese soil. Scenes like these—the sallow evening light, the old Indian cropping grass, the creak of the cartwheels, the streaming egrets—were more native to him than England. He had sent deep roots, perhaps his deepest, into a foreign country.

George Orwell, Burmese Days, 1934

Elephant positioning teak log for the downstream journey

(above) One of the Mandalay Palace's impossing twelve gates, sadly the interior buildings were almost entirely destroyed in fierce fighting towards the end of the Japanese occupation of the city; (below) The Chhaganlalgalliara Memorial Hall, built shortly after Orwell's Burmese Days *was published*

MANDALAY

> For the wind is in the palm trees, an' the temple-bells
> they say:
> Come you back to Mandalay,
> Where the old Flotilla lay...

In fact Rudyard Kipling never went to Mandalay, but he did capture the romance, mystery and intrigue which the name conjures up.

Mandalay's magic is not immediately apparent; for most of the year the town is hot and dusty, and for the rest chilly and damp. The majority of houses are wooden, with the occasional rather grand stucco mansion—remnants of colonial days. Though in recent years the city landscape has changed somewhat. Many of the rich merchants whose new wealth springs from trade with China have built themselves large mansions. The city has a spacious feel; each home has its earthen yard, either front or back. The Burmese are inveterate gardeners: lush bougainvillea tumble over fences, their startling pinks and oranges glowing against the dust-brown of the houses. But only the Palace walls and a number of religious monuments survive to remind us of Mandalay's past as Myanmar's capital.

Although relatively youthful as Burmese cities go (it was built between 1857 and 1859), Mandalay is indeed worthy of its exotic reputation. The 'Gem City' was the scene both of incredible splendour and of appalling cruelty. In 1879, during the staging of a three-day *pwe* (entertainment) for his subjects, King Theebaw had 80 of his close relatives murdered because he thought they were conspiring to depose him, while noisy music helped deafen the sound of butchery. Enclosed in red velvet bags (red velvet to mask and absorb the blood, the sight of which would have horrified the Burmese) these royal corpses were then deposited in the Ayeyarwady River.

Today, Mandalay has settled down and, with a population of approximately 1.2 million, is Myanmar's second-largest city. It continues to be an important Buddhist centre, not only boasting possession of the much fought-over Mahamuni Image (see page 157) but also the Kuthodaw Pagoda and the sacred Peshawar Relics, which are on display in the U Khanti Museum (in the U Khanti Monastery). It is also the main market town for Upper Myanmar, a place for the hill tribe peoples to gather, and the gateway to the mountain strongholds of the Shans and Kachins. The overland trade route to China also begins here.

Unlike Yangon, Mawlamyine or Taunggyi, where so much evidence of colonialism lingers, Mandalay feels purely Burmese. For the traveller it is the centre of a vast amount to see: nearby are the former capitals of Ava (modern day

Inwa), Amarapura and Sagaing, as well as the interesting towns of Mingun and Pyin Oo Lwin (formerly Maymyo). In fact Mandalay and its surroundings are worthy of a week's visit in themselves. Sadly, however, it is often relegated to a single day's sightseeing.

HISTORY

In 1853 King Mindon ascended the Lion Throne of Upper Burma. (Following the first and second Anglo-Burmese Wars the British controlled Lower Burma.) In his capital of Amarapura on the banks of the Irrawaddy, Mindon heard tales of the growing importance of Rangoon, so to restore the diminished glory of the Kingdom of Ava, he planned a new capital, although he cited religion as the reason for the move. According to Buddhist legend, during his life on earth, the Buddha had stood with his disciple Ananda at the top of Mandalay Hill and prophesied the building of a religious city on the plain below. Thus by building a new capital rich in religious monuments the devout Mindon could at the same time commemorate the 2,400th anniversary of the Buddha's death and fulfill the prophecy, as well as provide the British with a reminder of his power.

The chief monks and soothsayers agreed on a site to the south of Mandalay hill, not too near the river. This suited Mindon excellently, for in his palace at Amarapura 'the noise of the foreign steamers disturbed the royal repose'. A plan was drawn up (the original, a beautiful scroll with the buildings painted in red and gold, can be seen in the Print Department of the India Office Library in London), and in June 1857 the move from Amarapura commenced. Mindon took up residence in a temporary palace at the foot of Mandalay Hill.

Historians do not agree on whether or not Mindon actually had a number of his subjects buried alive under the four corners of the city's foundations. (The basis for this age-old Burmese practice was that the victims' spirits would protect the city from its enemies.) If indeed he did, the antidote did not prove effective against the British, who overran Mandalay in 1885. By 1859 the Gem City was fully inhabited, a royal proclamation having decreed that all citizens of Amarapura were to move with the king and his court (the Chinese merchants were the only ones to refuse). 1879 saw the death of Mindon and the accession of his son Theebaw.

The new king—Burma's last—was a weak creature, entirely under the control of his shrewish queen, Supayalat, and her mother. For statesmanship or the welfare of his subjects Theebaw cared little, although he was a devout Buddhist. The royal couple lived an idle, decadent life in their gilded palace. Meanwhile, the Anglo-French conflict reached its climax with the annexation of Mandalay by the British in 1885. On 29th November the king and queen departed from their palace

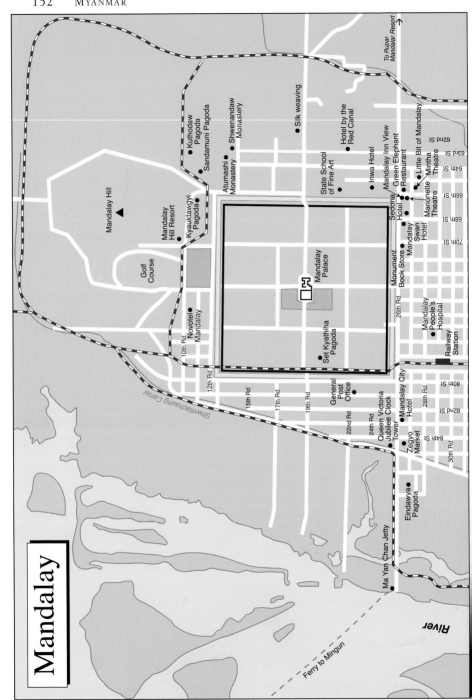

Mandalay

To Rupar Mandalar Resort →

Silk weaving

Hotel by the Red Canal

Shwenandaw Monastery

Kuthodaw Pagoda

Sandamuni Pagoda

Atumashi Monastery

State School of Fine Art

Inwa Hotel

Mandalay Inn View

Green Elephant Restaurant

Little Bit of Mandalay

Mintha Theatre

62nd St
63rd St
64th St
66th St
68th St
70th St

Kyauktawgyi Pagoda

Mandalay Hill

Mandalay Hill Resort

Golf Course

Sedona Hotel

Marionette Theatre

Mandalay Swan Hotel

Monument

Mandalay Book Store

Mandalay Palace

26th Rd

Mandalay People's Hospital

Novotel Mandalay

Set Kyathiha Pagoda

Railway Station

80th St

10th Rd
12th Rd
15th Rd
17th Rd
19th Rd

General Post Office

Queen Victoria Jubilee Clock Tower

Mandalay City Hotel

22nd Rd
24th Rd
28th Rd

Zegyo Market

82nd St
84th St

30th Rd

Shwetachaung Canal

Eindawya Pagoda

Ma Yan Chan Jetty

Ferry to Mingun

River

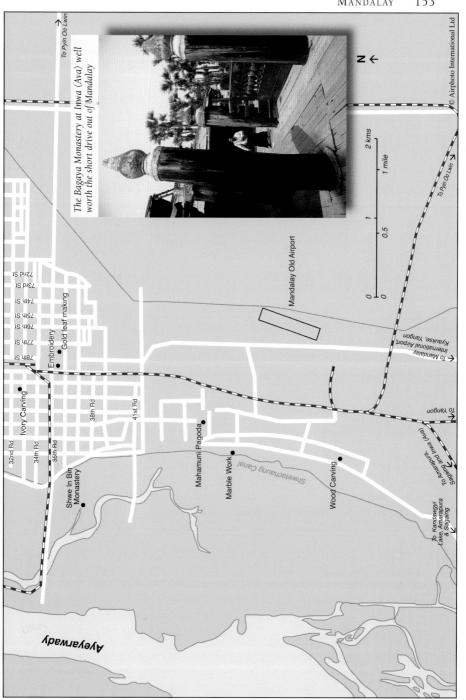

The Bagaya Monastery at Inwa (Ava) well worth the short drive out of Mandalay

© Airphoto International Ltd

N

To Pyin Oo Lwin

To Pyin Oo Lwin

To Pyin Oo Lwin

To Mandalay International Airport Kyaukse, Yangon

To Yangon

To Amarapura and Inwa (Ava)

To Kandawgyi Lake, Amarapura & Sagaing

Sagaing

Mandalay Old Airport

2 kms

1 mile

0   0.5   1

Ayeyarwady

72nd St
73rd St
74th St
75th St
76th St
77th St
78th St

Embroidery

Gold leaf making

Ivory Carving

32nd Rd
34th Rd
35th Rd
38th Rd
41st Rd

Shwe In Bin Monastery

Mahamuni Pagoda

Marble Work

Shwetachaung Canal

Wood Carving

by ox-cart. Remaining at least true to her thick-skinned character, the remarkable Supayalat seemed as unimpressed by the ignominy of her downfall as she had been oblivious to her royal obligations during her years of power. Arriving at the Irrawaddy quayside on her journey into exile, she leaned out of the cart holding up her cheroot, whereupon 'there was a general rush to supply her with a box of matches. Smiling, the Queen accepted a light from a delighted Tommy'.

The City of Gems was to see many changes. The Lord of the White Elephant, deprived of his kingdom and palace, soon died. With Burma now a province of British India, the Mandalay Palace was renamed Fort Dufferin, after the then Viceroy of India, who was later to become the Marquis of Dufferin and Ava. The fort was used as the administrative headquarters, while the Hall of Audience became the church, an altar being set up in front of the Lion Throne.

For the next 50 years the city prospered, river trade boomed, and when the railways were extended into Upper Burma, Mandalay served as the northern terminus. Although Mandalay enjoyed a calm unknown in the time of Theebaw, the excitement and intrigue of former days was missed by some: colonialist Sir George Scott lamented, 'There are no agreeable scallywags. There are Cooks tourists instead during the three cool months of the year.'

April 1942 brought an end to the calm with the arrival of the invading Japanese army. For three years they used Mandalay as their northern headquarters, and Allied planes repeatedly bombed the city. As the majority of the buildings were wooden, the resulting fires were horrendous. In March 1945, Gurkha and British troops stormed the city and, after fierce fighting, took the Japanese strongholds of Fort Dufferin and Mandalay Hill. During their occupation the Japanese had built an intricate web of concrete-lined tunnels in the pagoda-covered hill. Unfortunately, the palace did not survive the Allied attack. 'The palace had been burnt down,' Field Marshall Slim recalled, 'whether fired by our shelling and bombing, although we had tried to avoid it, or by the Japanese to destroy the stores they had in it, I do not know.' Since then Mandalay has not managed to escape further fires, which break out in different parts of the city with distressing frequency. The worst of these occurred in the spring of 1985.

The fortunes of Mandalay changed dramatically during the 1980s, when the border with China was re-opened. Free as well as black market trade moves back and forth along the old Burma Road. The markets buzz, some young entrepreneurs have discarded their *longyis* for Western dress, buildings both public and private are—by decree—given frequent coats of paint and pots of flowers decorate the roadsides. Roads have been mended, new ones built, new joint-venture hotels constructed, and a new airport that has the capacity to take jumbo jets is completed. All in all, Mandalay is now a boomtown. To quote a local, it has acquired 'a little bit of a face-lift'.

SIGHTS
MANDALAY PALACE

The Hall of Audience with its seven-tiered golden spire stood at the 'Centre of the Universe', as the palace was called, surrounded by the other throne halls: the Duck Throne, where foreigners were received; the Elephant and Deer Thrones, employed for purposes relating to the Lord White Elephant; and the Lily Throne, where the Chief Queen received guests on feast days. In all there were 133 apartments (Mindon had 49 recognized wives and many concubines who between them produced 50 sons and 64 daughters) within the massive, pink, crenellated walls. The palaces were built of teak, lacquered, gilded and, in some instances, such as the Glass Palace, entirely covered with mosaics of coloured glass. To the Westerner, there was however an eyesore—the corrugated iron roofs 'the invention of which must rank among the major crimes of the Western world'. But to Mindon they were both practical and almost the ideal colour (traditionally a king was supposed to live beneath silver roofs), and they were reminiscent of the Great Khan's fabled palaces of shining roofs. The lotus-covered moat was spanned by white bridges leading to the 12 gates. There were three gates on each of the two-kilometre (one-and-a-quarter-mile) sides of the square. Guarding every gate was a delicate wooden spire (*pyathat*). The main entrance was the eastern gate which was reserved exclusively for the use of the king and the royal family. Foreigners and condemned men were relegated to the inauspicious western gate. Two little tricks were employed to remind foreigners of court protocol. First, the lintel on the western gate was so low that the visitor had to bend to enter. Second, nails were

A 19th-century carved wood and gilt samari *figure from one of the nine royal thrones in the palace at Mandalay. It has a lion's head on a bull's body, with the hooves and horns of a deer. The end of the tail is carved separately, and is movable, a feature common to such figures*

Karen maidens wearing Burmese court dress, each coiffed in a traditional hairstyle. This dress was in vogue until 1886, when the British dissolved the court of King Theebaw and Queen Supayalat. Today, it is often worn as a costume by female dancers at pwes *(evening entertainments)*

placed in the floor of the Duck Throne Room, their points surreptitiously poking up through the polished teak boards. It being de rigueur to remove footwear in the palace, this forced wary barefooted foreigners to remain bent in supplication.

To visit the 809 hectares (2,000 acres) of the palace grounds today a guide is required, as units of the Burmese Army are stationed within its walls. There is a scale model of the palace as it was—but until recently all that remained of the original were some foundations, King Theebaw's palace (without its roof), the original plinth of the Lion Throne (the throne itself is now in the National Museum in Yangon), and a reconstructed version of the Glass Palace. Then, a few years ago an extensive and costly renovation programme was ordered by the government, with the divisions of Mandalay, Sagaing shouldering the burden of finance—though many a voice has suggested that the money would have been better spent elsewhere. As one enters the palace complex a sign proclaiming 'Tatmadaw (army) and the People co operate and crush all those harming the Union', is a reminder of the army's presence. A number of the palace buildings have been reconstructed, but although they are accurate copies of the originals, much of the detail is missing, so the visitor is denied the sense of majesty that must have formerly existed. It is now possible to climb up the helter-skelter-shaped watchtower, from where there is a fine view of the city.

On the south-west side of the palace site stands the Set Kyathiha Pagoda, a peaceful haven and home to a serene golden Buddha image. Away from the 'new' palace buildings, the visitor can wander among the remaining ruins and scrub jungle, and with a keen sense of imagination visualize the exotic elegance, the other-worldly calm, the tragi-comic pride and intrigue of the court of King Mindon.

SHWENANDAW MONASTERY

The only palace building to survive World War II intact was the Shwenandaw Monastery (Shwenandaw Kyaung). King Theebaw thought it was inauspicious (his father King Mindon had died in the building) and, on his accession in 1879, had it moved to its present location east of the palace, not far from the foot of Mandalay Hill. This beautiful building is surrounded by a teak platform supported on wooden pillars topped with marble lotus flowers. The outer walls are finely carved, some panels decorated with mythical animals, others dancing figures; the rest a lace-like trellis carving of vines and flowers. The weather, which has given the teak a soft greyish-brown patina, has dealt savagely with the reliefs, many of which are crumbling and pitted. Inside the building are two massive halls. The main hall contains a copy of the Lion Throne, a Buddha image commissioned by Theebaw with the features of his father, and a gold couch that Theebaw is said to have used during meditative visits here. This room retains echoes of its courtly past. Each massive pillar is a single trunk of teak still showing remnants of vermilion, lacquer, gold and filigree decorations. Around the ceiling base are fine carvings of *nats* worshipping the Buddha; the ceiling itself is painted with golden sparrows. This ornamentation is lit rather charmingly by a single neon strip complete with dangling cobwebs.

Shwenandaw Monastery is a beautiful wooden building decorated with exquisite carvings. It was originally the living quarters of King Mindon within the Mandalay Palace. After his death, his son King Theebaw moved the building out of the palace compound to its present site. A lucky move, as the rest of the palace buildings were destroyed by incendiary bombs during World War II

In the run-up to Visit Myanmar Year 1996 many of Mandalay's best buildings were over-restored. Sadly this stunning monastery is one of the casualties. Once the head monk died the Shwenandaw Monastery was closed, the young monks were sent elsewhere and the building was declared a 'heritage site'. Much of the old roof carvings have been replaced with workman-like reproductions and a heavy hand has plastered the whole of the exterior with a thick coat of creosote. Luckily, the occasional pieces of gold lacquer on some outside relief carvings have been preserved. The renovations to the exterior have meant that the monastery has lost some of its depth, as the new carvings are somehow one-dimensional. And without the monks living in the building much of its spiritual soul has evaporated. However, the interior, with the living quarters of the monks gone, is perhaps more as it would have been when King Mindon used it as his palace. The one positive element of the renovation is that the second main hall is now open. A huge grand space, the walls and ceiling are covered in faded gold leaf. The room is dissected by vast wooden pillars and the cornice is decorated with stories of the *Jataka*.

For the first-time visitor, the Shwenandaw Monastery is of course still a fascinating building. But it is sad that the restoration was not carried out with more attention to preserving all of its charm and beauty. Though visiting the building again some twelve years later the weather has removed much of the harsh creosote and the magic of the palace is very much intact.

ATUMASHI MONASTERY

The Atumashi Monastery (Incomparable Kyaung) stands beside the Shwenandaw Monastery and was, until recently, a shell of stairs and foundations. Completed in 1878, it was the last great religious edifice constructed by King Mindon. It housed four valuable sets of the Tripitaka (Buddhist sacred texts) and a nine-metre- (30-foot-) high standing Buddha with a huge diamond set into the forehead. On the evening of 29th November, 1885, the night following King Theebaw's surrender to General Prendergast, Mandalay was overrun by dacoits (bandits) and the diamond was stolen—some say by British soldiers. It has never been recovered. In 1890 the monastery was destroyed by fire, but what remained of the stucco carving was quite fine. Unfortunately, nothing of this quintessential 'pleasure of ruins' now stands. The whole building was torn down and reconstructed in preparation for Visit Myanmar Year. The vast new edifice was built to the original plans, but unfortunately the workmanship was not very good and the exterior of the building and surrounding terrace is already cracking. You enter the former monastery up a grand staircase and into a huge empty space except for a Buddha image—totally out of proportion to the area. At least the majestic trees, which surround the compound, have been left.

KUTHODAW PAGODA (MAHA LAWKAMAZIN)

In 1857 King Mindon built the Kuthodaw Pagoda, a copy of the Shwezigon Pagoda in Pagan (modern day Bagan), which itself had been completed in 1087 during the reign of King Anawrahta. At the entrance to the pagoda visitors were gently reminded of Burmese custom: 'Prohibited Footwearing Cycling Umbrella Holding'—but sadly the sign has now vanished. A long, cool corridor leads to the pagoda itself which stands in a beautiful setting surrounded by little white stupas and huge, spreading star-flower trees—though several of these trees are now showing their age. As so often in Myanmar, the simple beauty of the stupa is marred by ad hoc wiring which supplies unattractive neon light (as opposed to the charming variety in the Shwenandaw) to the *hti* (umbrella)—a nightmare for keen photographers. Another victim of Visit Myanmar Year was the removal, by the entrance to the pagoda platform, of several early 20th-century clockwork sideshows: one would climb some wooden steps, place a coin in the open mouth of a cat, and around came models of Myanmar's hill tribes. This was a typical Burmese mixture of religious and secular life found within a pagoda. Perhaps the greatest tragedy that has emerged from the rush to smarten up as many of the country's great buildings as possible, in readiness for the Visit Myanmar Year, has been the introduction of what is locally called 'Japan *shwe*'. This form of synthetic gold paint from Japan has found its way onto many of the country's smaller stupas. For centuries these would have been white-washed, with the larger ones perhaps topped off with a golden *hti* (umbrella). Unlike real gold, this synthetic paint has no depth or life, so the stupas no longer twinkle in the sun. Indeed the beautiful Kuthodaw stupa was white but today's visitor will find it gilded—the top with real gold the lower portion with 'Japan shwe'. Some of the small stupas at the base of Kuthodaw have fallen victim to this unattractive paint.

Kuthodaw is often called 'the biggest book in the world', for surrounding it are 729 marble slabs inscribed with the Tripitaka texts (the index is to be found beside the main entrance). In 1871 King Mindon convened a meeting of 2,400 monks from all over the country to discuss the Buddhist texts. After several months of deliberation a new 'authorized' version was agreed on. The texts were then carved on to the marble slabs and this became the authentic version of the Tripitaka. Mindon felt this would safeguard the scriptures, which were otherwise highly vulnerable (as indeed proved the case at the Incomparable Monastery) for they were traditionally recorded on palm leaves.

SANDAMUNI PAGODA

Sandamuni is another pagoda surrounded by inscribed marble slabs, in this case housed in mini-stupas, whereas those of the Kuthodaw are in square houses with a twirl of icing-sugar plaster on top. These slabs record commentaries on the Tripitaka. Mindon moved in June 1857 from Amarapura to a temporary palace on this site to oversee the building of his new Gem City. The site also bears sad associations. It was here that Mindon's half-brother and confidante, Crown Prince Kanaung, is buried. In gratitude for the Prince's help in overthrowing his predecessor, King Pagan Min, Mindon made Kanaung crown prince. On 8th June, 1866, two of Mindon's sons, aggrieved at being excluded from the succession, planned to assassinate both their father and uncle. They consulted the ponnas (Brahmin soothsayers) who suggested an auspicious day on which the

The arduous climb up Mandalay Hill is rewarding. Half-way up, a glorious view of the plain unfolds. In the foreground is the fine sight of the Kuthodaw Pagoda surrounded by 729 mini stupas, each housing a portion of the holy Buddhist texts, the Tripitaka

ponnas knew Mindon was to visit his temporary palace, leaving Prince Kanaung in charge. The rebel princes stormed the palace, killed Kanaung, and then set off for the temporary palace intending to murder their father. Mindon, however, managed to escape and returned safely to the Gem City. The princes had left only a solitary guard to watch for the king, and Mindon's loyal slaves made quick work of him. This tragedy is probably the reason Mindon failed to appoint another successor, thus making it possible for the scheming Central Queen, mother of Supayalat, to persuade the King on his deathbed to acclaim his weakling son, Theebaw, as successor.

KYAUKTAWGYI PAGODA

At the foot of Mandalay Hill stands the Kyauktawgyi Pagoda. The covered corridor leads through a garden, where images of Buddha's 80 disciples (20 on each side) stand guard, each in a little house. A painted fresco around the end of the corridor illustrates 16 dreams of King Kawsala (an Indian king and contemporary of Gautama Buddha)—premonitions which were predicted to come true on the

2,500th anniversary of the Buddha's death, which by Burmese reckoning fell in 1952. (There is much variation in the records as to when and for how long Gautama Buddha lived, though common belief is that he was born in India in 566 BCE and lived for 80 years.) One of the fresco panels tells of the world's women fighting for liberation.

Originally Mindon planned for this pagoda to be styled after the Ananda Temple in Bagan, but the finished version bears no resemblance to it. Instead of four colossal Buddha images, it houses only one. This is crafted from a single piece of the palest green marble quarried at Sagyin, some 18 kilometres (12 miles) up the Ayeyarwady. It was rafted downriver to Mandalay, but there was no way to transport it over the last leg, across dry land. A canal was dug but, the story goes, there was not sufficient water to sustain the giant raft. So 10,000 conscripted labourers were ordered into the canal, thus raising the water level sufficiently to allow the great marble slab to be floated to its destination, where it was then carved into its present form. It is a beautiful image, and—for one so large—conveys profound serenity. The head is decorated with delicate gold filigree. The dress and shawl are inlaid with jewels, all of which, save for the central diamond, are said to be synthetic. To remind one of the 20th century a green telephone in a padlocked box stands close by.

Mandalay is a logging centre. Huge teak logs are unlashed from the raft and then trunk by trunk, hauled out of the river by water buffalo. These stately animals work in pairs: yoked together they drag the vast trunk on to the mud bank, obeying the authoritative voice of the handler. Once the trunk has been loaded on to the lorry, the buffalo flop back into the river, yoke and all, for a well-earned wallow while awaiting their next turn

MANDALAY HILL

Two enormous lions guard the foot of the southern staircase leading up the sacred Mandalay Hill. The best time to visit is early morning, before breakfast, avoiding the heat of the day. The view from the top is spectacular. To the south and east lies the city of Mandalay, Mindon's 'Cluster of Gems', and beyond it early morning mists roll off the huge Ayeyarwady. (Sir George Scott knew this view well and noted how, 'The river glitters like diamonds in the patches that catch the early sun.') If it is not too misty the Inwa Bridge and the barren, pagoda-crowned hills of Sagaing will be visible. To the north and west, the broad rice-growing plains meld into the Shan Hills. Of the religious monuments themselves, the first pagoda on ascending the hill contains the Peshawar Relics (now exhibited at the U Khanti Museum on the west side of Mandalay Hill). These relics are said to be three bones of the Buddha originally given to the king of Peshawar (now in Pakistan) by the great King Ashoka around CE 235 and passed on in turn to the Burmese Buddhist Society by the British in 1908. By then Peshawar, once a Buddhist centre, had long since become predominantly Islamic.

Further up, the huge golden Shweyattaw Buddha stands guard over the city. It is here that the Buddha, accompanied by his disciple Ananda, is thought to have stood and prophesied the building of a great religious city. Before commencing his 'City of Gems', Mindon erected this statue in memory of the Buddha's prophesy. This figure is unusual in that, unlike most Buddha images, his hands are not portrayed in the traditional *mudra* position; rather, his right hand points to the city below. Nowadays it is no longer necessary to climb the some 1,728 steps, as a road has been built up the west side of the hill, as have an escalator and a lift. At the top of the Hill stands the Sutaungpyi Pagoda glistening with bright blue and silver glass mosaic cladding. Much of the money for the new mosaic was raised abroad. The names of the donors, such as 'the Famigilia Belfiore Restaurant, Roma Italia' are inscribed around the building. The terraces of the pagoda have been greatly enlarged to accommodate the hundreds of tourists, both local and foreign, who gather every evening to watch the sun set over the Ayeyarwady. The viewing terrace is edged with high bar stools—no where near enough for the visitors— interspersed with a few telescopes.

SILK WEAVING

A pleasant interlude to a pagoda-packed day is to visit the silk weavers in the street opposite the eastern entrance to Mandalay Palace. You know you are approaching the correct location when you hear the 'clack-clack' of the looms, on which the traditional wedding *longyis* for both men and women are woven. Two girls work at each wooden loom passing the 100 to 200 different bobbins to and

fro as they thread them through the silk, with a mirror near at hand to check the pattern. Today the silk yarn is imported from Japan, and the dye mainly from Britain; formerly vegetable dyes would have been used. One of these beautiful *longyis*, 1.1 metres (44 inches) wide and 1.8 metres (two yards) long, should cost between 3,500 and 5,000 kyats. At the back of the workroom is a large shop, which sells the silk *longyis* and other locally made garments.

STATE SCHOOL OF FINE ART

Just south of the silk weavers' street is the State School of Fine Art. Here you can watch young hopefuls being coached in the Burmese performing arts: dance, music, puppetry and acting. The discordant crashes and wails of the music can be trying to the untrained ear, but the fluid, elegant movements of the dancers are a pleasure to behold. The Burmese are also highly skilled at puppetry, which has a tradition dating from the 11th century. Mandalay boasts some fine professional puppet troupes, one of which is Mandalay Marionettes Theater on 66th Street, between 26th and 27th Street (www.mandalaymarionettes.com). Each evening at 8.30pm, puppet master Daw Ma Ma Naing's show begins in the small theatre with some lithe young graduates from the School of Fine Art performing a few classical dances. Then come the puppets (marionettes), accompanied by a small orchestra. One popular piece shows Zawgyi, the magic and mystic alchemist, searching for medicinal roots in the forest and encountering adventures on the way. The action includes Garuda, the mythical bird, fighting the Naga (King of the Serpents)—their acrobatic movements never fail to delight the audience. The costumes and the staging are excellent. As in live theatre, the acts are often based on stories from the life of Buddha and from the Ramayana (the Hindu epics).

Mandalay is famous for its artisan guilds set up by King Mindon in 1857, when he was building his new capital. The embroidery master sews next door to the family who craft the papier-mâché dolls so popular as 'nirvana goods' at pagoda stalls

Around the corner from the Mandalay Marionettes Theater on 27th Street between 65th and 66th Street is the Mintha Theater (www.minthatheater.com). Each evening at 8.30pm they present a varied programme of classical dance accompanied by live music. The performance will include some twelve different short stories beautifully presented. The supple elegant dancers are dressed in regal costumes. One has to marvel how the female dancers manage the 60-centimetre train as they execute their often complicated routine—they simply flip the train around, seemingly with great ease and never tumble.

ZEGYO MARKET

At the centre of the town, within walking distance of the major hotels, stands the Queen Victoria Jubilee Clock Tower, next to which is Zegyo Market. Mandalay is the main market for the surrounding region and Zegyo is a large, bustling affair. The original, rather fanciful arched building, designed by the Italian Count Caldari in 1903, has been replaced by a solid 1990s affair. At dawn, farmers with towels wrapped around their heads to ward off the early morning chill, start arriving, carrying enormous baskets brimming with fresh produce. Considerable time and effort is spent in laying this out with each variety of merchandise in its allotted section. The resulting display provides an everyday demonstration of the Burmese sense of style and design: a pyramid of glossy tomatoes on a flat basket, a round of green chillies with young eggplants as the centrepiece and, interspersed among these brilliant colours, mounds of tea, bundles of cheroots and neat stacks of the cosmetic *thanaka* wood. *Thanaka* powder is popular as a cosmetic with women all over Burma for its astringent and cooling, as well as aesthetic, qualities. As well as the fresh produce sections, manufactured consumer items, both legitimate and smuggled, are available. There is also a night market on 84th Street, on the east side of Zegyo Market. For the visitor who would like a memento of Burmese music this is the place to buy tapes.

MANDALAY MUSEUM AND LIBRARY

To the north-east of the market, on 80th Street between 24th and 25th Streets, is the Mandalay Museum and Library. It has an interesting collection of royal garments, probably those left behind by King Theebaw and Queen Supayalat, and a variety of ethnological exhibits, but on the whole it is not as interesting as the museum in Taunggyi. This is now rather a forgotten place as the most prized items of their collection have been moved across to the museum in the Mandalay Palace. Nonetheless it still has some beautiful Buddha images.

EINDAWYA PAGODA

Due west of Zegyo Market is Eindawya Pagoda. It was built by King Pagan Min on his accession to the throne. His home had been on this site while he was Crown Prince. Pagan Min was deposed, though spared, following the palace revolution of 1853. He lived out his life in a monastery on this site, eventually dying of smallpox. This golden pagoda of lovely proportions (sadly the base has recently been covered in mosaic) was built also in memory of Theebaw's only son, who died in infancy, also of smallpox.

MAHAMUNI PAGODA

Mandalay's most fabled religious monument is the Mahamuni (or Arakan) Pagoda. It was originally built in 1784 by King Bodawpaya to house the Mahamuni Image, but was destroyed by fire in 1884 and immediately rebuilt. The 3.8-metre- (12.6-foot-) high seated image of the Buddha has a legendary origin and a complex history (see page 32). Three times the Burmese tried to steal it from the Arakanese, but only in 1784 were they finally successful. According to an inscription in the pagoda, Bodawpaya coaxed this Buddha image to Mandalay by the 'charm of piety'. The history books, however, tell of a bloody battle. They do not divulge how this massive sculpture was transported over the steep, pathless mountain sides. Some, to this day, ascribe the feat to supernatural powers. One hundred and twenty families accompanied the image on its long journey to Mandalay and remained to tend it.

A devotee places some gold leaf on the revered Mahamuni Buddha image in Mandalay. This seated image supposedly was sculpted in the presence of the Buddha during a visit to the kingdom of Arakan in 500 BCE. When the image had been completed by the 'heavenly sculptor', the Buddha is said to have breathed on the image to ensure the likeness was exact. Then addressing his likeness he announced: 'I shall pass into Nirvana in my eightieth year but you, instinct in my essence, will live the 5,000 years which I have prescribed for the duration of the religion.' This legend is described in great detail by Maurice Collis in The Land of the Great Image

Even today the image's face is washed and its teeth cleaned at 4.30am every day—for the early riser a fascinating ritual to watch. The shape of the body is greatly distorted as each day the faithful paste on more and more little squares of gold leaf. Sometimes it is necessary to apply a thin layer of lacquer to the body to enable the gold leaf to stick, and this is done as part of the early morning ablutions. Women believers are not allowed into the inner sanctum and have to pass their gold leaf to a man dressed in white, who is in charge of the Buddha's welfare. Another man is employed solely to collect the fallen gold leaf, which reputedly amounts to as much as 2.7 kilograms (six pounds) a year. The inner square of the pagoda, the section which houses the Mahamuni image, is decorated with a red lacquer base and a thin layer of gold leaf on top. The whole area once exuded a warm glow. Now these bottom sections have been faced with cold, plum-coloured tiles, covering up the red lacquer. A practical move as far as maintenance is concerned, but an aesthetic disaster.

In a separate building to the north of the main pagoda are six bronze Khmer statues. These are all that remain of 30 bronzes also plundered from the Arakan by Bodawpaya. One hundred and twenty years earlier, the Arakanese King Razagyi had removed these statues from the Burmese kingdom of Pegu. The Burmese had taken them from the Siamese capital of Ayutthaya, and the Siamese had in turn looted them from their original home in Angkor Wat in Cambodia in 1431. King Theebaw had the other 24 bronzes melted and cast into cannon for his fight against the British. The bronze statues are very worn, no doubt from their many arduous journeys but also from incessant handling. If one is ill, it is believed that touching the appropriate part of one of the statues will cure the corresponding organ of one's own body. A small museum is also situated in the courtyard, housing a strange mixture of regalia, wax models of King Mindon, Queen Supayalat and King Theebaw, as well as a beautiful crystal bed brought from France by Mindon at the cost of 18,000 silver coins. Some of the exhibits have now been moved to a new museum in the reconstructed Mandalay Palace.

Perhaps the most fascinating part of the Mahamuni Pagoda is the long, shop-filled colonnade that leads to the famed Buddha image. It was along this colonnade that sumptuous daily offerings from the royal palace used to pass. Today it hums with trade; shopkeepers ('heavenly merchants') sell every variety of Nirvana goods—lacquerware, Buddha images of all shapes and sizes and the eight items of a monk's paraphernalia: three pieces of robe, one belt, one water strainer, one razor, one offerings bowl, one needle and thread. Much of what one can buy here is made in the workshops on the south side of the colonnade. This is an excellent place for the keen shopper. Several stores have good embroidery, both old and new. The new

The Prince and Princess of Wales visiting the Arakan (Mahamuni) Pagoda, 17th February, 1906. In the foreground are Burmese nuns, seated beside urns containing votive offerings. The pagoda enshrined the Mahamuni image, the imposing brass statue of Buddha over which many wars were waged

pieces tend to be the most expensive, so remember to bargain. This is also the best place for waxed umbrellas of all sizes. Some of the really large ones are extremely colourful.

THE ARTISAN GUILDS

Not far from the Mahamuni Pagoda, also in the south of the city, are the Artisan Guilds. In 1857 when Mandalay was being built, King Mindon set up these guilds, which today form the backbone of Myanmar's craft industry. On one side of the street are the alabaster and marble carvers, and the forecourt and workshops are strewn with Buddha images of different shapes and sizes, in varying stages of completion. Opposite are the shops of the wood carvers, where one can find charming small Buddhas carved from sweet-smelling sandalwood. Several workshops specialize in 'instant antiques'—bronzes cast using the lost-wax method. In the forecourt of the establishment craftsmen model, while in the rear yard heaps of dry cow-dung smoulder. From these workshops emerge exquisite little bronze Buddhas, to which an instant chemical 'age patina' is added. The finished product may well find its way to the Thai antique market: buyer beware. Perhaps the guild's most idiosyncratic work of all is the production of gold leaf. Gold nuggets from the mines of north Myanmar are first flattened to paper thinness and then placed between layers of bamboo paper wrapped in deer skin (which does not stretch). In a small hut forbidden to women stand two men, each wielding a long-handled sledge hammer. For ten minutes at a time these muscular characters pulverize the small leather packets, rendering their contents so thin and delicate that 28 grams (one ounce) of gold covers an area of about 10 square metres (12 square yards). The gold leaf will later be sold to devotees to paste onto Buddha images.

SHWE IN BIN

Monasteries abound in and around Mandalay, so visit only the best. One such is the Shwe In Bin, in Pe Boke Tan Street, south of 35th Street. This beautiful teak building (constructed some 80 years ago by a rich Chinese jade merchant, though many of the carved panels date from an earlier period), raised on cream stucco foundations, stands in its own compound shaded by mature trees. Its mud floor, baked to a soft brown, is constantly swept by the young monks. The interior is characteristically multicultural: beautiful carved doors in the Burmese style, Victorian crystal paraffin lamps, as well as an interesting series of paintings depicting General Prendergast and Colonel Sladen negotiating with court ministers prior to King Theebaw's exile. Another set of paintings show negotiations for the sale of the Mogok ruby mines to the French.

THE MIDDLE FAIR WAY

Nigel Melville, 1988

If the search for the middle way through the temples of Myanmar proves elusive, some travellers may find a form of Nirvana at Pyin U Lwin (formerly Maymyo) Golf Club. Here the golfer's dream—that every drive comes to rest in the middle of the fairway and the rare one that disappears deep into the trees is found in a clearing with a perfect lie and sight of the green—may be fulfilled. The fairways may be rather unkempt and the greens somewhat bumpy, but you are unlikely to score better at St Andrews or Augusta.

The golf club is a legacy of the British, now largely enjoyed by Burmese army officers who, like their colonial predecessors, occupy the grand houses and messes surrounding the course. Whether the views across the course fill them with equal nostalgia for Surrey is uncertain, but they seem to show the same enthusiasm for golf and set off every afternoon in pursuit of the perfect score. The course is more than 6,400 metres (7,000 yards), par 72 with varied and interesting holes lined by trees and interspersed with ditches and ponds.

Roger Moore (no relation to the actor but equally dashing) and I were accosted by a horde of enthusiastic young boys long before we had reached the clubhouse and were led to caddymaster U Toe Maung. We paid green fees and hired clubs and caddies at a total cost of 100 kyats. Having reduced the number of our supporters to three each (one to carry the clubs, one to go on ahead to locate the ball and one with general but unspecified responsibilities), the caddymaster insisted on accompanying us. At the first hole, a long tree-lined par four, my opponent hit a strong but sliced drive which disappeared into the trees on the right. My shot was similar but pulled to the left. We set off down the fairway with our entourage to find after about 210 metres (230 yards) a pair of boys standing beside our balls in the middle of the fairway—'Hit a tree and bounced back, sir.'

When we eventually found the green, we were offered a multiplicity of advice on the line and speed and were given five-foot putts as 'unmissable'.

We continued round the course with remarkably good scores, having miraculously avoided any trouble, until the short 13th hole where a raised tee meant that we could all see that my opponent's severely hooked shot had not rebounded on to the fairway. Leaving my ball safely on the green, we all set off into the trees and undergrowth without much hope. After a few minutes searching a cry of 'here it is' brought us back to a path (which I am certain I walked down) leading straight to the green and the ball perched up on a convenient tuft of grass allowing a full swing. My opponent gained little merit from me but took full advantage and lobbed the ball to the heart of the green to loud applause to halve the hole.

After playing 18 fine holes during which the length of our drives, the symmetry of our swings, the delicacy of our chips and the precision of our putting had all been extolled, we returned to the clubhouse. The only disappointment there was that the bar was rather short of beer (which was apparently something to do with the celebration of the centenary of the establishment of Mandalay Brewery in 1886—the British demonstrating their priorities in building up the infrastructure after occupying Northern Burma in 1885).

Tips did not seem to be compulsory but the six new balls which we had brought with us were greatly appreciated. We were encouraged to return and if possible bring the apparently much prized possession of a gold umbrella from Lillywhites, Piccadilly (supplier of sports equipment to many generations of colonial officials). Group photographs and exchanges of addresses concluded an unscheduled but thoroughly enjoyable interlude in our Burma itinerary.

MANDALAY'S SURROUNDINGS

AMARAPURA

Some 11 kilometres (seven miles) south of Mandalay is the town of Amarapura, the 'City of Immortals'. In its heyday a city of some 200,000 inhabitants, it now has a population of a mere 10,000. The leisurely 'clack-clack' from the looms of the cotton and silk weavers has replaced the noisy bustle of this former capital. The town stands on slightly elevated ground which in the flood season forms a long peninsula.

HISTORY

In 1782 King Bodawpaya, fifth son of the great Alaungpaya, ascended the Lion Throne at Ava. His passage to the throne had been sufficiently blood-stained for his *ponnas* to advise a move of capital. This was not such a radical suggestion as it would have been in the Western world. Although Burmese cities and palaces were ornate and grand, the majority of the buildings were constructed of wood and relatively easy to dismantle, move to a new site and reassemble. So in 1783, the court was moved a short distance north to Amarapura.

During its brief tenures as capital (1783–1823 and 1841–1857) Amarapura hosted two British embassies, that of Captain Michael Symes in 1795 and of Sir Henry Yule in 1855, each of which was excellently documented. Sir Henry Yule travelled with a cartographer, a painter and, for the first time ever for a foreign mission, an official photographer (the unforgettably named and highly competent Linneus Tripe), so we have a clear view of contemporary life in the City of Immortals. The city, true to Burmese tradition, was laid out four square, bounded by a defensive wall some four metres (12–13 feet) high with a battlemented parapet. Pagodas on the four corners still stand and are visible from U Bein Bridge.

SIGHTS

PALACE RUINS AND TREASURY

All that remains of the palace is the yellow stuccoed treasury building and the record office, which was built by King Tharrawaddi (1837–1846). Formerly it had been 'crowned with the gilt pavilion which serves as a Belvedere where the king occasionally amuses himself at eventide with his spyglass.' Nearby stand the old watchtower and the tombs of King Bodawpaya and his grandson, King Bagyidaw.

PAHTODAWGYI PAGODA

This white pagoda was built by King Bagyidaw in 1820. Around the pagoda's base are tablets illustrating the Buddha's previous lives. One of the finest views of this pagoda is from the U Bein Bridge across the Taung Thaman Lake.

U BEIN BRIDGE

At the southern end of the town, in a grove of majestic trees, forgotten pagodas crumble. Two large monasteries remain, as does the massive Taungmingyi Buddha Image erected in around 1846 by Pagan Min (King Mindon's deposed brother). This image was originally exposed to the elements, but in 1949 it was roofed in. In 1847 King Pagan Min allocated funds for the building of a bridge across Taung Thaman Lake. The mayor, one U Bein, obviously had an eye for a quick penny: he appears to have pocketed the money and re-used timbers from the abandoned Ava Palace. The king saw through the ruse, however, and the mayor was charged with fraud.

The long bridge passes over fertile rice fields. It used to be that during the winter months the lake bed stayed dry long enough for two harvests. Then, in the rainy season, from the Pahtodawgyi Pagoda in the north to the Ava stream south of Amarapura, the land floods to form the Taung Thaman Lake, and the farmers would become fishermen. However, due to the recent construction of a dam, the farmers have been forced to become full-time fisherman, the lake is now a constant. Take a stroll over this lovely old bridge and arrive at the small sleepy village of Taung Thaman.

KYAUKTAWGYI PAGODA

At the far end of the U Bein Bridge, in a grove of trees, stands the Kyauktawgyi Pagoda. This is a much smaller copy of the Ananda Temple in Bagan and was built in 1847 by King Pagan Min. A brick path lined with deliciously fragrant frangipani trees leads to the entrance of this white pagoda. Instead of the Ananda's four standing Buddhas, however, it has a single seated image, and is also noted for its 19th-century murals. The amble across the bridge to the pagoda is itself worthwhile. There are plenty of places to linger and enjoy the ravishing view, and to watch the fishermen casting their vast nests. At the lake's edge a few remaining farmers balance on the cross-bars of their wooden harrows, softly whispering words of encouragement to their oxen as they labour up and down the field.

NAGAYON PAGODA

On the outskirts of Amarapura is a pagoda built in the shape of a *naga* (a mythical serpent)—hence its name. The body of the *naga* is wound around the back of a vaulted building, its head erect like that of a hooded cobra.

MAHAGANDAYONE MONASTERY

One of the most prestigious monasteries in the Mandalay area is Mahagandayone, the home of some 1300 orthodox monks and novices. The monks run a primary school as well as a meditation centre. Due to the renowned status of this monastery an individual or group of donors often provides their daily meal. This means the monks do not have to go out every morning to gather alms. The food is cooked in the monastery's clean but basic 'cook house'. Four huge steamers cook the rice, whilst vast blackened woks hold the bubbling curries. One of the cooks stirs the curry with a long pole; another makes sure there is enough wood under the wok. When the food is ready the gong, a hanging piece of old rail, is hit to summon the monks to the courtyard. The donors and their family stand beside the great vats of steaming rice, the monks file past in silence, taking the lid off their lacquer bowl to receive a large dollop of rice. A monk stands by to brush up any rice that has dropped onto the brick floor of the courtyard. With the lid back on the bowl a piece of pink sponge cake is popped onto the top. The monks file into the dining hall where they sit cross-legged, the curries, vegetables and some *lapet* having been placed on the table. The abbot and senior monks sit at one end with the novices at the far end. When the meal is finished each monk leaves the table taking his bowl with him; anything that remains will be his breakfast the following morning. Nothing goes to waste in the monastery, as surplus food is in turn passed on to any locals in need, or re-heated for the next day's meal.

INWA (AVA)

South of Amarapura is Inwa, the once mighty capital called Ava, but now just a sleepy village whose inhabitants specialize in making lacquerware offerings bowls for monks. In 1855 Sir Henry Yule found the remains of Inwa much as they are today: 'The ramparts still stand though in decay, the greater part of the interior area is a mere mass of tangled gardens and jungle.'

The journey to Inwa is a pleasure in itself. Just before reaching the Inwa Bridge, which crosses the Ayeyarwady, one leaves the main road and lurches along a small road, until the Myitnge River. Here one boards a flat-bottomed ferry, most probably sharing it with an ox-cart or two, bicyclists, chickens—in fact a veritable mini-Noah's Ark. On the far side of the river one continues by pony trap, the only four-wheeled vehicle in Inwa being a very elderly fire engine.

The interior of the Bagaya Kyaung at Inwa,
which is badly in need of renovation

HISTORY

Ava is first noted in records in 1364 as a Shan capital. It served as capital of Upper Burma until 1634 when, during the Second Burmese Empire, it became capital of the whole of Burma. Apart from the brief move to Amarapura, Ava remained the capital until a strong earthquake in 1838 persuaded King Tharrawaddi Min and his *ponnas* that the site was inauspicious and it was abandoned for good. However, right up until 1886, when the Burmese royal family went into exile to Ratanagiri, near Bombay, the 'Kingdom of Ava' continued to be the formal name of the Burmese state.

SIGHTS

NANMYINT WATCHTOWER

King Bagyidaw's watchtower still stands, slightly tilted, 'as the earthquake left it, greatly out of the perpendicular and with the massive verandah and pillars round its base staggering hither and thither.'

MAHA AUNGMYE BONZAN

This monastery is unusual in that it is totally constructed of brick and stucco and thus survived the passage of time better than most of its contemporaries. It was built in 1818 by King Bagyidaw's chief queen for the abbot, Nyaungyan Sayadaw, who was reputed to be her lover. It is a large, pale-yellow building, decorated with fine bas-reliefs of mythical animals, gargoyles and beautiful arches.

JUDSON MEMORIAL

Nearby and east of Maha Aungmye Bonzan, a memorial to the Christian missionary Dr Adoniram Judson stood until recently. It was on this site that he and other Christian prisoners were held captive during the last six months of the first Anglo-Burmese War in 1826. His wife, Anne Judson, camped in 'a little filthy room half full of grain' and cared for the prisoners. A few years ago, the authorities dug up the memorial slab and buried it somewhere in the vicinity.

BAGAYA MONASTERY

Bagaya Monastery (Bagaya Kyaung) is perhaps the most beautiful of the monasteries in the area. Famous for its 267 teak pillars, it is set in the middle of Le Daw Gyee, the great royal rice fields. The nicest way to approach this exquisite little wooden monastery is to walk along a narrow path across the paddy— although there is now a small, as the Burmese say, 'all-weather paved road' to the building. The carving on the doors and walls is well preserved. The main hall stands on a platform apart from the monks' quarters and the other buildings. It is constructed so that there is a space between the walls and roof, which keeps the hall light and cool throughout.

LACQUERWARE FACTORY

Inwa features a lacquerware factory, where the monks' handsome black offerings bowls are made. In common with all Burmese crafts the ancient methods prevail; it is said that 'the supreme test of excellence for a offerings bowl of lacquer is when the sides will bend in till they touch without cracking', the construction being of woven horsehair rather than cheaper bamboo wickerwork.

INWA BRIDGE

For many years the Inwa Bridge was the only bridge to span the Ayeyarwady throughout its entire length. When present construction up and down the river is completed there will be five bridges. This iron rail and road bridge was built by the British in the 1930s. In 1942 part of the bridge was blown up by the British as they retreated from the advancing Japanese. It was not repaired until 1954. Now the old iron bridge is un-used as a new one was opened in 2008.

SAGAING

In the 1930s, the writer Maurice Collis stood on the eastern bank of theAyeyarwady and gazed across at Sagaing prior to taking up his post as its Deputy Commissioner. 'Behind the town with its mat and wooden houses was a cluster of yellow hills,' he wrote, 'on top of each a golden pagoda with monasteries in profusion. There bathed in sunshine, secret and still, was Buddhist Burma.' Today there are said to be no fewer than 554 monasteries, home to some 6,000 monks and nuns.

HISTORY

Sagaing served as the earliest recorded but the shortest lived capital in Upper Burma. From 1315 to 1364 the Shans made it their capital. Some 400 years later, King Alaungpaya, the victor over the Mons and founder of the third and last Burmese Empire, moved his capital here from his native Shwebo before eventually settling in Ava. Sagaing also figured briefly in the dynastic history of another great Asian nation: the last emperor of China's Ming Dynasty is said to have lived there for a short period after fleeing the Manchu conquest of his homeland.

SIGHTS

KHEMATHAKA CONVENT AND LWANZEDI

In his marvellous 1855 work, *Mission to Ava*, Sir Henry Yule warns, 'Readers of this narrative are probably tired of pagodas before now but in Burma people do get very tired of pagodas.' In Sagaing take heed of this warning and enjoy the spectacular view in addition to visiting monasteries and pagodas. In the centre of Sagaing's village street is a friendly teashop; the mildly adventurous might try the sugarcane juice. (The cane is crushed by a Heath-Robinson contraption with a large iron wheel.) The teashop also provides a fine observation

Looking across the Ayeyarwady from the 'pagoda sprinkled heights of Sagaing' to where once stood the 'cockpit of kingship' Ava (Inwa). The sight, with the background of the huge dark Shan Hills to the eastward, is striking and beautiful in the extreme,' wrote Sir George Scott in 1886

point from which to watch monastic life go about its unhurried business: nuns dressed in their pale pink habits with (rather fashionable-looking) long narrow sleeves, folded bleached saffron cloths shielding their shaven heads from the sun. Nuns in Myanmar, unlike monks, do not seek offerings of food, nor is it required of the Burmese female population to spend a certain length of time in a convent. Many do, however, and it is quite common to see little girls of four or five dressed in nuns' habits, often in the same establishment as an aunt or elder sister.

Once refreshed, turn left at the T-junction at the end of the village and then left again up a flight of stairs which leads to Khemathaka Convent. Continue your climb through the convent, a collection of fine teak buildings, until you come to the main stairway and turn right up the hill. Some way up on the left will be the Lwanzedi Pagoda (if you get lost, any passer-by can show you the way). This pagoda, though in itself of no particular artistic merit, provides a superb vantage point from which to revel in the pure beauty of the surrounding countryside. Pagodas of all shapes and sizes dot the landscape. Scattered among them are fine European-style stucco buildings. Through the middle of this picture glides the Ayeyarwady, and beyond it the spires of Mandalay Hill gleam, while on the horizon way to the north-east the huge dark Shan Hills rise up. The picture is 'striking and beautiful in the extreme'.

SOON U PONYA SHIN PAGODA

The Soon U Ponya Shin Pagoda also enjoys a splendidly elevated position, the difference being that there is a road up to it, so for those less inclined to exertion this is the place to enjoy the panorama. It stands slightly apart, however, and you will miss the pleasure of the village scene.

U MIN THONSE (THIRTY CAVES PAGODA)

Another interesting pagoda to visit on the Sagaing hill is U Min Thonse a semicircular colonnade housing 43 seated Buddha images, their hands in the 'calling earth to witness' mudra. Thought to have been built during the 11th century there are 30 openings along the colonnade, so as you enter the space light floods in from the left and illuminates the 43 seated images on the right. Either end of the colonnade stands a large Buddha image as if on guard, the significance of 43 images alludes to the 43 years that Buddha spent giving sermons. The pagoda has recently been renovated; shiny mosaic tiles cover the walls with small plaques acknowledging those who have made donations—many from abroad.

KAUNG HMUDAW PAGODA

Ten kilometres (six miles) west from the Inwa Bridge is the Kaung Hmudaw Pagoda. Its shape is unusual for a Burmese pagoda in that it is an enormous dome, about 275 metres (900 feet) in circumference and 45 metres (150 feet) high, and topped by a small *hti*. It was built in 1636 by King Thalon to celebrate the founding of Ava as the kingdom's capital. Local folklore suggests that the shape represents a certain queen's perfect breast. The pagoda is also a copy of the Mahaceti Pagoda in Sri Lanka, and is alleged to contain a tooth of the Buddha brought from Kandy. The base of the pagoda has small *nat*-filled niches, as well as some 800 pillars, each 1.5 metres (five feet) high with a niche for an oil lamp. The annual Kaung Hmudaw Pagoda festival is held at the November full moon. As always at festival time, a market springs up around the pagoda; this one is renowned for pottery.

YWAHTAUNG VILLAGE

On the return journey from the Kaung Hmudaw Pagoda to the Inwa Bridge one passes through Ywahtaung village, the home of the silversmiths' guild. These silversmiths produce extremely fine work, using the ornate patterns of traditional designs. The silver betel boxes and bowls in the shape of monks' offerings bowls, which are to be found in most Burmese homes, are likely to have come from Ywahtaung.

MONYWA

The old town of Monywa lies 122 kilometres (76 miles) west of Sagaing. Monywa earned a footnote in Burmese history as an indirect consequence of the attempted assassination of King Mindon in 1866. The quick-witted slave who foiled the attempt was rewarded by Mindon, first with the appointment as his slipper bearer, and later as governor of Monywa. One of Myanmar's more colourful temples, Thanboddhay, is here. Constructed from 1939 until 1958 this is said by locals to be an extremely lucky site—during WW11 many bombs were dropped in the area but never exploded on this building. Today the temple is a riot of colour with Buddhas images from the tiny to the large everywhere, some 500,000 in all. Monywa is a centre for traditional embroidery as well as modern work with sequins. The nearby village of Kyauk-ha is famous for lacquer. There are several newish hotels which make an overnight stop a possibility. Across the Chindwin River from Monywa are several other interesting sites, Po Win Taung and Shwe Ba Taung (Hill) both are collections of sandstone caves full of Buddha images and murals.

For the hardy traveller a drive of some 4 hours to the west of Monywa, along very bumpy road lies the 1605 sq kilometre (620 sq. miles) Alaungdaw Kathapha National Park. Myanmar boasts 9 National Parks with this being the largest and the oldest, it was first named a Nature Reserve in 1893. The Park is home to many

The remains of the King Bodawpaya's folly: a pagoda, which if it had been finished, would have stood some 150 metres (500 feet) high. After seven years of frenetic building, the project was halted as the King's astronomers warned: 'The great pagoda is finished, and the country is ruined.'

species of mammal including elephants, thamin, wild pig, clouded leopard to name a few, a great variety of birds—eighteen species of woodpecker alone and wonderful orchids. The park is administered by the Forestry Commission and the NGO FREDA (Forest Resource and Environmental Development and Conservation Association). It is possible to stay at one of their guesthouses or cabins—elephant is the mode of transport once within the Park. To arrange a visit a permit is needed so it is best to be in touch with an agency that specializes in eco-tourism (see page 257).

MINGUN

A boat ride up the Ayeyarwady River lies Mingun, where you will find 'King Bodawpaya's folly'. It is a delightful half-day trip from Mandalay.

HISTORY

King Bodawpaya founded a new capital at Amarapura, after conquering the Arakan (modern day Rakhine State) and carrying away their prized Mahamuni Image. In 1790 he began constructing a mammoth pagoda on the western banks of the Irrawaddy. First he built a temporary palace on Nandaw Island in the middle of the river opposite the site. (It was on this same island that Captain Symes was

virtually imprisoned for 40 days during his second mission to Ava in 1802.) But in 1797 the king abandoned the project. There are different theories as to why: one goes that soothsayers had warned him that if the building were finished his life would end; another suggests that he went through a period of religious disbelief; a third posits perhaps the most realistic reason, that the project was immensely costly—Bodawpaya is said to have spent more than 10,000 viss (about 17.5 tons) of silver on it. And, of course, it was hardly prudent of the monarch to be living on a small island away from his capital.

A corner of Settawya Pagoda built by King Bodawpaya at Mingun. This striking white pagoda is said to have been built while the plans for the huge Mingun Pagoda itself were being finalized

SIGHTS

PONDAWPAYA PAGODA

From the landing stage turn right (upstream) and near the water's edge, is a scale-model of what the Mingun Pagoda would have been had it been completed. Seeing this helps one to understand the true enormity of Bodawpaya's folly.

SETTAWYA PAGODA

Walk on and the Settawya Pagoda comes into view. This attractive white pagoda surrounded by huge terraces is said to be the first pagoda built by King Bodawpaya in Mingun, presumably for use while he was building his folly. A central staircase leads down into a vault which houses a footprint of the Buddha.

MINGUN PAGODA

A focal point of Mingun is an open piece of ground with a huge banyan tree encircled by a seat at the centre. A perfect place to stop and have a cool drink of water or Coke, there will be countless vendors on hand to provide the necessary. On the river side sit the remains of the huge pagoda's guardian lions. The grey stone haunches of these majestic statues are clearly definable whereas the rest is a heap of rubble. The ground around the lions has been mown and so it is easy to admire the statues at close quarters.

On the other side of the banyan tree an enormous pile of bricks is all that remains of Bodawpaya's grandiose scheme. The square ruin stands on three terraces, the walls of some of which are 48 metres (160 feet) high and pedimented and pilastered in the Pagan style. An earthquake in 1838 wrought considerable damage. The roof (it never reached the stage of having its stupa) fell into the vaulted basement area where the pagoda's relics were interred.

If permitted the climb is easy, notwithstanding going barefoot as one must, as a brick staircase has been added up one side. It is quite steep and for a modest tip an enthusiastic child will be your guide. At the top one is rewarded with a superb view of the Ayeyarwady River and the Hsinbyume Pagoda, as well as the haunches of the guardian lions. Bodawpaya himself is said to have collaborated with the architect on the complicated engineering of the building. According to Captain Hiram Cox, the then British Resident, a series of quadrangular lead-lined pits were prepared for the treasures, then roofed with lead tiles each 13 centimetres (five inches) square; this device was one of 'His Majesty's own conceptions'. However, it seems that the hapless architect was murdered lest he pass on his knowledge of the vault's design.

MINGUN BELL

This bell, one of the world's largest, (more than four metres (12 feet) high and five metres (16 feet) wide at its base, and weighing 90 tons) was cast by the lost-wax process on Nandaw Island. It was transported across the Ayeyarwady back to the mainland on two catamarans (these craft are now in the Sagaing Fort Museum). The bell was originally erected on teak uprights, but these gave way during the 1838 earthquake. It seems that it was the ubiquitous Irrawaddy Flotilla Company who re-hung it on its present steel pillars.

HSINBYUME PAGODA

This is a most attractive white pagoda, which was built in 1816 by Bodawpaya's grandson (later King Bagyidaw) in memory of one of his wives. Around the base are seven concentric circular terraces. The structure itself is symbolic of Meru, the cosmic mountain, while the undulating terraces symbolize the Seven Seas of Buddhist cosmology. On the eastern side a staircase climbs up the centre of the terraces above which is a fine vaulted roof. This staircase was reserved for royalty, while on either side are plain steps for lesser mortals. Around the terrace base are niches housing *nats*, ogres and *nagas* all protecting the pagoda. The view of the surrounding countryside from the top terrace is stunning.

WATCH THE AYEYARWADY DOLPHINS

Some 4 hours upstream from Mandalay is an area where it is possible to see the Irrawaddy dolphin (Orcaella brevirostris). The dophin is on average around 2.3 metres (8 ft) and very friendly. Hire a boat (with a help of an eco-tourist agency see page 257) and take a picnic or sign up for a two day special tour. As you near the area the boatman will talk to the local fishermen to see where the dophins are on that day. It is necessary to transfer into a fisherman's kayak. The fishermen and dolphins have a history of collaboration. The fishermen use two canoes and by tapping a bamboo stick on the side of their craft call to the dolphins who then allegedly drive the fish into the nets—they also communicate by using the dolphin guttural call. Sadly the numbers of dolphins have declined so now 74 kms of the river is protected.

PYIN OO LWIN (MAYMYO)

One of the nicest excursions from Mandalay is to drive for two and a half to three hours—depending on the vehicle—east of Mandalay up into the hills to the town of Pyin Oo Lwin (formerly named Maymyo). For the first half hour the drive is through paddy fields with the blue Shan Hills ahead. Then the climb starts and the landscape becomes wild. Huge mango and acid plum trees are interspersed with towering bamboo fronds, and with toddy palms—bamboo ladders strapped to their trunks—awaiting harvest time. (Toddy wine is well worth sampling.) Following a succession of dramatic hair-pin bends the halfway point is reached; many of the older cars stop, bonnets are raised amid much hissing of over-heated engines, and water is splashed onto tyres. As well as the usual drinks the teashops sell packets of delicious nuts and home-made crisps. Pyin Oo Lwin is 1,095 metres (3,510 feet) above sea-level and is delightfully cool after the hot plains. Sweaters are essential for the evening.

HISTORY

In 1886, following the exile from Mandalay of King Theebaw and the subsequent British takeover, Maymyo became an army base. Colonel May (hence Maymyo) of the Bengal Infantry led operations to quell rebel fighting in the Shan States from here. These campaigns took place over a ten-year period, long enough for the climatic advantages of Maymyo to become apparent to the British, and it grew into a popular hill station.

SIGHTS

THE BOTANICAL GARDENS: NATIONAL KANDAWGYI PARK

The splendid 175-hectare (432-acre) botanical gardens were laid from 1915 whilst Sir Harcourt Butler was Governor of Burma. It was reclaimed from virgin marshland by Turkish prisoners of World War I. The gardens are beautifully maintained and stocked with fine specimen trees, with borders overflowing with annual herbaceous flowers. In the past few years many attractions have been added, a marvellous orchid house and outside orchid walk, a jungle walk, a little museum and the bandstand is back in operation. On holidays there are concerts in the park and there are plans afoot to add some overnight accommodation. This is a perfect spot for an afternoon stroll. All manner of English 'cottage garden' seeds are for sale in charming packets marked 'Create garden to promote happiness'.

PYIN OO LWIN TOWN

To the south and east of the town centre stand English-style houses, each surrounded by a garden (many now used by Burmese government officials), and an 18-hole golf course. A good way to see this area is by bicycle, which one can hire from the Thiri Myaing Hotel (the former Candacraig Hotel, itself a fine red-brick, beamed building. The clock tower marks the centre of Pyin Oo Lwin: a sure sign of British colonial town planning. The buildings here are Burmese in style but the shop names still have a colonial ring, such as The Crown Confectionery with its regal crest. Public transport is by beautifully decorated horse-drawn carriages. Pyin Oo Lwin is still very much an army town but experiencing a re-brith as a hill-station. The successful local businessmen of Mandalay are building themselves houses to which they can escape the searing heat of Mandalay in summer. So the town has an injection of new life, little restaurants, guest houses and shops have sprung up all over town

PYIN OO LWIN MARKET

From the sightseer's point of view, Pyin Oo Lwin has one of the country's best markets. Mouthwatering fruit and vegetables are laid out with consummate style, an extra decorative touch provided by small sprigs of flowers; in January mahonia flowers are used, their sweet smell overpowering the pungent odour of *ngapi* (fermented fish paste). The covered section of the market sells clothes, local fabrics and embroidery, and has several good antique stalls. At the time of writing, this section of the market was being reconstructed. When you are exhausted from shopping, visit the café, which specializes in milk shakes—the avocado and strawberry ones are particularly delicious. In finest Burmese style, pots of orchids are arranged outside, while within, each little round table has its own floral decorations. The owner, his rigid posture recalling years of service with the British Army and dressed in an impeccably cut dark blue coat, tells stories of days gone by. Or why not pop into 'Liquor Corner' a wine shop and café selling Ayethaya locally grown wine? A group of westerners with the help of the Ministry of Agriculture and Irrigation imported some 13,000 vines from France in 1999 and today produce good red, white and rosé wines.

The early morning light illuminates a horse-drawn carriage waiting outside the market at Pyin Oo Lwin. This hill station, formerly called Maymyo, was once a centre of colonial life and host to the Governor's summer residence. Leslie Glass (an ICS officer pre-war) sets the scene: 'Once a year Maymyo celebrated the gala of Polo Week, during which teams from British and Indian regiments, from the Police, from the Forest Service, and from the big firms battled for trophies in between dances, tennis tournaments, gymkhanas and other festivities.'

PWE KYAUK AND ANISAKAN FALLS
For those with a taste for lazy days and picnics these falls are worth visiting, though it must be admitted there is nothing particularly distinctive about them.

GOKTEIK VIADUCT
This spectacular railway viaduct is 55 kilometres (34 miles) north-east of Pyin Oo Lwin, and a must for train enthusiasts. The easiest way is to catch the 8.20 train which will have climbed up from Mandalay (having left at 4am!)—this old train with wooden bench seats in Ordinary Class will continue the journey slowly along the mountain track reaching the viaduct around 11 o'clock. As the tracks winds around the hills it is possible to see the magnificent viaduct from afar. Continue on the train to either Naung-pein or Hsipaw and hire a car or take a bus back to Mandalay, perhaps stopping off in a Shan village enroute.

PEIK CHIN MYAUNG CAVES
Some 12 miles out of Pyin Oo Lwin on the Lashio road are the Peik Chin Myaung Caves. Similar to the Pindaya Caves near Inle Lake, these too are filled with Buddha images, only these are new ones. Worth a visit as the drive to the caves is pleasant.

KYAUKSE
Once a year at the time of the October full moon the town of Kyaukse, about one hour's drive south of Mandalay, is host to the Elephant Festival. Legend has it that in the 11th century King Anarawtha returned home from a trip to India bearing two relics of the Buddha. The relics were put on an elephant who was allowed to roam until he settled naturally—and present-day Kyaukse was the place he came to rest. The Shwe Tha Laung Pagoda was then built on the hill to enshrine the relics and each year the winner of the Elephant Festival goes up the hill to the pagoda to pay respects to the relics. Kyaukse is surrounded by paddy fields and gentle hills so is a glorious setting for the festival.The festival announces itself as you near the small town as the noise is phenomenal and attracts people from far and wide. The competition has a history of 75 years. The contestant elephants are made of papier mâché highly decorated with fabric and sequins, inside the papier mâché carcass are two young men. Whilst waiting for their turn to perform the elephant team is atop an open lorry with a live band blaring—so as many teams compete the noise level is awesome. When called to the arena their mahout leads the dance which can be very complicated full of twists and turns with the elephant pirouetting on its 'would be' hindlegs. The dexterity with which the two young men make this papier mâché elephant perform is extraordinary and must be exhausting. Though once having finished their 15-minute routine they pop out of the papier mâché elephant to take their bow in front of the judges, looking none the worse for wear.

(above) This classic Dennis fire engine still stands ready for any emergency in downtowm Mandalay; (bottom) further restimony to the British colonial administration, this bungalow at Loimwe once housed the commander of the military station of the region

This dramatic photo from space is from ISS
Expedition 27, photo courtesy Image Science
and Analysis Laboratory, NASA-Johnson Space
Centre.
Photo shows the older areas of the city of
Yangon cradled by the Yangon River. Note the
Shwedagon Pagoda in the center of the image,
and lower right, the densely formed grid
pattern of streets that make up Yangon's
remarkable heritage district.

The elaborate Hti or crown atop the Taungkwe Zedi (Pagoda) at Loikaw

The Mekong River curls through the Golden Triangle

Tachilek on the Thai border, famous for its duty free shopping

One of the four approaches to the Shwedagon Pagoda

BAGAN (PAGAN)

The remains of the old capital Pagan, modern-day Bagan, are scattered across a vast semi-arid plain. They positively exude antiquity and mystery. One visits individual monuments and each has its own special qualities, but it is the whole that is magnificent. In the early morning mist the pagodas seem to 'loom, huge, remote and mysterious, like the vague recollections of a fantastic dream', as Somerset Maugham wrote in 1930. Approaching midday the sun burns the colour from the landscape, leaving the red-brick pagodas stark and desolate. A column of dust marks the passage of an occasional ox-cart across the dry plain. With the declining day the colour creeps back, the trees and scrub turn from dull grey back to lively green. The sun sets behind the hills on the far side of the Ayeyarwady, filling the sky with a reddish glow.

The pagodas recall an age of former greatness. Once a vast and populous city, it became a straggling village living off sales of lacquerware and the steady trickle of tourists. The peace of the village was shattered one morning in 1990 when, to their surprise, the Bagan villagers were given notice to move their houses and shops immediately. Some of the village houses were thought to be built over the site of the old palace where excavations were about to start. So with a Government handout of building materials some 6,000 villagers were forced to move to the new site located in the south of the Bagan area, near the beautiful Lawkananda Pagoda. At the start, the loss of the village in among the monuments was upsetting, but now everything seems to have settled down. The village of New Bagan feels well established and the scar of the old village has more or less disappeared. However, new signs of modernization have crept onto the plain though they too have now diminished with time. As dusk descends, a series of unattractive neon lights which swathes the tops of the buildings illuminates—what is more, they stay alight until after dawn. A grey tarmac road sweeps through the centre of the site, replacing the dirt track of old. This strip of tar shines in both the sun and the rain, and disturbs the visual quality of the scene. The road was built to whisk the then President Suharto of Indonesia from the airport to the Thiripyitsaya Hotel during his state visit, and is thus nicknamed 'Suharto Avenue' by the locals. The last visual blot on the landscape is the newish museum. The shape of a large pink wedding cake, it is so large that it blocks part of the view of the Ayeyarwady River and dominates the east side of the site. The most significant change to the landscape has been the 'greening' of the Bagan plain. Gone is the dry desert feeling as trees have been planted and allowed to grow—in fact it is not permitted to cut branches off the trees when they get in the way of the farmers. At night the pagodas and museum are ablaze with fairy lights. All this means that some of the serenity and tranquillity of the Bagan plain has been lost forever—but the magic is still intact.

HISTORY

The Burmese founded the Kingdom of Pagan in CE 849, but it was not until King Anawrahta ascended the throne in 1044 that Pagan entered its golden era. By 1056 Anawrahta had unified the country and had given it a national religion. From the moment that he returned from his victorious campaign against the Mons, bearing 32 copies of the Tripitaka scriptures, the building frenzy began. First he built a library, the Pitakat Taik, to house the scriptures, and then, soon after, the fine Shwesandaw Pagoda. The style of Anawrahta's early buildings was influenced by the Mon architects whom he had brought back to Pagan following his victory at Thaton. These square, squat constructions with arches and complex patterns of brickwork—temples rather than pagodas—belie the Indian origins of the faith that inspired them. Perhaps Anawrahta's most famous monument is the Shwezigon Pagoda. By the time this pagoda was started, towards the end of his 40-year reign, a distinctly Burmese style had evolved. The stark power of the earlier buildings had dissolved into softer, more fluid lines, complexity into fantasy, the golden stupa apparently weightless and ready to float up to the heavens.

Pagoda and temple building continued with unabated enthusiasm for the next two centuries. There is no record of the actual number of religious monuments built during this period, the height of Pagan's power. King Narathihapati, the last King of

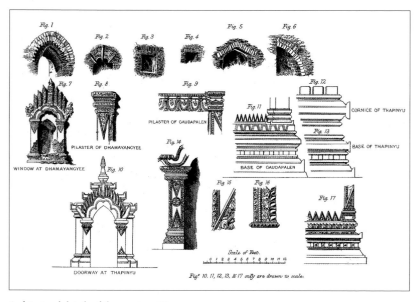

Architectural details of the remains at Bagan

Pagan, allegedly tore down 10,000 buildings in order to defend his capital against an imminent Mongol invasion. At the approach of the great Khan's army in 1287, the king left the capital, earning himself the ignominious title of 'The king who ran away from the Chinese'.

From that date the city took on the role it plays today, as a monument to a Buddhist renaissance of astonishing creativity and vigour. The constant felling of trees to feed the greedy brick kilns throughout more than 230 years of construction left the hills eroded and barren. Probably by 1287 it was becoming difficult, even with the intricate irrigation systems begun by Anawrahta, to sustain the large population. No trees, no topsoil, no rain, no food, thus no people. Pagan could not survive the harsh logic of nature.

In 1975 a fierce earthquake struck Pagan, destroying many small monuments and severely damaging some of the larger ones. Funds for restoration were made available by the United Nations, and the work was carried out to a high standard under the loving and expert eye of curator, the late U Bo Kay. After his death the restoration continued and now the majority of the pagodas and temples have had their pinnacles and destroyed sections restored—this goes for the largest down to the smallest buildings.

As well as a zealous restoration and in some cases total reconstruction programme of the damaged temples and pagodas, the landscape is also undergoing a huge change. What used to be the arid plain of Pagan is now becoming the green

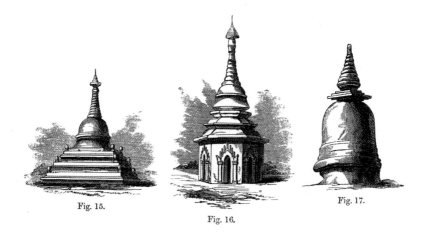

Fig. 15.

Fig. 16.

Fig. 17.

All kinds and forms are to be found in the temples of Bagan: the bell-shaped pyramid of dead brick-work, then the same raised over a square or octagonal cell containing an image of the Buddha, and the knob-like dome with the square cap, similar to ones found in India

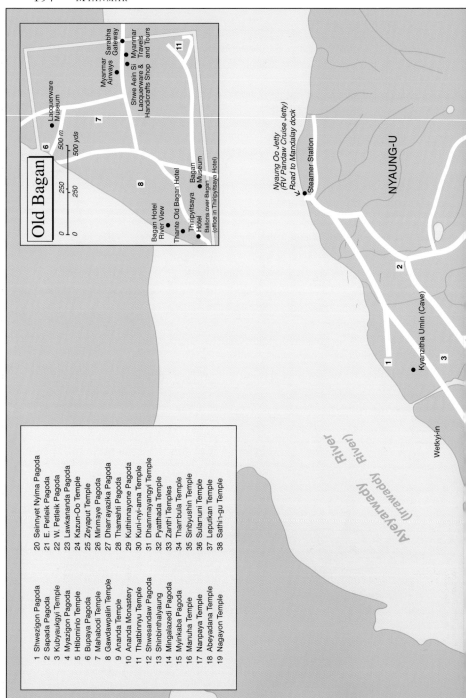

Old Bagan

0   250   500 m
0   250   500 yds

6
7
8
11

Lacquerware Museum

Myanmar Airways   Sarabha Gateway
Shwe Aein Si Myanmar Travels
Lacquerware & and Tours
Handicrafts Shop

Bagan Hotel River View
Thante Old Bagan Hotel
Thiripyitsaya Hotel
Bagan Museum
Ballons over Bagan (office in Thiripyitsaya Hotel)

Ayeyarwady (Irrawaddy) River
River

Nyaung Oo Jetty (RV Pandaw Cruise Jetty)
Road to Mandalay dock
Steamer Station

NYAUNG-U

2

Kyanzitha Umin (Cave)

3

1

Wetkyi-in

1 Shwezigon Pagoda
2 Sapada Pagoda
3 Kubyaukgyi Temple
4 Myazigon Pagoda
5 Htilominlo Temple
6 Bupaya Pagoda
7 Mahabodi Temple
8 Gawdawpalin Temple
9 Ananda Temple
10 Ananda Monastery
11 Thatbinnyu Temple
12 Shwesandaw Pagoda
13 Shinbinthalyaung
14 Mingalazedi Pagoda
15 Myinkaba Pagoda
16 Manuha Temple
17 Nanpaya Temple
18 Abeyadana Temple
19 Nagayon Temple
20 Seinnyet Nyima Pagoda
21 E. Petleik Pagoda
22 W. Petleik Pagoda
23 Lawkananda Pagoda
24 Kazun-Oo Temple
25 Zeyaput Temple
26 Minmaye Pagoda
27 Dharrayazika Pagoda
28 Thamahti Pagoda
29 Kuthinnayone Pagoda
30 Kuni-nyi-ama Temple
31 Dhammayangyi Temple
32 Pyatthada Temple
33 Zanthi Temples
34 Tharrbula Temple
35 Sinbyushin Temple
36 Sularuni Temple
37 Leputkan Temple
38 Sathi-gu Temple

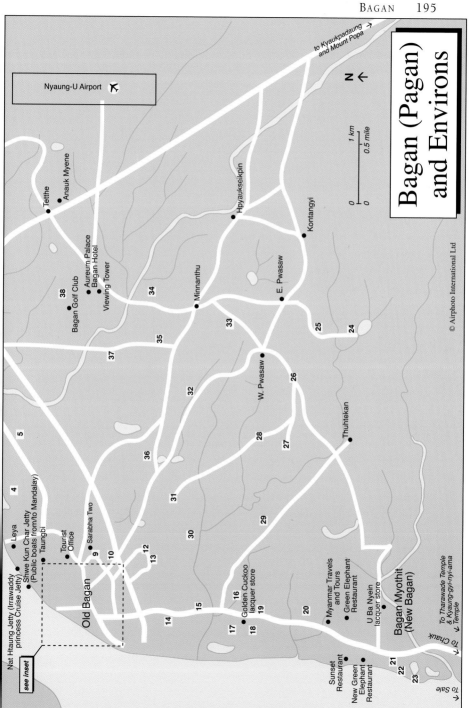

Bagan (Pagan) and Environs

N ←

to Kyaukpadaung
and Mount Popa →

Nyaung-U Airport ✈

0   1 km
0   0.5 mile

© Airphoto International Ltd

Tetthe
Anauk Myene
Bagan Golf Club
Aureum Palace
Bagan Hotel
Viewing Tower
38
Hpyaukseikpin
Kontangyi
Minnanthu
E. Pwasaw
34
33
35
37
W. Pwasaw
25
24
32
26
5
36
28
27
31
Thuhtekan
29
30
Leya
4
Shwe Kun Char Jetty
(Public boats from/to Mandalay)
Taungbi
Tourist
Office
Sarabha Two
9
10
12
13
Old Bagan
Nat Htaung Jetty (Irrawaddy
princess Cruise Jetty)
see inset
15
14
16
Golden Cuckoo
lacquer store
19
17
18
20
Myanmar Travels
and Tours
Green Elephant
Restaurant
U Ba Nyein
lacquer store
Bagan Myothit
(New Bagan)
To Tharawade Temple
& Kyaung-gyi-nyi-ama
Temple
To Chauk
21
22
23
Sunset
Restaurant
New Green
Elephant
Restaurant
To Sale

plain of Bagan in a very successful scheme to re-green the landscape. A wide variety of trees now grow up between the monuments, crops are cultivated in small fields, and the whole landscape is now green. Once the trees mature the whole feeling of the Bagan plain will change dramatically.

KINGS OF PAGAN'S GOLDEN ERA

Name	Relationship	Period
Anawrahta	Son of Kunshaw	1044–1077
Sawlu	Son	1077–1084
Kyanzittha	Brother	1084–1113
Alaungsithu	Grandson	1113–1167
Narathu	Son	1167–1170
Naratheinkha	Son	1170–1173
Narapatisithu	Brother	1173–1210
Htilominlo	Son	1211–1234
Kyaswa	Son	1234–1250
Uzana	Son	1250–1255
Narathihapati	Son	1255–1287

SIGHTS

Most travellers will have only a couple of days in Bagan and must therefore be selective. If you are not travelling with a group, hire a pony cart, jeep or bicycle. If you arrive by air, go straight to the Shwezigon Pagoda in Nyaung U near the airport, and then spend the remainder of the day around the central Bagan area. On the following day take your transport south and visit the pagodas on the way to the villages of Thiripyitsaya and Bagan Myothit. Most importantly, equip yourself with a good map; the Ministry of Hotels and Tourism has prepared an excellent one. It is available in most hotels as well as at some of the pagoda shops.

The monuments in Bagan can be divided into two distinct types: temples and pagodas. Put simply, a temple is a hollow building containing one or more Buddha images. Several storeys high, the receding terraces are usually topped by a small stupa-like campanile. The best views of Bagan and its changing moods are to be seen from the top of the large temples. Unfortunately it is now prohibited to climb most of these. The constant flow of visitors up and down the brick stairways was thought to be causing erosion and damage. However, monuments such as Shwesandaw Pagoda, Minglazedi and a few others are still climbable. Another way to appreciate the incredible landscape is to take the dawn hot-air balloon courtesy of 'Balloons over Bagan', ask your hotel for details.

A pagoda is a solid structure, built atop several narrow terraces and usually enshrining relics of the Buddha or a particularly revered monk. For an excellent and detailed explanation of the variety of architectural styles found among Bagan's monuments, see the official *Pictorial Guide to Pagan*, on sale at all the major pagodas.

SHWEZIGON PAGODA

Construction of this great golden pagoda was begun by King Anawrahta and finished by his son, King Kyanzittha, in 1087. The Shwezigon holds a special place among Burmese pagodas for two reasons: it was the first major monument built in the Burmese (as distinct from Mon) style following the country's conversion to Theravada Buddhism, and was the first pagoda to have *nat* images allowed within its precinct—a decision that was fundamental to the rapid adoption of Theravada Buddhism during Anawrahta's reign. The Shwezigon is said to contain important relics of Gautama Buddha, two bones and the copy of a tooth.

One enters the pagoda along a covered corridor filled with shops selling the usual mixture of Nirvana goods and antiques. Half-way along is a fine sign on pagoda etiquette, 'Request to Myanmars and Foreigners. Bagan is Myanmar's traditional culture that's why if you stop on the pagoda platform it is not allowed to wear the short pants, shameless dresses and not good looking dresses'. A little further along on the right is an instant photograph stall. U Sein Win photographs his clients in front of the Shwezigon Pagoda and then repairs to his 'smallest darkroom in the world'. He sits in the tiny box processing the picture then hands it out to his helper, who dries it over an old-fashioned electric fire. The golden stupa rises from five terraces (three square at the base, then two round) each symbolizing a different stage of Nirvana. Around the base of the terraces are glazed plaques that illustrate the former lives of the Buddha. The pioneering *nats*, 37 of them, are housed in a rather insignificant building at the north-east corner of the pagoda precinct. To reach it you have to pass a charming sideshow, a Burmese-style wishing well. A *hti* (an umbrella device normally placed on the top of the stupa) revolves in a cage, while around its base there are bowls, each marked with a wish: 'May you pass your examination'; 'May you meet the one you love'. A *nat* image beside each bowl bows as the *hti* creaks around. For those intending to make a wish there is even a special counter nearby where you can change your notes into coins.

The Shwezigon Pagoda's annual festival falls during the November full moon. Pilgrims travel from far and wide and the pagoda and its environs are a veritable hive of activity—a splendid time to visit the Shwezigon.

KUBYAUKGYI TEMPLE

This early 13th-century temple, near Wetkyi-in village, displays strong Indian influence. Its spire is not the usual cicada shape but straight-sided and tapered like that of the Mahabodhi Pagoda in Bagan village. The Kubyaukgyi Temple was restored in 1468. Inside are the remains of tempera wall paintings, including a charming one of Gautama Buddha during his incarnation as a hermit walking with his mother, as well as a frieze of the 28 Buddhas (24 are from previous cosmic worlds, while the last four are from the present world cycle, Gautama being the 28th Buddha). Each one sits under a different tree, for each enlightenment took place under a different species.

SARABHA GATEWAY

The Sarabha Gateway marks the eastern entrance to the old city of Pagan. This and the small section of brick wall on either side are all that remain of the ninth-century rampart. Each side of the gate contains a niche housing Bagan's guardian *nats*, 'Mister Handsome' and his sister 'Golden Face', known collectively as 'Lords of the High Mountain'.

ANANDA TEMPLE AND MONASTERY

The Ananda Temple was completed in 1091, soon after the Shwezigon. Of the 'four great temples' of Bagan, to which local folklore attributes various superlative qualities (Gawdawpalin, the most elegant; Ananda, the most beautiful; Dhammayangyi, the most massive; and Thatbinnyu, the highest), Ananda holds the greatest fascination. Distinguished from the rest by its whitewash (except for the top of its stupa which has now been gilded) and shaped like a perfect Greek cross, it rises in graduated terraces to a height of some 52 metres (170 feet).

One enters along a wooden colonnade, at the far end of which a shaft of light falls on the face and shoulders of a beautiful gold Buddha (unfortunately the soft natural light has recently been augmented by a spot light). This image, 9.5 metres (31 feet) tall, stands on a carved lotus pedestal. Around the central core of the temple are three other statuesque Buddhas of similar size encircled by two concentric

(top left) Oxen cross the sand banks at dusk and wade into the water, where their masters fill up their barrels. Sadly this is a scene now becoming more rare. The advent of 'ad hoc' pipes and pumps along the Bagan shores of the Ayeyarwady has usurped the evening role of the oxen; (top right) The beauty of many of the Bagan temples are their interiors. Row upon row of Buddha images are seated, while in the niches are nestled more images depicting the life of the Buddha; (bottom left) One of Bagan's smaller pagodas recently restored privately. Only within the past few years have individuals been allowed to restore some of Bagan's monuments and thus collect their due merit; (bottom right) One of the four corner stones of the Bagan plain is the golden Shwezigon Pagoda. It was the first pagoda built by King Anawrahta after the country's conversion to Theravada Buddhism in the 11th century. It was also the first pagoda to welcome nat images into its precinct

and lofty corridors. Lining these corridors are hundreds of tiny images housed in niches, where one can study 80 sandstone reliefs illustrating the life of Gautama Buddha from his birth to his enlightenment. Unfortunately these exquisite sandstone sculptures have recently fallen foul of the 'Japan *shwe*' and have been painted with this terrible gold paint. The four large images represent the four Buddhas of the present world. Gautama, the most recent Buddha, was apparently placed on the western side to give him a view across the Ayeyarwady to the Tan-kye Hill and Pagoda, where he had stood with his favourite disciple, Ananda, and predicted the future building and greatness of Bagan.

Retrace your steps through the great doors along the colonnade, turn left and on the left is a small red-brick building, Ananda Monastery, its walls covered in delightful frescoes depicting scenes from the Buddha's life. If you are not accompanied by a guide you will have to ask a pagoda official at the colonnade entrance to let you in and turn on the lights. In a shed just opposite, to the left of the monastery, is a charming 11th-century standing bronze Buddha. These days the shed is locked, but just ask the nearest stallholder for the key and with any luck they will find the right person. A huge new monastery will soon be in place next door to the shed so maybe the Buddha image will be moved, but for the present the Buddha image is still in situ.

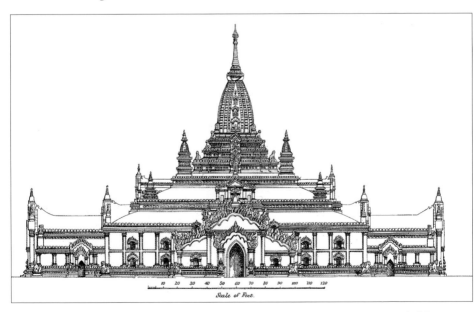

The Ananda Temple is one of the four great Buddhist monuments in Myanmar. Distinguished from the others by its whitewash, it is shaped like a perfect Greek cross and rises in graduated terraces to a height of some 52 metres (170 feet)

The January full moon marks the Ananda Temple festival. The approaches to the temple are crowded with stalls, pots of all shapes and sizes and rows of old black umbrellas hanging like bats. Men wander around with what look to be clown-like hats which, on closer inspection, turn out to be piles of tea strainers. The place is alive with sideshows, marionettes, *nat* puppets, and even a stall where one can dress up in drag to have a picture taken. A Ferris wheel is operated by hand. A crowd of children betray the whereabouts of the cotton candy man whose pink delight is produced from a strange barrel-shaped contraption. In the evening a *pwe* is staged.

HTILOMINLO TEMPLE

Htilominlo is a two-storey red-brick temple built by King Mantaungmya around 1211. On the outer walls are fragments of the original frieze and mouldings, and around the base some glazed tiles remain. Inside, four Buddhas face the cardinal points on both levels. These Buddha images sadly have had a major make-over; gone are the calm facial expressions and the hair is now jet black with tufts sticking up. If allowed, climb up the narrow, vaulted internal staircases for a good view of Bagan from the north-east.

DHAMMAYANGYI TEMPLE

Bagan's most massive temple, Dhammayangyi, was built by the wicked King Narathu. In 1167 Narathu succeeded to the throne by smothering first his father, King Alaungsithu, as he lay sleeping in his favourite temple, Shegugyi, and then his brother, Minsthinsaw, in the Palace. Soon thereafter he began the construction of this temple, no doubt to gain some much-needed merit. The ground plan is similar to the Ananda's but lacks its elegance, although the brickwork is fine. It is said that if on the king's visits to the site, he was able to stick a pin between the bricks, the mason in question would have his hands cut off prior to being executed. Not surprisingly Narathu himself met a bloody end. One of his queens (a Hindu princess and a former wife of his father whom Narathu had forced into marriage) had displeased him with her hygiene rituals and so he had her executed. In revenge in 1170 the princess's father sent to Narathu's court eight assassins disguised as Brahmin priests. They quickly dispatched Narathu, and the temple was never finished.

SHWESANDAW PAGODA (GANESH PAGODA)

North-west of the Dhammayangyi Temple stands the Shwesandaw Pagoda. This is said to be the first monument built by King Anawrahta after his conquest of Thaton and the Mons in 1057. Probably because of this, the pagoda displays a strong Mon influence. Each of the four corners of the building is guarded by Ganesh, the patron saint of the Mons. It is thought that some sacred hairs of Gautama Buddha, which

Anawrahta carried as booty from Thaton, are enshrined here. Two square red-brick terraces lead up to three white stuccoed terraces. A steep stairway dissects each of the terraces, and from the upper levels there is yet another superb view of Bagan.

SHINBINTHALYAUNG

In the same compound is a low red-brick building which contains a long recumbent Buddha image, which is thought to date from the 11th century. This reclining image faces east, with its head pointing south, unlike that of the Manuha Temple, which faces west with the head to the north—the traditional position of Buddha prior to entering Nirvana.

SULAMUNI TEMPLE

Just beyond Dhammayangyi stands the red-brick Sulamuni Temple. It was built in 1174 by King Narapatisithu, a son of King Narathu, again no doubt as an atonement. One enters the temple precincts up a brick mounting-block and through a gateway in the surrounding brick wall. The light inside is particularly striking: the sun's rays shine through the outer arches onto the central core, radiating a soft terracotta glow. The walls are decorated by murals dating from the 12th to 19th centuries. All but those on the south have been badly damaged by the weather due

Standing 60 metres (200 feet) high, Thatbinnyu Temple is Bagan's tallest building. It is a white stucco building dating from the reign of King Alaungsithu during the 12th century

to the vaulted openings along the outer walls. Those on the south side depict 17th-century life. On the eastern side in a recess is a huge seated Buddha, larger than those at the other cardinal points, as the eastern entrance is reserved for royalty. The vaulted stairways to the terrace are glossy, again lit by the 'terracotta' light. The Sulamuni Temple is a favourite haunt of hawkers selling antiques; take particular care before buying any of the gems offered and in all cases bargain determinedly.

(left) The terracotta walls glow as sunlight pours in to the corridors of the Sulamuni Temple. A perfect escape from the blazing heat of the midday sun

A corner of the great Thatbinnyu Temple. With the evening light falling on the building, it is possible to see where the top sections of the spires have been replaced. The Bagan plain was badly hit by an earthquake in 1975 and many pagodas and temples were damaged. Since then an intensive restoration programme, aided by the United Nations, has been in operation

THATBINNYU TEMPLE

The Thatbinnyu Temple is a white stucco building dating from the reign of King Alaungsithu (1113–1160) and at 60 metres (200 feet), is Bagan's highest pagoda. Thatbinnyu is indeed a fine building, but its main attraction is the view from its terraces, spectacular both at dawn and dusk. It is also, owing to its central position, the most popular vantage point in Bagan, which can be a disadvantage for those inclined to solitude. The Ayeyarwady River forms a great elbow on two sides with a strange spur of hills to the east, and into the distance the plain erupts with pagodas of all shapes and sizes and degrees of decay. Sadly, due to the erosion of the brick it is now no longer possible to climb this temple.

Beside Thatbinnyu stands a small replica known as the Tally Pagoda. For every 10,000 bricks used in the main building one went towards the Tally Pagoda. The site of the 11th-century royal palace is nearby and today serves as a football pitch.

There is one beautiful old wooden monastery remaining in Bagan, Nat Taung Monastery. It is approached along a dirt track and is hidden in among a copse of mature trees. Walk across the well-swept dirt courtyard to the 200-year-old building, up the stone stairway and through the wooden doors decorated with two rather cross-looking devas. Inside the main hall, propped up against the wall are some lovely carved panels, saved by the monks from other buildings that have disintegrated. The interior is simple, and great teak pillars divide the space, the occasional Buddha image, the monks' belongings. A smaller room holds a collection of red-and-gold lacquered chests containing the monastery's palm-leaf Tripitaka texts. There is a great peace and serenity about this place.

GAWDAWPALIN TEMPLE

This temple, which was built during the reign of Narapatisithu (1173–1210), is a thinner and slightly shorter version of Thatbinnyu. It sustained severe damage during an earthquake in 1975, but has now been thoroughly restored. The views of this most elegant of Bagan's temples have been seriously impaired by the construction of the new Bagan Museum. From the south, the huge 'wedding cake' museum completely blocks out the neighbouring temple.

BAGAN MUSEUM

The old Bagan Museum is housed in a small, hexagonal building just across the road to the south of Gawdawpalin. This museum is to remain open alongside the new one. It is abundantly stocked and contains some fine pieces, including small bronze 10th- and 11th-century Buddha images, an 11th-century stone Buddha image of classic, simple lines, and a series of exquisitely carved small dolomite reliefs depicting the Buddha's life. However, the Museum's most prized possession is a large stone tablet (on display in Gallery 3), dating from 1113, inscribed in four contemporary languages, namely Pyu, Mon, Pali and Burmese. The stone was discovered in 1887 in the Kubyaukgyi Temple (now called Myinkaba). The importance of this piece (sometimes called Myanmar's Rosetta Stone) is that it has furnished scholars with a code to the Pyu script, hitherto indecipherable. Some of the above have been moved to the museum at Nay Pyi Taw the country's new capital. Though a collection of the stone sculptures (both originals and copies) now stand in the main hall of the new museum with the remainder in a first floor gallery. The design of the new three-tiered museum is in the traditional Burmese style, though the colour is not. Painted in several tones of pink and mauve with a little synthetic gold here and there, the structure is visible from all over the Bagan plain. It is even larger than Dhammayangyi, Bagan's 'most massive' temple. What a shame that the architects did not try and meld the building into the landscape—though now some fourteen years since its opening both the weather and the 'greening' of Bagan have made the building less conspicuous. Another large building, the state guest-house, which is situated around the curve of the Ayeyarwady to the east, next to the Thiripyitsaya Hotel, has been painted a mixture of greens and browns. So if watching the sunset from the terraces of nearby Shwesandaw Pagoda, the guest-house does not upset the eye.

Some 2,000 objects are on display in the museum's exhibition galleries. The space is huge and even with the large amount of exhibits the museum feels empty and stark. Also, perhaps in an attempt to try and fill the space, some of the exhibits are not up to standard.

As visitors are no longer allowed to climb some of the major temples to watch the sunset and sunrise, the government architect has incorporated a large terrace, at third-storey level, around the new museum building. Visitors will be encouraged to view the magnificent plain of Bagan from this vantage point. The museum is open daily (except Myanmar New Year holidays) 9am–4.30pm.

THE ROAD SOUTH
MYINKABA AND THIRIPYITSAYA
MINGALAZEDI PAGODA

Mingalazedi was built by Narathihapati, 'The king who ran away from the Chinese', and was completed in 1284, just three years before Kublai Khan's invasion. As such it was the last major pagoda built in Bagan. It is noted for the glazed terracotta tiles around its terraced bases. These are apparently much prized by art thieves, which is why the pagoda is enmeshed in chicken wire.

KUBYAUKGYI TEMPLE (MYINKABA)

This Mon-style temple was built by Prince Rajakumar, the only son of King Kyansitta, in 1113. It was not in fact until the king was in old age that he came to know of Rajakumar's existence. The boy's mother had left the court while pregnant. She had been given a valuable ring by the king on the understanding that, if the baby was a boy, she should return to the court with her son and the ring, but if the baby was a girl, she should sell the ring. Many years later Rajakumar returned with the ring. His father's delight at the discovery of a son was tempered by the awkward fact that he had meanwhile promised the throne to his daughter's son, Alaungsithu. Instead, the king gave Rajakumar some land. Rajakumar was a pious man and, on his father's death, he sold the land and built the temple. The inner sanctum is decorated with frescoes, which have been restored. Under each painting is an account, in ancient Mon script, of the tale it depicts.

MYINKABA PAGODA

On the left, as one enters into the village of Myinkaba, is an inverted bowl-like pagoda built by King Anawrahta in memory of his predecessor and half-brother, Sokkade, whom he had killed and tossed into a stream. It is sited beside the very watercourse down which the victim's corpse floated on its way to the Ayeyarwady.

MYINKABA VILLAGE

The most notable features of Myinkaba village are the huge stacks of bamboo one sees everywhere. Bamboo is the raw material for the plaited matting which serves as the walls of houses all over Myanmar. Stop and watch this intricate manufacturing operation in progress: the bamboo is first split into strands, then deftly woven into large squares.

The village is also famous for its traditional Mon-style lacquerware, the secret of whose manufacture has been passed from generation to generation since King Manuha brought his artisans with him into exile here more than 900 years ago.

MANUHA TEMPLE

At the southern end of Myinkaba village is the Manuha Temple complex. When in 1057 King Anawrahta returned victorious to Pagan, it was here that the captive King Manuha was brought to live. By 1059 Manuha had built himself this two-storey square white temple and through it conveyed a melancholy message. The three Buddhas are uncomfortably large for their enclosures, thus illustrating his captivity and mental stress. The facial expressions of the two seated images are grim. That of the one reclining Buddha, on the other hand, is smiling and serene. He faces north and is therefore on the verge of Nirvana and release from the transitory world.

The midday sun bakes all around. Undeterred, a group of young men with paint pots slung round their waists clamber up a pagoda in the middle of New Bagan village and administer a 'spring' paint

NANPAYA TEMPLE

Beside the Manuha Temple is the charming brick-and-mud mortar Nanpaya Temple. This was King Manuha's residence, and later became a temple. Inside, the central plinth is empty, but on the four central pillars are beautiful stone carvings of Brahma, the Mon patron saint. The Mon people had originally been Hindu, hence the Rama goose was the emblem of the Mon Kingdom. At certain times of the day the light comes through the perforated windows, illuminating sections of the carving (but take a flashlight along). The outer walls are crenellated, and some of the sandstone friezes remain intact. A modern concrete path surrounds the temple; make sure not to leave it, as the rough ground harbours some prickly briars.

ABEYADANA TEMPLE

Further south along the road on the right side is Abeyadana Temple. Legend tells us that Kyanzittha, while fleeing from his elder brother, King Sawlu, had planned to meet his lover, Abeyadana, where the temple now stands. She was late so he wandered off and fell asleep nearby. When she found him, an enormous *naga* was hooded over the sleeping Kyanzittha protecting him. She screamed, waking Kyanzittha, and the *naga* was frightened away. Kyanzittha took the *naga's* action to be a sign that he would become king. When he finally ascended the throne in 1084, he built this temple, naming it after Abeyadana, now his wife. It houses a large seated Buddha. Around the corridors are many small Buddha images in the niches, and there are also some good Mahayanist and Hindu frescoes.

NAGAYON TEMPLE

Just across the road is the Nagayon Temple. King Kyanzittha built this temple on the site where he slept protected by the *naga*. Indeed, the large Buddha image in the inner shrine is protected by a hooded *naga*. Again many of the corridor niches contain Buddha images, and part of a series of wall paintings depicting the life of the Buddha decorates the entrance.

EAST AND WEST PETLEIK PAGODAS

At the entrance to Thiripyitsaya village stand the East and West Petleik Pagodas. Some 50 years ago when these 11th-century pagodas were in disrepair, it was decided to clear the debris from around their base. This operation revealed rows of unglazed terracotta tiles illustrating scenes from the *jataka*, the story of the Buddha's previous lives. Sadly, many of these plaques have since either been stolen or have fallen prey to the weather. As a result they are now surrounded by a rather unsightly fence and roofed over.

LAWKANANDA PAGODA

On the far side of Thiripyitsaya village the road comes to an abrupt end in a grove of trees. There above you, on a little hill overlooking the Ayeyarwady, is the Lawkananda Pagoda. This handsome white stupa, the top portion of which has been recently gilded, was built by King Anawrahta in 1059 and marks the southern boundary of Bagan. It is said to contain a replica of a tooth of Gautama Buddha. Poised high above the Ayeyarwady, it commands excellent views to both the north and south. Below it there used to be an anchorage for large trading vessels, which was used when the water level was too low for them to dock at Bagan proper.

Near this pagoda is situated the village of New Bagan (Bagan Myothit). In the early days of its building there was an air of impermanence about the community, but it is now thriving. To begin with there were no trees and the bougainvillea that grows so well in arid Bagan had not yet made its mark. Now the village feels quite settled. Most of the lacquerware businesses have re-located and opened new operations here, along with the antique shops. Several guest houses are open to foreign visitors. Perhaps some of the calm, contented and shaded atmosphere of the previous village is lost, but the identity of New Bagan is blossoming.

BUPAYA PAGODA

Bagan's other riverside pagoda and a landmark for sailors is Bupaya Pagoda. It is about eight kilometres (five miles) upstream from the Lawkananda and is just within the ancient city's northern limits. This fairy-tale pagoda sits on top of semicircular terraces. The foundation wall rises sheer from the river's edge and is topped by a large and pleasing scallop design. It is thought that the original 'pumpkin pagoda' dated from the third century. What one sees today, however, is a recent reconstruction, the original stupa having tumbled into the river during the 1975 earthquake.

The best time to visit Bupaya is at sunset. Evening is also the time for collecting water, and from the pagoda one can watch as oxen drawing elegant carts proceed across the sandbanks and wade out into the stream, where their masters ladle water into large barrels. After the sun has dropped behind the Tan-Kye Pagoda, on the far side of the Ayeyarwady, the colours intensify—red, orange, magenta; no two evenings are the same. It is now necessary to hunt for the ox carts which collect the river water during this magical hour of an evening. A series of Heath Robinson-style pumps

On a bend of the Ayeyarwady, high up stands the Bupaya or 'pumpkin' pagoda. A welcome and important landmark for confused sailors of many generations and nationalities: 'The width of the apparent river was excessive, and it was difficult to guess where the proper channel lay,' recorded Captain Baker of the East India Company in the mid-18th century

and pipes have largely replaced the trusty oxen and their handlers. If there are none below Bupaya walk along the river shore and you will probably see one or two traditional water-carriers. There will be plenty of other river-shore activity going on as families take their evening bathe, do the laundry and generally enjoy a social gathering in and around the water.

SALE (SALAY)

For anyone who enjoys chugging along the river, a trip to Sale (formerly Salay) is suggested. Hire a boat (easily arranged by your hotel) and sail down the Ayeyarwady to Sale, which is some 20 miles (15 kilometres) south of Bagan. The small wooden craft will probably leave from the riverbank just below the Bupaya Pagoda. A ladder is propped up against the bow, and once you are on board and settled into the over-sized armchairs, complete with padded neck cushions, the journey begins. The boat will dodge the sandbanks and hug the shore. This is a beautiful stretch of river. Little pagodas perch on the hills, majestic trees punctuate the river bank, some of their roots are elevated and spread out like huge hands. There is much life along the bank. Farmers stand on the back of their wooden ploughs, pulled along by oxen, as they prepare little squares of very fertile alluvial soil—pulses and peanuts are the main crop here. Groups of children drop their baskets to wave at the passing boat. Fishermen stand in the water casting their nets, while others dangle a line from their canoe. The boat glides on past Chauk, one of the original oil fields, which still produces oil today. A collection of nodding 'donkeys' (oil-well pumps) stand by the river bank, relentlessly grinding away. Once the oil is extracted it is shipped downstream to the refineries at Thanlyin.

Large boats called hnau *used to commonly ply the rivers. The most peculiar part of the vessel was in the spars and rigging. The mast consisted of two spars, and above the mainyard the two pieces ran into one, forming the topmast. The sail was suspended on rings like a curtain outwards both ways from the mast. These boats could scarcely sail of course, except before the wind*

If you feel a little peckish during the one and a half hour boat trip, refreshments sit on a little table. The *lapet* (pickled tea leaves) and the accompanying crispy fried garlic, sesame seeds and chopped nuts are all in a traditional lacquer container, as well as some good sweets made from tamarind, all washed down by Burmese green tea.

On arrival at the Sale jetty, it is a five-minute drive to the Yoke Sone Monastery, a fine teak building decorated with some beautifully crafted reliefs. The monastery was commissioned by a local 'billionaire' in 1882. Permission for the felling of the necessary tress was granted by King Theebaw in Mandalay. Unfortunately, within three years the British took control of Upper Burma and so the permission was revoked. It then took the benefactor another seven years to regain the permits from the British and for the monastery to be built. When, several years ago, the last head monk died, the 116-year-old building was put under the control of the Archaeological Department, with the remaining monks moved across the courtyard to another building. The monastery, now renamed the U Pon Nya Museum, has been well restored and has so far avoided the dreaded heavy coat of creosote.

Mythical lions form the bannisters up to the main entrance. Inside, the main hall has been converted into an exhibition space. A large central table is covered in antique lacquer pieces, some fine wooden reliefs are propped up against a wall and the ceiling of this room is also finely carved. A large standing gilded Buddha image, dating from the Mandalay period (18th century) dominates the 'Beautiful Hall'. In the 'Connecting Hall' the prize is a vermilion-and-gold standing Buddha. However, the real gems are the 45 carved reliefs on the outside of the front of the building—there are none on the back, as the donor ran out of money. The figures are carved with great style and artistic merit, and the expressions on the faces are full of character. Each relief tells a story. The theme of each piece is the curbing of sexual desire in order to live a better life. Under some of the carvings is a translation, perhaps—'son of rich man taking pleasure' followed by 'son of rich man incarnated as a tree nat'. The U Pon Nya Museum is open every day except Monday from 9am to 4.30pm.

Sale is a perfect small community to wander around. A host of small white stupas interspersed with some Italianate monasteries, stand near the museum. Walk along beside them, up some stone steps to the right and another wooden monastery will come into sight. The Tha ta na Kyaung (Lay thar Monastery) is not as fine as the U Pon Nya but well worth a visit. Inside, the layout is traditional.

(following pages) Every evening as dusk falls a domestic scene unfurls on the shores of the Ayeyarwady River at Bagan. 'There is in Burmese life a beauty that delights the eye and a dignity that makes one feel proud of the human race.'

There are still monks living here, so the trappings of daily life are present—an orange telephone covered by a white antimacassar. Their tripitaka texts are housed in a large red lacquered cabinet, the doors of which are decorated with squares of brightly coloured woven cloth, each telling a *jataka* tale. Inside the cabinet each set of the Tripitaka is individually wrapped in an antique piece of fabric.

From Sale to Mount Popa is around a one-hour drive, thus making a day-trip to Sale a perfect sandwich between Bagan and Mount Popa.

MOUNT POPA

Some 50 kilometres (30 miles) south-east of Bagan, in the middle of the scorched Myingyan Plain, rises up lush Mount Popa, home of the *nats*. The drive from Bagan to Popa takes around one hour along a new road and passes through toddy palm groves. Long bamboo ladders are tied to tree trunks. Look up at the crown of the tree where there will be little black buckets suspended. In the cool of the early evening an agile young man will shin up the tree and collect the little pots, by then filled with the toddy juice. Sugar is made from this, as is a rather potent liquor. If feeling strong and adventurous, stop at one of the mat sheds beside the road and try a little toddy wine.

Popa means 'flower' in Sanskrit, and Burmese legend tells that the mountain was originally the home of beautiful ogresses who played hide-and-seek on its tangled slopes. These curious characters emerged in recorded history in the form of rebels and brigands preying on travellers on their way to Pagan. It was at Mount Popa that King Anawrahta amassed his army before marching on Pagan to regain his throne.

The chief mythical inhabitants of Mount Popa are a brother and sister, together known as Min Maha-giri (meaning 'Lords of the High Mountain') who are said to have lived just north of Pagan during the fourth century. Their story epitomizes both the violence and essential morality inherent in *nat* beliefs. The brother bore the nickname 'Mr Handsome' and was a 'mighty blacksmith', whose hammer could cause the earth to quake. This was too much for the neighbouring king, who vowed to assassinate him. But the blacksmith was forewarned and escaped to the forest. The king then seduced Mr Handsome's beautiful sister, and made her his queen. 'I no longer fear your brother, because he is now my brother also. Invite him to Tagaung and I shall make him governor of the city.'

Mr Handsome accepted the king's invitation, only to be seized, tied to a *saga* tree and burned alive. His sister, heartbroken, leapt onto the burning pyre and perished with her brother. Only her face was not burnt, and hence she became known as 'Golden Face'. The two were transformed into mischievous *nats* and lived in the *saga* tree. To avenge their murder, they killed anything that ventured into the shade of the tree. The king felled the tree and threw it into the Irrawaddy. When the log reached Thiripyitsaya, King Thinlikyaung pulled it from the river and carved on it images of the brother and sister. With much pomp and ceremony this was transported to Mount Popa where a shrine was built and remains to this day.

The climb up Mount Popa is recommended for the cool of the day. A partially covered staircase goes all the way to the top, sections of which are quite steep—those who suffer from vertigo have been known to descend on their bottoms. At the summit sits a pagoda and several other small halls all surrounded by a wide platform, the view across the plain of Bagan and beyond is spectacular. It is possible to stay in the monastery at the foot of the hill.

The Mount Popa area has recently been designated as a National Park and as part of this environmental awareness there is a stunning hotel Popa Mountain Resort (see page 264) on the peak opposite Mount Popa. It is a perfect place for those interested in the wildlife of Myanmar. The group that runs the resort (and several other adventure resorts), arranges treks up to an extinct volcano, bird-watching and so on—they are deeply committed to eco-tourism. The hotel itself is beautifully designed with separate, comfortable but simple individual chalets all perched on the hill with magnificent views across the ravine. As you arrive at reception, the first thing that catches the eye in the foreground is an inviting swimming pool. When the resort first opened the pool was purely for show, since it stands higher than the pagoda atop Mount Popa, and one monk complained that they should not be looked down upon. Thankfully this problem has now been sorted out, so swimming is allowed. A beautiful resort hotel and a perfect place to take a few days' rest from the rigours of sight-seeing. Relax and enjoy the natural surroundings, sip a cool fresh lime soda under the shade of a fine monk's umbrella by the pool, look across at Mount Popa and watch the enormous butterflies as they flit around the assorted flowering shrubs.

Colonialist Sir Henry Yule describes how he was entertained by a pair of dancing elephants and their masters: 'Not the least amusing part of the performance lay in the gestures of the mahouts, who on each side went violently through the actions and dances which they intended the elephant to imitate...'

INLE LAKE

The Inle Lake area is stunning, and to appreciate it properly a good two to three days is needed. Unfortunately, this is one place where the inadequacy of Myanmar's transport system can become a distinct disadvantage. In bad weather planes do not land at nearby Heho. In such circumstances, the only way to leave the valley is a bumpy six-hour bus ride to Thazi, followed by a train journey of perhaps ten or even as much as 20 hours to Yangon. Nevertheless the lake, the Shan capital of Taunggyi, and the magical quality of the area make the risks well worth taking.

HISTORY

The Intha people, who are of Mon rather than Shan descent, originated from the south-east of Myanmar around Tavoy (modern day Dawei). When or why the migration took place is unclear. Some say it was during the reign of King Narapatisithu (1173–1210). A wealth of stories surround this king. He was thought to have travelled to Tavoy on a religious mission, and there he founded a city. He is also alleged to have repulsed a vast invading Chinese army in the Inle Lake valley. Today on the bed of the lake are rows of posts, supposedly pillars of his palace. Another theory suggests that the Inthas were convicts expelled from Tavoy in the 17th century; and still another story holds that they simply became fed up with the constant battling between the Mons and the Burmese. In any event the Inthas (literally meaning 'Sons of the Lake') not only survived in their remote mountain environment, but prospered. The lake, some 32 kilometres (20 miles) long and at its widest just five kilometres (three miles) across, now has 200 settlements and a total population of some 150,000, many of whom live on floating islands of vegetation.

SIGHTS
THE LAKE

Inle Lake reveals itself gradually to the approaching visitor. One advances down narrow streams hedged with high rushes, probably aboard a long canoe propelled by a lusty outboard, which whisks along at terrifying speed. After several miles one emerges from this maze of waterways into a more tranquil world on a mirror of water, its glassy blue reflecting the occasional cloud. To left and right the picture is framed by serried green mountains with the centre a continuous blue.

Other than the growl of canoe buses as they whip to and fro, the silence and stillness are only disturbed by fishermen. The fishermen of Inle Lake have

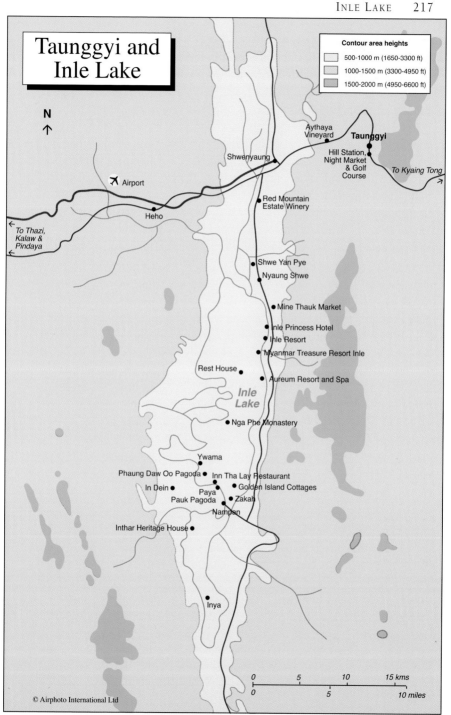

Taunggyi and Inle Lake

N

Contour area heights

500-1000 m (1650-3300 ft)
1000-1500 m (3300-4950 ft)
1500-2000 m (4950-6600 ft)

Aythaya Vineyard

Taunggyi

Hill Station, Night Market & Golf Course

To Kyaing Tong

Shwenyaung

✈ Airport

Heho

Red Mountain Estate Winery

To Thazi, Kalaw & Pindaya

Shwe Yan Pye

Nyaung Shwe

Mine Thauk Market

Inle Princess Hotel

Inle Resort

Myanmar Treasure Resort Inle

Rest House

Aureum Resort and Spa

Inle Lake

Nga Phe Monastery

Ywama

Phaung Daw Oo Pagoda

Inn Tha Lay Restaurant

In Dein

Paya Pauk Pagoda

Golden Island Cottages

Zakah

Nampan

Inthar Heritage House

Inya

0   5   10   15 kms
0   5   10 miles

© Airphoto International Ltd

evolved an eccentric method of rowing and fishing specially suited to local conditions (the water being both shallow and very clear). By propelling their craft from the bow, they can watch for approaching patches of tangled weeds and, more important, are able to see tell-tale bubbles and then pounce on the unsuspecting fish. And with only one limb engaged in providing locomotion the rest of the body is free for the business at hand: the fisherman uses his legs to push home the conical-shaped net.

Skimming along, one soon comes upon rows and rows of floating gardens bursting with an abundance of flowers and vegetables. These have been gradually built up over the years by cutting strips of dense weed from the lake floor. The tangled mass is consolidated with earth and eventually forms one of the most fertile growing media imaginable. New areas are constantly being 'grown' in shallow water: grass cuttings and weed form the foundation, then comes a layer of earth and finally top soil. When the layers of weed and earth have become integrated, strips some six feet wide and perhaps as long as a football pitch are cut loose and poled to their destinations, where they are pegged to the lake floor with long bamboo staves.

The Intha people are facing a problem. The water-level of the lake has dropped considerably over the years, so much so that it has been known for the main channel in Ywama to dry up. Apart from a drop in the level of rainfall, the encroachment of the dreaded water hyacinth has exacerbated the problem. A dredging programme is being implemented, both by machine and by hand–the US$5 now collected from all visiting foreigners when entering the Inle Lake area is going towards the preservation of the lake and their community. However the advent of many new tourist hotels on the lake cannot have helped the environment.

YWAMA (HAIRYA YWAMA)

The largest village built on the lake is Ywama. Its streets are a web of canals, each piece of 'land' connected by arched wooden bridges and causeways. This is a rich community, and its teak houses are generally handsome, two-storey affairs. They are constructed on large wooden poles driven directly into the lake bed, the space below the first floor being used as a boathouse. Each dwelling has its own landing stage, often no more than a floating pavement of grass, pegged by bamboo (which doubles as mooring for visiting craft). On the plot surrounding the house are the trappings of domestic life: a tidy vegetable patch, a water pen for ducks, washing hung out to dry. At one end of the plot a small area of the canal, the size of a bath tub, is encircled by a bamboo fence; this is the scene of the family's daily washing ritual. It contains wooden planks both for sitting on as well as for use as a scrubbing board, and a large bowl for rinsing, though for the younger members a splash in the canal is preferred. From the back of the house a walkway leads to an elevated lavatory. Despite in many cases the absence of plumbing, the problem is mysteriously disposed of, and the air is purity and fragrance itself. Most of the larger houses and the new hotels have now installed septic tanks. Apparently even the dead are buried in the lake.

A pivot of social life is the morning's floating market, which congregates on Ywama's broadest canal, alongside the village store and *nat* shrines. Here, under the protective shade of their straw *khamouts* (conical-shaped hats), chattering businesswomen manoeuvre elegant canoes filled with all manner of produce. Now that the market has become so popular with visitors, the majority of craft will be piled with antique boxes, pipes and so on. As soon as a tourist boat approaches, one or two of the marketeers will row like fury to be the first to come alongside the visiting boat. A terrible 'boat jam' results as everyone jostles to sell their wares. Alight and visit the many stalls on the floating village. Hard bargaining is advised as the prices asked are astronomical. On shore are some traditional stalls selling vegetables, lake fish and of course the smelly fish paste, *ngapi*. The Inthas' wealth is derived not only from their market gardening activities, but also from lucrative craft industries, notably weaving of Shan shoulder bags, beautiful thick Shan *longyis* as well as the production of fine and delicate silverware. Indust-

rial methods, however, tend towards the quaint to say the least: The blacksmith's bellows operator—his grandmother—sits perched on a small platform behind two long thick bamboo tubes, alternately pulling in and out long feather dusters, causing a very effective air draught.

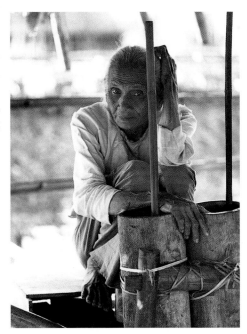

Grandma has a rest from her bellows. At a signal from the blacksmith, she will pull up and down on the two bamboo sticks. On the end of them is a mop of chicken feathers

At the end of a side canal on Inle Lake is this charming collection of stupas

(above) Far across the lake an Intha fisherman surveys the water, looking for fish. To date the lake remains unpolluted, so he should be able to spy any likely victims

(below) Rising from the waters of Inle Lake is Phaung Daw U Pagoda. One of the three principal shrines in Myanmar, it is home to five small famous Buddha images

PHAUNG DAW U

The lake is as richly endowed with pagodas and monasteries as anywhere else in Myanmar. In particular, the Phaung Daw U Pagoda is regarded (with the Shwedagon in Yangon and the Shwezigon in Bagan) as one of the country's three principal shrines. Along the corridor leading to the pagoda are a variety of stalls, some selling Shan handicrafts, others various antiques and knick-knacks. This pagoda houses five small Buddha images whose original forms have long since been lost under years of plastering with gold leaf by pilgrims. Once a year, at the September full moon, there is an elaborate festival during which the Buddha images are rowed around the lake to visit outlying pagodas. They are conveyed in a magnificent copy of a royal barge (*karaweik*) shaped like the golden swan (symbol of Buddhist royalty). The minute Buddhas sit under white royal umbrellas. Nowadays only four of the Buddhas make this regal progress. Some years ago the barge capsized with all five aboard; their distraught guardians were only able to recover four images but, on returning to the pagoda, they found the fifth miraculously in its normal position. It has not been moved since and now guards the pagoda during the others' annual outing. On the day of the actual full moon the procession accompanying the images returns to the Phaung Daw U Pagoda and once safely back in the pagoda a series of leg-rowing races takes place. A riotous affair with the audience bobbing around on their boats, or standing crammed into the buildings along the shoreline. They shout encouragement to their favourite team—great guffaws of laughter erupt when a team capsizes. If spending the whole day on the lake, try any of several good restaurants (see page 276) beside the Phaung Daw U pagoda.

PAYA PAUK PAGODA

When travelling on the lake near the Golden Island Cottages (see page 267), on the south of the lake the stupa of a pagoda entices. It is the Paya Pauk Pagoda. As you alight from the boat the steps lead into the adjoining Paya Pauk Myauk Monastery. In the late afternoon the visitor will be greeted by the chanting of children reciting their prayers to the monks. The pagoda has an open chamber in the side of the stupa, which houses a large seated Buddha image some 50 metres (165 feet) high. A ladder rests up against the wall—each morning a devotee will climb up to wash the Buddha's face. The screen behind the figure has been covered in mosaic and fairy lights—the scene is a strange mixture of the serene Buddha and the pulsating fairy lights. To the right of the chamber lies a beautiful Buddha in alabaster, very simple. Walk around the stupa, also covered in mosaic, and enjoy a wonderful view of the lake, the stupa of the Phaung Daw U pagoda rising up in the distance.

INTHAR HERITAGE HOUSE

On the edge of Inpawkhon Village is a two-storey former rice mill—a beautiful teak building recently restored and now the home to pedigree Burmese cats and an organic restaurant. So a perfect place to stop for lunch after a morning on the Lake. The owner of this Heritage House has a mission to restore pure bred Burmese cats to Myanmar. A fascinating video explains the breeding programme and the owner's world-wide hunt for some pure breed animals—success was found in London's Harrods Store. The cats occupy the bottom portion of the building and are very beautiful animals. The building itself has been lovingly restored all but 20% of the wood is recycled and it has the feeling of a real home—indeed the owners often stay there. So eating a delicious organic lunch, on the terrace overlooking the Lake and Paya Pauk Pagoda is like eating at home, indeed many of the recipes are from the owner's Intha grandmother.

INDEIN

A canal on the south-west of the lake leads to the village of Indein—a lovely forgotten area with profuse vegetation—wild cosmos and ginger plants flowering in March. Once off the boat walk through the village and across a couple of fields to the 16th century Indein Pagoda which itself is of no particular architectural merit, but it is the area which is full of atmostphere. The hill-side was once the site of some 2042 pagodas and small stupas with today around 1054 remaining. They are mostly built of the local sandstone bricks in the Shan style—in all states of repair, some crumble whilst others have been restored. It is said that the area has good feng shui hence the large collection of pagodas—and certainly the views are spectacular across the countryside to the surrounding hills. Local legend has it that the 11th century King Anawrahta visited. Once back in the village after a hot and exhausting trudge around the ruins, stop off at the Star Restaurant. Try their delicious, cool fresh lime juice or milk shake.

ZAKAH

This village, also in the south of the lake, houses the boatyards, both for new craft and repairs. Everywhere is the tap-tap of hammers and the noise of saws. It takes a boat-builder four days to make the dug-out canoes and four weeks for the long boats. The boats are constructed exactly as they have been for centuries—and with no plans. No nails are used but instead 'mangrove' plugs. The teak comes from the forests of the nearby Kayah State. Once the boats are launched they are used for three to four months before their owners return to the boatyard, where two coats of lacquer will be applied. The engines are all imported from China.

(top) A procession of boats leads the karaweik barge with is precious cargo of four tiny Buddha images. Once a year, at the September full moon, there is an elaborate festival during which the images are rowed around Inle Lake to visit outlying pagodas; (centre and bottom) The four small Buddha images aboard the karaweik barge arrive at Nyaung Shwe. The fifth Buddha remains on guard at the Phaung Daw U pagoda, considered one of Myanmar's three major Buddhist shrines. Once safely installed in the pagoda, the boat races begin. With great speed and dexterity the long boats, their oarsmen standing career towards the finishing line. Incredible balance is required for the whole contingent to remain standing as they speed along. Much to the delight of the spectators, there are many who capsize

NGA PHE MONASTERY

One of the most eye-catching sights on the lake used to be the Nga Phe Monastery. A large many-sided wooden building, it rose out of the calm, blue water of the lake, its corrugated roofs sparkling in the midday sun. Now that the water level has dropped so dramatically, the monastery is surrounded by vegetation and is practically on dry land during the dry season. The pleasing large interior space remains intact, with the wide, polished teak boards. Although the magic has evaporated it is still an interesting building to visit. The resident monks take pleasure in making their large cat population jump through hoops—hence it is sometimes called 'jumping cat monastery'.

MINE THAUK MARKET

For those who would like to visit a more authentic local market than the floating market, now so commercial, stop at Mine Thauk on the way back to Nyaung Shwe. A large and bustling market, each vendor sits on the ground, shaded by a large umbrella, their goods arranged around them in style. Piles of lotus leaves carefully folded in four sit beside a lady selling tomatoes. A customer approaches, and the required amount of tomatoes is weighed with the help of exquisitely carved brass opium weights. A lotus leaf is then opened flat into which the tomatoes are poured, and the package is handed over to the customer—how much better than using a plastic bag. At one side of the market, cattle and oxen are bought and sold. A host of small restaurants, shaded by mat sheds serve their patrons bowls of tasty *mohingha*, Shan noodles and other small

eats. This colourful market, full of different ethnic groups, is a perfect place for the keen photographer to spend a happy hour or so.

During the week-long 'royal' visitation of four of the Buddhas from the Phaung Daw U Pagoda to the village of Nyaung Shwe, a festival takes place. Food stalls are set up, and an old-fashioned funfair complete with Ferris wheel operates. The highlight of the festival is the all-night pwe

NYAUNG SHWE

The village of Nyaung Shwe is the best jumping-off point for a trip on the lake. It is a pleasant place to wander in, and the restaurant beside the main jetty is a good place to sit, eat and watch the water traffic. The cold and wet traveller (one sometimes gets very wet on the lake) could do worse than revive his or her spirits with Mandalay rum and tea. One can also get good biscuits and bread from the local bakery. The early-morning market here is worth a visit, particularly for those interested in Shan goods, beautiful *longyis* and bags. If possible, a visit to Inle Lake should coincide with the late-September, early-October pagoda festival. The stately golden *karaweik* bearing the four precious Buddha images is a breathtaking sight, as it proceeds across the lake surrounded by a flotilla of small boats, all manned by leg-rowers. Once the small Buddha images from the Phaung Daw U Pagoda have been safely deposited in the pagoda at Nyaung Shwe (they rest there for three days) the festivities begin. During the highly competitive boat races there is much uproarious shouting and screaming, as many a leg-rower tumbles from his perch. On shore a fairground is set up with side-shows and an old Ferris wheel, probably still operated by man-power. The narrow streets are lined with food stalls, cooking up all sorts of 'small eats'. As night falls, people will start to flock to the temporary theatre for the *pwe*, which will continue throughout the night. During the festival the noise makes it difficult to sleep, so for those seeking a tranquil night, travel back on to the lake and stay on the water in one of the lake-borne hotels (see page 265).

SHWE YAN PYE

The road out of Nyaung Shwe is a narrow causeway, lined with spreading trees, which cuts through the middle of very fertile fields. Centuries ago this land was part of Inle Lake. After a few miles, the road passes a fine wooden monastery some 110 years old. Built by a *sawbwa* (prince) of Nyaung Shwe on a site of a former palace, this monastery has a lovely simple gilded interior and possesses a peaceful feeling—even though a devotee has given the head monk a noisy, chiming electric clock. The ceiling and the pillars of the building are covered in mosaic, a gentle grey colour. Beside the monastery stands a pagoda of simple lines, its stupa also decorated in silver-grey mosaic.

TAUNGGYI

Taunggyi was founded by Sir George Scott—the Superintendent of the Shan States around the turn of the 20th century, who adapted the Burmese name Shway Yoe— as the seat of the Shan government over which he presided. It was sited 1,430 metres (4,690 feet) above sea-level to provide the colonial British civil servants with a refuge from the heat. A few of the typical hill station houses remain and the Taunggyi Hotel is one such. Be sure to have a flashlight in Taunggyi, as there are frequent power cuts, and also a raincoat, as it can be very wet. During the cooler months it can also be very chilly. The journey from Taunggyi down to the plain and Inle Lake takes about an hour. As long as it is not raining (as it frequently is) this is a spectacular drive. One of the draws to Taunggyi in October is the annual Balloon Festival—stunning to look at the individually decorated balloons as they take to the air during the 3 day festival. Though a form of hot-air balloon they are made of paper so no baskets underneath for passengers.

SIGHTS

TAUNGGYI MARKET

There is a market every day in Taunggyi, but every fifth day it swells enormously as the regional market rotates among Taunggyi, Nyaung Shwe, Ywama, Heho and Kalaw. On these special days the market is crowded with the ethnic minorities decked out in all their finery.

TAUNGGYI MUSEUM

This is an excellent small museum of ethnology and well worth a visit. There are displays showing the different ethnic groups in their costumes, models of their houses, farming methods and so on.

KALAW

Kalaw, another favourite hill retreat of the British colonials, lies between Taunggyi and Thazi. (Thazi is the junction for the Yangon–Mandalay train.) Many of the stockbroker Tudor-style houses remain, surrounded by English gardens with the occasional overgrown tennis court. The old Kalaw Hotel is one such grand house, where you can stop for tea or a drink.

The 1,400-metre (4,600-foot) altitude makes warm clothing necessary, especially as power shortages are also frequent here, and Mandalay rum is the only source of central heating. Around Kalaw lives the colourful Palaung tribe (see page 62). If you are lucky enough to be in Kalaw on the regional market day you will be treated to a veritable feast of colour as the hill-tribe people throng to market, buying and selling food and wares of every description. Trekking from and around Kalaw has become popular and is the start of a two- day walk to Inle Lake, a guide is essential. If pre-arranged walkers can spend the night in local houses, the guide will buy food at one of the markets enroute and then cook it in the host house. Several routes can be taken and the most interesting arrives at the south-west end of the lake at Indein.

PINDAYA CAVES

A beautiful drive of some 45 kilometres (28 miles) to the north-east of Kalaw brings one to the Pindaya Caves, the home of countless Buddha images as well as interesting stalagmites. Your flashlight will come in handy here. A covered stairway leads to the cave entrance. Uncharacteristically, there is no local legend as to why the images are there, nor indeed how long it has been thought to have been an auspicious site. Once in the cave there are some 6,000 Buddha images of all shapes and sizes to see. This is not a place for those who suffer from claustrophobia. To reach some of the caves in this underground maze it is necessary to take to the hands and knees—and everything is very damp. There are two other places of interest at Pindaya: the Shwe Ohn Hmin Pagoda and the Padah Lin Caves, where archaeologists have excavated a Neolithic site. Parts of the caves are decorated with murals, so again have a flashlight handy. It is not always possible to gain access to these caves; it depends if the archaeologists are working. It is now possible to stay overnight at Pindaya in one of the new good hotels.

A group of mischievous looking young monks

One of three remaining cone-shaped pagodas, Payagyi was built by the Pyu people at their capital of Srikshetra during the fifth century CE. Said to have been used as both watchtowers and religious monuments, these strange constructions erupt out of the plain

OTHER OPEN PLACES IN MYANMAR
PATHEIN (BASSEIN)

The most interesting way to reach Pathein, formerly called Bassein, is by boat. (The alternative is to fly or take the train). From Yangon one travels for 18 hours, first along the Twante Canal and then through the myriad waterways of the Ayeyarwady Delta. The 'express' ferry takes between 14 and 15 hours. With a population of 145,000, Pathein is the delta's main town and the principal market for the surrounding 'rice bowl' of Myanmar. A characteristic Burmese town of wooden houses and dusty streets, it is famous for its pottery and its hand-made umbrellas and parasols—there are around 20 factories within the city.

It appears that until the European traders became interested in Burma, Pathein was only a sleepy fishing village. Ralph Fitch, the English merchant chartered by Queen Elizabeth I, landed at 'Cosmin', thought to be present-day Pathein, in 1586. In the 16th century the East India Company set up a 'factory' (ie trading post) here and at neighbouring Cape Negrais. When, in 1852, Lower Burma was annexed by the British, King Mindon pleaded unsuccessfully that he be allowed to keep the port of Bassein 'either territorially or so that he might have free and unrestrained intercourse by that port with the rest of the world,' for he 'felt as if imprisoned, landlocked in Upper Burma'. However, with the growth of the port of Rangoon and its less tortuous route to the Irrawaddy, Bassein's importance diminished.

SHWEMOKTAW PAGODA

There are three main pagodas in Pathein, all of which are reputed to have been built by the lovers of a Muslim princess named Ohnmadani: Tazaung Pagoda, Thayaunga Yaung Pagoda and Shwemoktaw Pagoda, the most impressive of the three, which stands at the centre of the town. A good way to view the town is to hire a little boat and sail along the waterfront. The two-storey stucco houses which line the water's edge have a colonial feel to them, the golden spire of the Shwemoktaw Pagoda stands in stately guard behind. Every May at full moon the pagoda hosts a festival. A large majority of the festival stalls sell pots, reflecting Pathein's major industry. Continuing the town's entrepreneurial traditions, many of the stall-holders at festivals up and down the country are from the Pathein area.

About 36 kilometres (22 miles) from Pathein, on the Bay of Bengal coast, sits the seaside resort of Chaung Tha. This beach does not boast the white coral sand of Ngapali, further up the coast, but is pleasant. There is a coral reef off shore which provides good snorkelling, though due to the closeness of the Ayeyarwady delta, the water is sometimes cloudy. As this resort only opened to foreigners fairly recently the accommodation is still fairly basic. Another beach resort worth visiting a little further south on the Bay of Bengal is Ngwe Saung, more silver sand, good snorkelling, delicious seafood with comfortable bungalow style hotels.

TWANTE

It is possible either to stop off at Twante for a day on the way to Pathein or to take a boat trip through the Twante Canal from Yangon. The journey of around two hours is more interesting than the destination, a quiet town whose inhabitants specialize in pottery. Wherever you turn in this town pots are being crafted—they are mostly terracotta and come in all shapes and sizes. The Mon-style Shwesandaw Pagoda offers a perfect respite of calm when one has finished pot-shopping.

THANDWE (SANDOWAY) AND NGAPALI BEACH RESORT

The village of Thandwe (formerly Sandoway) is a charming spot, with the usual market and tea shops, several of which serve delicious food. It also boasts a nine-hole golf course. The village is used as a resort by top Burmese officials and foreign diplomats, whose tasteful villas stand along the waterfront.

Down the coast from Thandwe lies one of the world's most beautiful beaches, Ngapali. A mere 45-minute hop by air from Yangon, Ngapali is miles and miles of silver sand lapped by the Bay of Bengal, with little villages clustered under the shade of the palm trees. Early morning sees the fishermen setting out or returning from an overnight trip, while the women spread out small fish to dry on bamboo mats—some are even tucked into their hats. At sundown the dried fish are transferred into baskets and carried home along the soft sands, coloured pink by the setting sun. These crystal-clear waters are a snorkeller's paradise. Over the past few years a collection of world-class bungalow style hotels have been developed along this beach. The architecture is discreet so the cottages meld in beautifully with the vegetation on the edge of the beach and the comfort is superb. After a day's snorkelling, a visit to Pearl Island, puzzling how the little sand crabs make their intricate patterns on the sand, visiting local villages or just relaxing with a good book—relax some more. As the light fades and changes colour with the setting sun, enjoy this beautiful natural light show sipping a delicious rum sour at one of the hotels bars which are set up on the sand each evening. Then for dinner go out to the road behind the hotels where there are a collection of truly good restaurants—much more exciting than the hotel food. They serve delicately steamed crab with a series of dipping sauces or spicy Rahkine curries with the taste of the ultra-fresh fish evident. One such is Min Thu behind the Aureum Hotel; Silver Star behind the Sandoway Beach Hotel should not be missed.

SHIN AUNG VILLAGE

Those who plan to spend several days in Thandwe should hire a jeep and explore the hinterland. A few miles inland are the foothills of the Rakhine Yoma. This is elephant country, where the animals work in the teak forests. Shin Aung village is one of many in the area where elephants are trained. An elephant costs roughly 90,000 kyats. Most are leased to the government. A one-year contract earns the owner 30,000 kyats. While the men work the elephants and till the land (though according to ancient tradition women plant rice, since rice is grown for the gods), the women spin and weave. On the terrace of a house one may see an old lady spinning, while underneath in the shed alongside the cows her daughter sits on the earthen floor weaving. This is a Chin village, so they specialize in thick cotton *longyis* similar to blankets, often coloured white. Elephant rides for visitors can now be arranged just ask for information at the hotel.

PYAY (PROME)

North of Yangon, on the eastern banks of the Ayeyarwady is Pyay, formerly known as Prome. A few miles north-east of the town is Srikshetra, one of Myanmar's most interesting early archaeological sites. As the Pyu people moved south from their Tibetan homeland around the first century CE, they are thought to have settled beside the Ayeyarwady's busiest ports. To visit Pyay and Srikshetra one can either hire a jeep from Yangon (a drive of about six hours), take the train from Yangon, or sail by boat downstream from Bagan.

The silken waters of the Bay of Bengal lap onto the silvery sand of Ngapali beach. The boat will ferry visitors to snorkel around the off-shore islands

Excavations at Srikshetra show that a wall enclosed three sides of the city, the sea the fourth. Three cone-shaped pagodas formed a triangle outside the city wall. These extraordinary buildings, which still stand, were used as lookout towers and fortresses to guard the city. Incorporated within the city walls were more watchtowers, only accessible by drawbridge from inside the city. On the three landward sides of the city was a broad moat. Parts of the palace site and moat have been excavated. The Pyu capital remained at Srikshetra until the eighth century when it was moved north to Halin. Around the mid-ninth century the Pyu dynasty foundered and Srikshetra itself was finally destroyed by the Burmese king Anawrahta in 1057 on his return from Thaton and his conquest of the Mons.

SIGHTS

SRIKSHETRA MUSEUM

Beside the small railway station of Hmawza—a delightful place reminiscent of an English rural station, complete with flowerbeds on the platform—is a museum. It is often locked, as the curator doubles as headmaster of the local school. The museum contains some interesting pieces excavated from the palace, including a Pyu-dynasty *thanaka-kyauk-pyin*. This is a stone on which the *thanaka* bark was ground to make cosmetic powder. Many of the better pieces, however, are now in the new Yangon Museum. Take a walk in the immediate vicinity of the museum and discover small pagodas hidden away, wooden monasteries shaded by great jacaranda and flame-of-the-forest trees.

PAYAMNA, PAYAGYI AND BAWBAWGYI PAGODAS

These extraordinarily shaped, vast pagodas erupt out of the flat Pyay landscape to form a triangle of defence around the city wall; for in addition to their religious functions they served as watchtowers. They are thought to have been constructed around the fifth century. In their heyday they would probably have been plastered and painted, but their red brick is now decorated with an assortment of vegetation. A tiny *hti* balances on the top of each one and there are no discernible entrances, which makes it hard to work out how they could have been used as watchtowers.

BEBE PAGODA

Near the Bawbawgyi stands the Bebe Pagoda, another strange-looking construction, cube-shaped with what looks like an inverted offerings bowl forming a hat on top. This pagoda is thought also to date from the fifth century.

SHWESANDAW PAGODA

Gautama Buddha is alleged to have preached a sermon on the site of the Shwesandaw, hence it ranks among Myanmar's most famed pagodas. The origins of the building are not clear. One version claims that the pagoda was first built by two merchant brothers soon after the Buddha's visit, then was rebuilt some 100 years later by the 'national hero king', Dwut-Tabaung, to enshrine a hair of the Buddha. What is certain, however, is that the pagoda has been damaged several times by earthquakes. It has survived and remains a beautiful gold stupa on a base of square terraces.

THE AYEYARWADY AT PYAY

At Pyay, the Ayeyarwady is wide, stately and busy. Some of Myanmar's newly developed oilfields are in the Pyay district, and many of the ships in port are extraordinary-looking oil transport vessels. At Toungoo, some 130 kilometres (80 miles) east of Pyay as the crow flies, is one of Myanmar's largest sawmills. 'Villages' of teak rafts (each one has its own little house for its pilot) are moored around the port awaiting transport to the sawmills.

Myanmar's forests account for approximately 76 per cent of the world's supply of teak. An estimated 4,000 elephants are used for extraction and haulage. Along the sandy banks around Pyay's port—hardly a crane and no suspicion of a container in sight—camp the families of the extra labour associated with the timber trade. Many of these are Chins and Kachins from the north who, in the cool of the early morning, are to be seen wrapped in their traditional thick cotton blankets. The mountainous river bank to the west is dotted with pagodas. One can visit the two most revered, Hsin De and Shwe Bontha, as ferries ply the river throughout the day.

MRAUK-U (MYOHAUNG) AND THE WEST

The magical region of the Rakhine State, formerly known as Arakan, is full of fascinating things to see. You can either fly direct to Sittwe (formerly Akyab), the jumping-off point for visiting the ancient capitals around Mrauk-U (formerly Myohaung), or stop off en route for a lazy few days or so at the beach resort of Ngapali.

HISTORY

This part of the Rakhine State is rich in archaeological remains. There were four Arakanese dynasties. The last dynasty, the Mrauk-U, which lasted from the 14th to the 18th century, was Arakan's golden age. During the 15th century Mrauk-U grew into an extremely rich city state, based mainly on its abundant rice production. With an annual rainfall of about 650 centimetres (250 inches) harvests never failed, while Mrauk-U's Indian neighbours suffered severe droughts. So Mrauk-U was fortunate to have a ready-made market for her surplus rice. It was during the 1660s that Father Manrique, the Portuguese Jesuit, lived for two years at the court of the dynasty's most famed king, Thiri-thu-dhamma, and left us with a detailed and intimate narrative of palace life and intrigue. Arakan's demise began in 1666 when the Mogul emperor Aurangzeb invaded Chittagong, then a part of the Arakanese empire. The loss of Chittagong was followed by a series of civil disturbances inside the Arakan proper. Constant rebellions and assassinations continued through the 17th and 18th centuries. Between 1666 and 1710 there were ten kings. In 1784 the Burmese king, Bodawpaya, finally took advantage of Arakan's weakness and invaded, bringing the Mrauk-U dynasty to an end.

SITTWE (AKYAB)

Sittwe, the capital of Rakhine State, stands on a small island at the tip of a spit of land jutting into the Bay of Bengal. It was built by the British after the annexation of Arakan in 1826 as their administrative headquarters. The site was chosen both for strategic and health reasons: it guards the mouths of the Kaladan and Magu Rivers, and the sea breeze was thought to stave off the ever-present threat of cholera. Gone are the days when visitors had to stay at the charming Tudor-style Circuit House, when one's fellow guests tended to be government officials on tours of inspection. There are now several passable hotels. (see page 268). Sittwe boasts excellent mohingha shops for breakfast and several good restaurants. The place makes up for its lack of important sights with an abundance of charm: wooden monasteries, mosques, two interesting museums the Rakhine State

Cultural Museum and the very different Mahakuthala Monastic Museum, an 'old curiosity shop' of treasures collected by the previous head monk in a grand slightly crumbling colonial house. In fact the town boasts many good-looking houses left over from colonial days and, dominating the town, a fine Queen Victoria Jubilee Clock. A leisurely stroll along Strand Road leads to the windswept promontory known as The Point. This is a lovely spot to come at sunset to admire the view. To the west are views over the Bay of Bengal, to the east the town itself and the mouth of the Kaladan River. All kinds of craft, many looking totally unseaworthy, grapple with nets and lines. At the point where the currents meet they have to drop anchor before tacking up the east coast.

MRAUK-U

The only way to reach Mrauk-U is by boat. The government boats wend their way upstream, first on the Kaladan and then the Lemro River, or travel by private boat. Little boats abound, some piled high with pots and miscellaneous wares. In the wider stretches of water strange, triangular nets suddenly rise from the water. How the fish are stopped from escaping before the fisherman ceases grappling with the pulleys is a mystery. Away from the coast, palms are replaced by great spreading trees, their gnarled roots often reaching into the river. As in most of Myanmar, hills frame the horizon. Arrival at the halfway stop is heralded by the sight of an enormous pagoda high on a hill guarding all around. If travelling on the government boat one's vessel nips down a side canal to reach the village. Here you can disembark, have a drink, and buy the locally grown nuts or beans baked and salted to a perfection of crunchiness. At each stop more and more people crowd on, so not only the two decks but also the roof are filled to capacity. There are likely to be soldiers on board en route to take up border duties; occasionally a particularly enthusiastic marksman will load his rifle and take a pot-shot at a passing bird. To approach Mrauk-U, the river steamer turns from the wide Lemro River and picks its way up a small creek, manoeuvring between many small craft and the huge trees that arch over the water. Green hills crowned with pagodas dominate the middle distance. A pleasant alternative to the crowded ferry is to hire a private boat to do the journey. Or twice-a-week a fast government ferry makes the journey non-stop in a mere two hours as against the 5 or more hours of the other boats. Ask around at the docks for boathire.

There is now plenty of good accommodation in Mrauk-U (see page 269), if staying at the luxurious Mrauk Oo Princess Resort (see page 269) they provide their own ferry service from Sittwe. Present-day Mrauk-U is a busy market town with the usual collection of monasteries, brown wooden and mat houses, a bustling very photogenic market. The best way to get an idea of how the town works is to climb one of the hills.

Some of Myanmar's most stunning beaches are found along the Rakhine State coastline. A windy day finds two monks enjoying a walk along the Sittwe promontory, which boasts amazing rock formations and black sand

A visit to the old city of Mrauk-U means a long boat trip first up the Kaladan and then along the Lemro River. Like all rivers in Myanmar they bustle with life, the small craft using time-honoured designs. As Rudyard Kipling suggested, 'it is the timelessness which is the essence of Burma'

Part of Mrauk-U's old city wall

SIGHTS IN THE MRAUK-U AREA

OLD MRAUK-U CITY

A huge amount of restoration has been carried out at Mrauk-U. Not only have some of the pagodas been restored but also parts of the old city walls. As at the Forbidden City in Beijing, the king's palace was an inner city forming the core of Mrauk-U. The city walls did not run in a continuous line but merely filled in the gaps between natural barriers of mountains and tidal rivers. A line of artificial lakes was constructed on the eastern city boundary, the most vulnerable to Burmese attack. In fact, it is said that in the 14th century a Burmese invasion was quelled by the opening of the sluice gates. As so often in Myanmar, nothing remains of the palace buildings, which were built of teak, just the foundations. Father Sebastian Manrique, the Portuguese Jesuit who lived in Mrauk-U from 1629–37 tells us it was lacquered and 'ornamented with carvings and gilt mouldings'. However, within the 'outer' city walls the plain is dotted with pagodas, some so long-forgotten that they are now little more than overgrown mounds, although the more important buildings have been restored. The geography of Mrauk-U is quite complicated so a good idea is to climb one of the hills to get an overall view. Sangha Taung Pagoda is a good place to start. Look down from beside the collection of grey stone stupas, below in the foreground is the domestic scene of the village with the river wending its way through the valley, dissected by the occasional wooden bridge. Beautiful trees punctuate the plain along with stupas everywhere but here they are grey, not white or gold and sturdier, completely different architecture to the rest of Myanmar—they just sit comfortably in the landscape.

Now thanks to the restoration programme there are many pagodas and artifacts to see in the Mrauk-U area, so the visitor has to be selective. On sale at most of the sites is a useful and informative guide book, "Famous Monuments of Mrauk-U". The first page is a reminder of the state of affairs in 2007 when it was published.

PALACE FOUNDATIONS AND MUSEUM

Beside the Palace foundations is a well-stocked museum, a light airy modern building. In a side room are some stunning Buddha images. Two which stand out are a bronze piece dating from the Wethali period (4–8 CE) with simple graceful lines on a decorated base. The other from the later Mrauk-U period (14th–18th century) a seated image in bronze but with remains of gold leaf on the body and unusually holding an umbrella. It is worth visiting the museum just to see those pieces however there are other things of interest including a relief map of the site.

From the museum just walk up onto the Palace site—the Palace itself was destroyed by fire in 1784 and has now been excavated enough so that it is possible to have an idea of where the royal quarters once stood. On the north side of the site a large brick stairway has been unearthed which would have gone over the moat leading to one of the Palace gates. A huge brick well still intact on the western side is now used as the village rubbish dump.

SAKYA MARAUNG PAGODA

Two fierce looking stone ogres and a sign proclaiming "Put off your footwear" welcome you as you enter through the gate of this fine brick pagoda. Built in 1629 the pagoda stands in the middle of the precinct with a series of brick stupas along the surrounding wall. An Ordination Hall stands behind the pagoda and houses a sand-stone image of the Buddha. The main stupa is plain and beautiful; it is a place with great feeling.

KOE THAUNG TEMPLE

Home to some 90,000 Buddha images this temple is not to be missed. It was built in 1553 by King Tikkha whose father King Mong Bar Gri built Mrauk-U's most renowned Temple Shittaung.

Another great grey square mass of a building but once inside it becomes much more refined. Corridors with avenues of arches unfold, the walls dotted with niches some filled with an object, some not—it could be a Buddha image or an animal or a female form holding one bare bosom 'wishing to feed the world'. Because it has not been extensively restored this temple still holds a feeling of the 'pleasure of ruins', stones are covered in lichen and wild flowers pop out here and there.

SHITTHAUNG TEMPLE

The Shitthaung Temple is a curious building, looking more like a huge, grey-stone wedding cake than a pagoda. Built in 1535 by King Min Bu, the Shitthaung, or 'Eight Thousand' Temple (so named on account of the many images it contains), stands in the north-west corner of the outer city. It was built by Indian workmen brought back by King Min Bin from eastern Bengal following a victorious campaign which saw the annexation of Chittagong. One approaches up a long staircase and enters through the great eastern door, which still has its original stone hinges. No mortar was used in the construction. Instead the bricks were fitted together like a jigsaw puzzle, then at regular intervals held in place by stone brackets. Inside are two concentric passages, the outer one decorated with a frieze of Arakanese musicians and the inner one by scenes from 550 stories of the Buddha's life. At the centre stands a 14th-century Buddha image carved from a single piece of stone, beautiful in its simplicity. As one walks along the cool outer passage, the occasional arch allows a view through to the inner sanctum. To the west is the Coronation and Meditation hall, where King Thiri-thu-dhamma was crowned on 23rd January, 1635. During World War II the Japanese used this massive pagoda as an ammunition dump.

ANDAW TEMPLE

King Min Bin also built the Andaw Temple, the architecture of which is of a style similar to that of the Shitthaung Temple—a square grey building surrounded by nine small stupas and Buddha images and topped by a solid dome. Again, no mortar was used. The inside plan is similar. Andaw Temple is said to have a wisdom tooth of Gautama Buddha enshrined in the inner sanctum.

HTUKKAN THEIN PAGODA

The literal translation of Htukkan Thein is 'lifting up heavy slabs of rock by using wooden levers', which is presumably how this and the other massive grey pagodas were built. Htukkan Thein was an ordination hall, and the niches in the inside corridor contain some fine stone Buddhas interspersed with carved figures displaying 64 contemporary Arakanese hairstyles. Originally these carvings would have been painted and on some the *longyi* pattern is still discernible. An hour or so before sunset is the best time to visit this pagoda. Shafts of evening sun are channelled through the arches and illuminate the Buddha images.

An old fashioned merry-go-round operated by hand

AROUND MRAUK-U

The countryside around Mrauk-U is filled with fascinating sights. Drive past the old Mrauk-U city gate (the White Elephant Gate) on to a vast plain surrounded by mountains. On top of one of the foothills in the village of Nagyan stands a monastery, once a centre for insurgents. From here there is a marvellous view of the Lemro River. Visit Laung Yet city (the last centre of the Four City States dynasty, 11th to 14th centuries), which is said to have housed 8,000 pagodas. Although most have disappeared, several survive in good condition and are worthy of a visit, in particular Laymyathna Pagoda, Lanr Pan Prauk Pagoda and Radanamanaung Pagoda, which was recently given a new grey dome.

WETHALI (VESALI)

The most interesting of the old cities is Wethali (third to tenth centuries), which has been excavated by Myanmar's archaeological department. The fort, with an outer wall 2.5 metres (eight feet) thick, is an impressive sight. It has been excavated into neat squares that expose the fine red brickwork. In peacetime it was used as an assembly and audience hall, the palace being nearby. The palace itself remains unexcavated, as a village presently occupies the site. A short walk away, on Thanya Yadana Hill, stand a pagoda and monastery, where the Second Buddhist Synod was reputedly held not long after the Buddha's death.

*Cattle amble home at sunset near
Bagan's Dhammayangyi Temple*

A convoy of bullock carts carries villagers to Bagan's Ananda Temple for its annual festival, celebrated during Pyatho (December/January). Thousands of pilgrims converge on the temple for the two-week festival, earning merit by making offerings to the hundreds of monks who gather for the event

Gaily decorated papier mâché animals and a troupe of young percussionists perform during the annual Myazedi Pagoda festival at Myinkaba village, Bagan

Boys in Nyuangbinwun village, Sagaing
Region, ride elephants to a ceremony at
which they will become novice monks.
Horses are the traditional steed at
novitiation ceremonies

Children at Bagan enjoy an exuberant
drenching during Myanmar's Traditional
New Year Water Festival, which is
celebrated in April

Gathering lotus stalks on Wet Thee Lake in Magway Region. The stalks are woven into expensive cloth, most of which is sold to Japanese buyers

Akha women winnow rice at Wonpon village, near Kyaing Tong (formerly Kengtung), eastern Shan State

Padaung women, easily identified by the brass rings around their necks, enjoy a kitchen chat in Pann-pat village, at Dimawso township, Kayah State. They were about six years old when the first brass rings were fitted around their necks

A novice monk at Bagan lights candles as part of a daily ritual. In the background is the Ananda Temple

Novice monks in the Saddan Cave at Hpa-an, the capital of Kayin State

An ox-bow lake beside the Ayeyarwady near the former riverside town of Ngazun, in Mandalay Region

Hot air balloons vie for prizes and glory during the annual festival held near the Shan State capital, Taunggyi. The festival is held in Tazaungmon (the Myanmar month roughly corresponding to November)

Climbing a toddy palm at Bagan to extract the sap used to make a potent beverage and a confectionary known as 'jaggery'

A tattooed Chin woman at Mindat, southern Chin State. Chin women were once known for their elaborate face tattoos but the tradition is dying out

A monk passes a cluster of chedis (stupas) near stairs leading to limestone caves at Pindaya, Shan State, in which there is the marvellous spectacle of thousands of Buddha images

Coco Island in the Bay of Bengal
was once a penal colony for
prisoners serving life sentences

One of Myanmar's rarest birds, pictured at
Bagan where it is known as a 'Yethugyi'

SINGUTTARA HILL

Perhaps Rakhine State's most fascinating sight is the fabled Singuttara Hill, which lies a day's river journey from Mrauk-U. Now it is possible to make the journey by jeep—a bumpy ride of 2–3 hours, but through beautiful countryside. Singuttara Hill was the original home of the sacred Mahamuni Image (now in Mandalay) and is still the home of the Yattara Bell. Its fascination lies not so much in its visual appeal as in the fact that the ownership of these two relics figured prominently in the region's history. It was believed that the Mahamuni Image, one of the five known actual likenesses of Gautama Buddha, was cast by a heavenly sculptor, the Lord of Paradise, while the Lord Buddha rested on Singuttara Hill after a week's preaching. So the Arakanese found themselves guardians of the oldest, most mysterious and most holy object of the Buddhist world. There is some scientific evidence to support the claim that an image has stood here since the time of the Buddha. Singuttara Hill stands within the ancient city of Dhannavati, whose walls are still traceable, and are said to date prior to the first century CE. The same antiquity is claimed for the remains of the original pagoda which housed the image. Magic was used to guard the image, it being held that its destruction or removal would herald the fall of the kingdom. On the Yattara Bell, which rests beside where the image once stood, are inscribed magical ciphers used to put invaders to flight by deranging their astrological chart and so placing them in jeopardy. Even the powerful Burmese King Bodawpaya took the precaution of employing experts to tamper with the ciphers before making his successful odyssey to secure the Mahamuni Image.

The pagoda now standing there is said to have been built in the 19th century in the Pagan style—the original was destroyed by the Mongols in CE 957. If visiting around the March full moon the pagoda festival will be in full swing with the pagoda packed with people. In the main hall is a copy of the Mahamuni image—though many local people believe this is the original with the one in Mandalay being a copy. Here donors give their gold leaf for the Mahamuni to a pagoda official who pastes it on the image. The Hall is very grand and gold, lit by ornate Victorian chandeliers. The terrace buzzes with people of all ages, sitting chatting, having their photographs taken which are immediately developed by complicated Heath Robinson looking printers; some people meditate whilst others pray. The atmostphere is of a merry fairground. Indeed below the terraces is a fair, a mass of market stalls, a ferris wheel and merry-go-rounds for children.Rahkine wrestling and 'ladies' tug of war, a riotous affair.

To visit the remainder of Myanmar's west, including the Chin Hills and the upper reaches of the Chindwin River, a permit is needed.

MAWLAMYINE (MOULMEIN) AND THE SOUTH

For second-time visitors to Myanmar, a trip to Mawlamyine (formerly Moulmein) is well worth the effort. Travel to Bago by road or rail, then on via Kyaiktiyo (see page 143) with its golden pagoda perched on top of a gilded boulder. Continue south through Thaton, the former capital of the Mon Kingdom and an early centre of learning. (Old Thaton has long since disappeared, but there are several interesting sights in and around the present-day city.) The approach to Mawlamyine is through the old town of Martaban whose hills are dotted with pagodas then onto the large bridge which spans the Thanlwin (formerly Salween) River and into Mawlamyine. It is possible to continue south to Kyaikkhami (formerly Amherst) and eventually, if you are very lucky, to Myeik (formerly Mergui). However it is easier to reach Myeik and Kawthaung at the southernmost tip of Myanmar and the gateway to the beautiful Myeik Archipelago via plane from Yangon. The reason being the activities of the smugglers who operate along the Thai-Myanmar border. This worries the authorities, so permission to drive further south than Kyaikkhami is difficult to obtain. It is also sometimes possible to fly to Mawlamyine, courtesy of Myanma Airways, two days a week.

Young boys frolic in the sea near the Kyaikthanlan Pagoda, made famous by Kipling: 'By the old Moulmein pagoda, Lookin' lazy at the sea, there's a Burma girl a-sittin'. And I know she thinks of me'

(right) The holy Golden Rock in Mon State, eastern Myanmar.

MAWLAMYINE

Mawlamyine itself is a charming city, built at the mouth of the wide Thanlwin River and the confluence of four smaller rivers, with the Mawlamyine Hill behind. The west of the city is protected from the Gulf of Mottama (formerly Martaban) by Bilugyun Island, but Mawlamyine nonetheless has the feeling of a seaside town.

Until the close of the first Anglo-Burmese War, Mawlamyine was a small trading post famous for pearl-fishing and teak, which was floated down the mighty Thanlwin River. With the signing of the Treaty of Yandabo in 1828, the Province of Tenassarim (including Mawlamyine) was ceded to the British, and it was the centre of the colonial administration until the end of the second Anglo-Burmese War in 1852 (and with it the cession of the whole of Lower Burma).

The wooden houses are often painted in pastel colours, and the iron balconies covered in flowering potted plants. A gentle sea breeze rustles in the palm trees. The atmosphere—perhaps something to do with the smuggling—is exciting and carefree. The town's traffic consists mainly of *tongas* (two-wheeled carriages) and vintage cars, to date there are no taxis in Mawlamyine though recently modern vehicles have appeared. Mawlamyine has recently undergone some regeneration so many of the old wooden houses have been replaced by modern square boxes— but the town still has the air of a 'sea-side' town.

THE STRAND AND THE MARKET

An evening stroll on the Strand is an exercise in nostalgia. This is a 19th-century promenade along the waterfront, probably constructed during Mawlamyine's British period between the first and second Anglo-Burmese Wars. It is lined with a few of the remaining rather smart stucco houses. The terraces of the Strand and Attran Hotels (see Page 271) are good places to enjoy an early evening drink, watch the sun go down and the world pass by. Mawlamyine has wonderful prawns and other seafood. At the northern end of the Strand is the market. The fishermen tie up their boats and unload their catch directly onto the stalls. Another large section of the market is given over to fresh flowers and vegtables.

KYAIKTHANLAN PAGODA

Rudyard Kipling made a two-day stop at Mawlamyine in 1889. Ever since there has been speculation regarding the identity of the pagoda in his famous lines:

By the old Moulmein pagoda, Lookin' lazy at the sea,
There's a Burma girl a-sitten'. And I know she thinks of me.

The most likely candidate seems to be Kyaikthanlan, a gilded pagoda set in the hills with wide terraces from which there are fine views over the city and harbour. One of the out-buildings houses the Thihar Thanna Throne, a beautiful gilded piece inlaid with glass on which the Buddha's tooth was carried from Kandy in Sri Lanka during King Mindon's reign. Near the pagoda is the Yadanar Bon-Myint Monastery, a huge wooden building constructed by one of King Mindon's wives, who became a nun after his death.

OTHER RELIGIOUS SITES

There is an abundance of religious monuments in and around Mawlamyine, the most notable being Uzena Pagoda with its figures of the Buddha in the different stages before attaining enlightenment, the cave of 10,000 Buddhas (Kawgaun) and the Hapayon Cave. But if your time is limited, I suggest a trip by one of the small craft you can hire in the harbour to Gaung Se Kyun ('Shampoo Island'). It was water from this island that was used for the ceremonial hair-washing of the king during the Buddhist New Year celebrations. The island sits at the confluence of five rivers. On it there is a monastery surrounded by stupas and an enormous statue of the Buddha looking back across the water to Mawlamyine and the Kyaikthanlan Pagoda. As you approach the Gaung Se Kyun its thin, white stupas sparkle against the green trees and the island seems to hover just above the water, giving rise to the belief that it was suspended from the heavens by a silken thread and that its surrounding water was sacred. Another nearby island worth an explore is Bilu Kyun ('Ogre Island')—in a private boat a 25-minute ride or there is a daily ferry—another excellent way to sample local life. There are some 64 villages on the island all with their small pagodas and little home industries to visit. The mode of transport around the island is a pony cart or fine old wooden buses. There are plenty of good tea shops where the visitor can sample a Mon dish or two before re-boarding the ferry back to the mainland, so a leisurely day trip.

KYAIKKHAMI (AMHERST)

The town of Kyaikkhami, once a British coastal resort known as Amherst, is about 90 kilometres (55 miles) south of Mawlamyine. It is sometimes declared out of bounds, owing to the activities of smugglers or rebels. But if possible hire a jeep and make a day trip. The main pagoda in Kyaikkhami, though of no particular architectural merit, enjoys an outstanding location, perched on rocks lapped by the sea and joined to the land by a covered causeway, which floods at high tide. Beside the causeway is a huge stone boat, apparently built by a retired British naval officer in the 1930s in which to live out his years of leisure.

THE JUDSON MEMORIAL

A few miles from the pagoda is the grave of Anne Judson, wife of Adoniram Judson, a Baptist and the first American missionary in the Far East. They arrived in Burma in 1813. Beside the grave is a memorial stone to their lives. Mr Judson compiled the first English-Burmese dictionary. In 2011 a new Memorial Hall was built with money from America and support from the remaining 6 Baptist families living in the area. During the week the Hall is a nursery school and on Sunday it is used as a church.

SETSE BEACH

Before starting the hot return journey to Mawlamyine, pause at Setse Beach for a refreshing swim in the clear waters of the Gulf of Mottama (formerly Martaban). There are miles and miles of white sand this beach was once a favourite playground of colonialists. Today it is popular with local residents as well as the occasional fisherman or coral diver. As this beach is south of the Ayeyarwady Delta the sea water here is brown, so not so inviting for a swim.

THANBYUZAYAT CEMETERY

Further north is the enormous war cemetery at Thanbyuzayat. Most of those buried here lost their lives working as Japanese prisoners of war on the Burma–Siam railway, the famous line that crosses the Bridge on the River Kwai in Thailand. The cemetery, immaculately kept by the Commonwealth War Graves Commission, is a garden filled with small crosses and grave markers with name, rank and age of the deceased, its beauty and calm rendering it the more poignant. Nearby is a small section of the original railway, with an engine and some rather menacing half broken life size statues of Japanese soldiers and two starving prisoners. Word has it that the railway is going to be reconstructed as a memorial to all those who worked on the 250-miles track as well as those who died.

MUDON

Just before Mudon, the last stop before arriving back in Mawlamyine, fantastic rock outcrops suddenly erupt out of the paddy fields. One such, topped by a pagoda, is named Mawlamyine Popa, after Mount Popa, home of the *nats*, near Bagan. The picturesque Kandawlay and Kandawgyi lakes beside the town of Mudon provide an ideal excuse for a tea stop and a leg stretch. The first lake is for the ladies to bathe in, the second for the men. On the far side of the lakes stand two white pagodas. Also in this area is the most extraordinary 180 ft high half-finished concrete Buddha image. It is a fantasy of the monk, U Kay-thra. Thus far the construction has taken 6 years and many million kyats. But this is not the only place the monk's dreams are being constructed; a few miles north of Mudon there is a huge monastery complex under construction. One reclining Buddha image is 170metres long and still unfinished; it is possible to walk into this image. But on the opposite side of the hill another reclining image is being started. Yet another image on the same site seems a colossal waste of money, why not build a hospital or school for the local populace instead. It is said that each time the venerable monk has a dream of a new image construction begins.

A necessary paint after the summer rains

One of the frustrating things about Myanmar is the vast number of fascinating places one is not allowed to visit for security reasons. Though in the past few years an increasing number of destinations have been opened, before planning a trip it is wise to check with a good travel agent. Though no longer out of bounds are several locations in the country's southeast such as Dawei, Myeik, Kawthaung and the Myeik Archipelago though they are an expensive option to visit. The visitor is required to fly to Dawei or Kawthaung to reach the Myeik Archipelago. Myanmar Andaman Resort on Macleod Island is the only place at present to stay in the Archipelago. As its manager is at pains to point out it is not a resort in the modern

(right) A monk strolls along the terrace of Kyaikthanlan Pagoda

sense of the word but an eco-lodge. It is expensive but a perfect place to dive (the only PADI resort in Myanmar), trek, enjoy the pristine beaches, spectacular snorkelling and so on. It is also possible to arrive from Thailand and a speed boat will collect you there for the journey to Macleod Island. The waters around these 800 islands of the archipelago are said to be a diver's paradise and are home to the Moken or Sea Gypsies, an ethnic minority found both in Myanmar and Thailand who spend most of the year on their boats but take to land during the monsoon season. At present various travel agents specializing in eco-tourism will organise groups to Lampi, one of the archipelago's largest islands. How often they manage to get permission for foreigners to visit is not clear—but it is worth a try for keen divers.

If the journey down south is too time consuming imbibe the area's atmosphere through the pages of Maurice Collis' magnificent book *Siamese White*, based on the life of the 17th-century adventurer and trader Samuel White of Bath, who became virtual king of Mergui (modern-day Myeik). Collis himself served as the British Resident in Mergui during the 1930s and developed an intimate knowledge of the area.

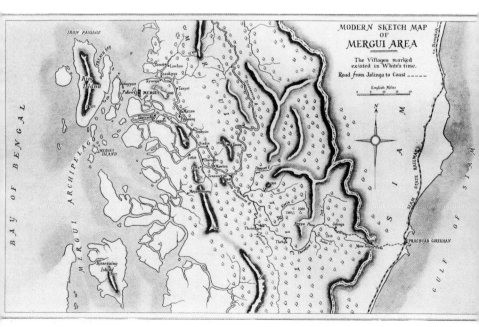

Map reproduced from the 1935 edition (Faber and Faber) of Siamese White
'A very ill man and a great Interloper and a great Enemy of this Kingdom in general.'—East India Company's opinion of White

EXTRANEOUS INFLUENCE

*M*oulmein was a town of strong baroque flavour. It was as if the essence of the Renaissance had finally reached it via Portugal, and after careful straining through an Indian mesh. There was a spaciousness of planning; an evidence of studied proportion about the old stone houses. Doors and windows were often flanked with heavy double columns. Much crudely stained glass was to be seen. Balconies were of wrought iron and from the eaves depended stalactites of fretted woodwork. The original roofs had been replaced by corrugated iron. It was as if an Indian architect had been responsible for this style, after spending perhaps a week in Goa. Crows alighted and perched swaying on the potted sunflowers put out on balconies. Rows of coconuts had been suspended from the eaves for the tutelary spirits' accommodation.

The Indians were here in strength and had brought with them their sacred cows, their 'medical halls', their 'select recommended gents' oriental tailors'. Business was done beneath fascia boards painted with ferocious tigers, firing howitzers and bombing planes. The cinema with the fine old façade was showing 'The Good Earth' and had distributed its advertising boards in various parts of the town. One leaned against one of the multiple trunks of a huge banyan tree, which was the home of one or more nats, for shrines were attached to it, and votive wooden horses hung from its boughs. Girls sat in a streamer-decorated shop and sewed shirts while a musician played to them on a mandoline. In the town lock-up, a little further down the street, a single prisoner balanced on one leg in a bamboo cage. At the other end of the town there had been an attempt at road repairs, but this had clearly been abandoned several years ago. Now the steamroller, which had been left where it stood, was already sunken to its axles. In a few more years it would probably have disappeared from sight, a rich find for the archaeologist of future centuries.

There was, of course, a festival going on, with booths and pavilions filling all the side streets and open spaces. Some of the citizens, anticipating the distractions of the evening, already carried hydrogen-filled balloons as they went about their business. The main street was jammed with bullock-carts and jeeps. All the latter had been vividly repainted and carried such names as 'Hep-Cat' and 'Lady for a Night'. Oh-oh's was called 'Cupid'.

Above the cheerful animation of the scene rose in majestic aloofness, the fabulous, almost unearthly, golden shape of the Old Moulmein Pagoda; so hateful to Malcolm, so nostalgically romantic to Kipling. It was all that remained without change of the magnificence of the East.

Norman Lewis, Golden Earth—Travels in Burma, 1952

The Ryugasaki Amateur Orchid Society proudly display their collection in their orchid garden on the shores of Inle Lake

THE EAST: KAYAH, KAYIN AND SHAN STATES

All of Kayah State, most of Kayin (formerly known as Karen) State and some of Shan State are out of bounds to the traveller. These are the areas where the authorities have been fighting protracted wars with armies of the minority peoples. At Burma's independence in 1947, the Karens, Shans and the other major ethnic minorities were persuaded to join the Union of Burma on the basis that the new Constitution gave them the option of their own autonomy. However, independence was not forthcoming and several minorities have been fighting for it ever since. Although in recent years many ceasefires have been signed between the ethnic groups and the government, but that is not to say the fighting has totally stopped and the authorities are understandably wary of letting foreigners visit unsettled areas. The pattern of fighting has been that the government forces advance during the dry season, and then minority armies consolidate and regain their position during the wet season. One of the most formidable forces has been the 10,000-strong army of the Karen National Union of the Karen people, many of whom are Christians. According to a senior military attaché in Bangkok, 'The Karens are the best guerrilla fighters in South-East Asia and among the best in the world. They are led by officers schooled in the British tradition and are highly disciplined and deeply motivated by nationalism.' Indeed their former general, Bo Mya, served with the Chindits during World War II, and their professionalism has attracted foreigners to fight alongside them for no pay. Their funds are very limited as, unlike some of the other armies, they refuse either to grow or trade in opium. Their revenues come from the border tax of five per cent which they levy on smugglers going to and coming from Thailand.

Much of the fighting between the government forces and the rebel armies has ceased. In 1996 the majority of the rebels agreed to a cease-fire with the authorities. However, there are still pockets of fighting and the refugee problem spawned by the prolonged conflict seems to be escalating rather than subsiding. Across both Myanmar's eastern and western borders there are vast refugee camps.

Kayah State is the country's smallest state and does not have an army of its own. It is on the fringes of Karen territory, and its people are called Red Karens, not for their politics but for their preference for red clothing. The capital of Kayah is Loikaw, where the Padaung tribe and their 'giraffe women' live (see page 64).

A slice of Shan State around the beautiful Inle Lake (see page 216) is open to tourists, but in much of the remainder of this extensive area of mountain and jungle, the government is fighting the few remaining Shan rebel groups and the drug warlords, who finance many of the minority armies. Opium growing still continues but the legendary drug lord Khun Sa has gone, he died in 2007. The former head of the Shan United Army and supreme warlord of Golden Triangle drug operations surrendered to the government in 1996. In his heyday he was said to have commanded a private army of 15,000, and would move his headquarters back and forth across the border, depending on the activities of the Burmese and Thai military. Khun Sa himself denied trafficking in narcotics and depicted himself as a freedom fighter trying to win autonomy from Yangon for Myanmar's two million Shans.

THE NORTH: MOGOK AND KACHIN STATE

As of September 2012 fighting was continuing in parts of Kachin State between Myanmar government forces and the Kachin Independence Army, the last of the main ethnic rebel groups to be resisting peace overtures from the government. The fighting resulted in train services between Mandalay and the Kachin State capital, Myitkyina, being suspended in early September 2012. The conflict has also resulted in the displacement of tens of thousands of Kachin, many of whom have sought refuge in camps across the border in China. At the time of publication much of Kachin State was off-limits to tourists, but the situation could change amid continuing efforts by the government to negotiate a peace agreement. After Kachin State re-opens to foreign tourists a sensible route would be to travel by train from Mandalay to Myitkyina, Myanmar's largest northern town, and then return to Mandalay by boat down the Ayeyarwady. During the dry season the low water level may make the Myitkyina to Bhamo section impassable; if so you could travel that part by jeep. It is by all accounts a beautiful stretch of jungle road.

THE ROAD TO MYITKYINA

Some 100 kilometres (60 miles) north of Mandalay the train passes through Shwebo. The great King Alaungpaya, 'a mere village headman', was born here and it was from Shwebo that he led his victorious forces against the Mons. For a brief five years, from 1755 to 1760, he made Shwebo his capital. This founder of the third and last Burmese empire is buried in his birth place, where his headstone still stands.

Mogaung, 100 kilometres (60 miles) south of Myitkyina, is the centre of Myanmar's jade mining region. The jade mined in this area has always been much sought after by the Chinese. It is high quality jadeite, as opposed to the less valuable Chinese nephrite. The mining methods are still primitive, including 'fishing for jade', whereby the miner paddles barefoot, feeling for the jade with his toes.

The railway runs up the western shores of the Ayeyarwady with Myitkyina being the northern terminus. The town stands on a scorching plain at the entrance to the narrow Hukawng Valley, the most 'fateful of all the ways of entry into Burma'. It was from Myitkyina along this valley (past the amber mines) that in the summer of 1942 thousands of refugees fled before the advancing Japanese. The monsoon rains arrived early that year and some 20,000 people died from malaria on the journey. Today, Myitkyina is a typical sleepy Myanmar market town, but if visiting in January the New Year Festival of the Lisu ethnic group will be enlivening the town. Bedecked and bejeweled in bright costumes the men show their bravery by climbing a long ladder of knives in their bare feet and much jollity and dancing is had by all. For bird lovers Myitkyina is a good jumping off point to Myanmar's largest natural Lake Indawgyi and bird sanctuary—a beautiful area and the home of many wetland species, ask one of the eco-tourist agencies to arrange a trip. The accommodation is still pretty Spartan.

If the Ledo Road had ever fulfilled its purpose (see page 39) it would instead have become a major entrepôt for goods traded between India and China. Above Myitkyina the upper reaches of the Ayeyarwady are a multitude of streams and riverlets. Just north of the town the river makes a boisterous emergence from the foothills and then spreads out and adopts the calm, noble personality that it will maintain for most of its 1,600-kilometre (1,000-mile) journey to the coast. There are, however, stretches south of Bhamo where the river banks become steep cliffs and the river bottom drops away to extreme depths. According to local legend these waters are inhabited by monsters (and no doubt by *nats*). The boat trip from Bhamo to Mandalay should take three days, but it has been known for boats to get stuck on sandbanks for several days.

A stop at Mogok, some 115 kilometres (70 miles) north-east of Mandalay, and its gem mines, would be fascinating. This is even more difficult to arrange, as the authorities have a major gem-smuggling problem to contend with and are apparently wary of inquisitive foreign eyes. Rubies are Mogok's most prized gems, though sapphires, emeralds and lapis lazuli are among the other precious stones mined in the area. (If you are a gem merchant, the easiest place to see Myanmar's gems is at the International Gem Emporium which is held in Nay Pyi Taw every year (see page 147). From Mogok it is possible to rejoin an Ayeyarwady boat, but it may be easier to continue south to Mandalay by road.

The furthest north destination is Putao right up in the mountains almost on the Indian border, a stunningly beautiful wild environment, perfect for the eco tourist. A variety of adventure excursions are on offer; trekking including local home-stays, kayaking, elephant trails, negotiating bamboo suspension bridges across ravines, local markets, beautiful butterflies and many varieties

of flora and fauna to be seen. For 'hardy' travellers Putao Trekking House offers various packages. For those who seek comfort go to the stunning Malikha Lodge (see page 271) where there are even open fires in the bedrooms and your every wish will be catered for. To visit Putao a permit is needed which your travel agent can organize 45-days ahead of the visit.

(clockwise from top) A Lisu man from China who arrived for the three-day Lisu Festival at Myitkyina in northern Myanmar in February 2011; the festival grounds where Lisu (who have come from near and far, including China) perform a traditional dance before a crowd of onlookers; Lisu sisters

(above & top right) Akha boys; (bottom right) Pa-o husband & wife, Shan State

Laughing grandmother and curious grandchild in a village near Kyaukme, Shan State

Pa O girl selling goods at a Pa O festival between Loikaw and Kalaw, Shan State

Fishermen during an island visit to take on fresh supplies in the Myeik Archipelago

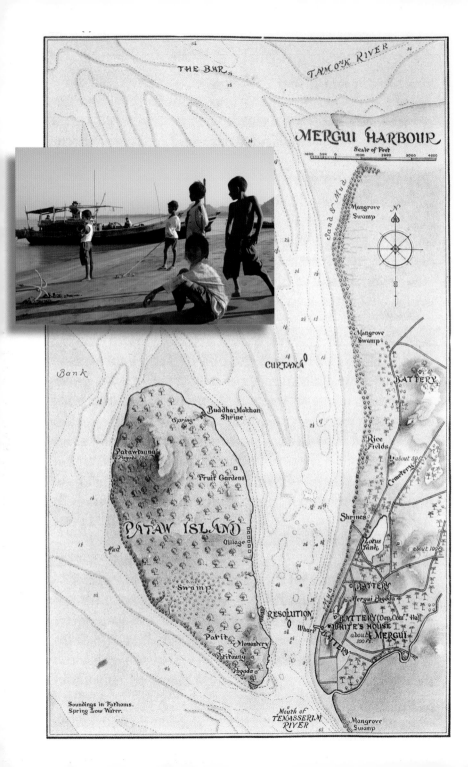

THE BAR

TAMOK RIVER

MERGUI HARBOUR

Scale of Feet

Sand & Mud

Mangrove
Swamp

N

Bank

CURTANA

Mangrove
Swamp

BATTERY

Buddha Makhan
Shrine

Spring

Rice
Fields

Patawraung
Pagoda 706

about 50

Fruit Gardens

Cemetery

PATAW ISLAND

Shrines

Village

Mud

Lotus
Tank

about 100

Swamp

BATTERY

Mergui Pagoda

Parit

Monastery

RESOLUTION

BATTERY (Dep. Com". Ho)

WHITE'S HOUSE

about

MERGUI

Urtaung

Wharf

100 ft

BATTERY

Pagoda

Soundings in Fathoms.
Spring Low Water.

Mouth of
TENASSERIM
RIVER

Mangrove
Swamp

'A very ill man and
a great Interloper and a
great Enemy of this Kingdom in general.'—East India Company's opinion of White

SIAMESE WHITE

'Mr. White is a civil worthy Gentleman
and I'll venture my life in his vindication.'—Captain Weltden's
opinion of White.

by

MAURICE COLLIS

FABER AND FABER LIMITED
24 Russell Square, London

A small fishing village in the Myeik Archipelago

*The Andaman Island Resort in the stunning and
untouched Myeik (Mergui) Archipelago*

Daily roadside market near Kalaw

(above) Burmese cheroots rolled in vine leaves. Loikaw
(left) Daily vegetable market at Loikaw

(top) A Kayah woman displays her wealth;
(bottom) Young nuns at a Yangon nunnery

(top) Older Padaung women often prefer to remove their brass necks rings for more comfortable living, but the woman proudly wears hers
(bottom) An older women of the widely dispersed Akha tribe, found in China, Thailand and Laos as well as Myanmar, take pride in their silver ornamentation. Especially valuable are the Edwardian silver rupee coins this woman wears in her headdress

Elaborately-costumed boys in a procession before their novitiation ceremonies.

(top) A modern Christian church near Loikaw; (bottom) "Tagundaing" Posts at Chikel village. These wooden sculptures celebrate ancient fertility rituals.

A golden cart carries a young boy to the monastery for his novitiation ceremony

This nunnery at Loikaw is also an orphanage. Many of these young nuns are orphans.

PRACTICAL INFORMATION
TRAVEL AGENTS

Travelling within Myanmar has become much easier since the authorities have allowed private travel agents to operate within the country. Some very good, competent agencies have sprung up. Once you have decided your travel dates, book your international flights and then contact an agent in Yangon. Give them an idea of your budget and they will then arrange all the internal details as well as provide well-informed English-speaking guides. There are numerous other tour operators in Yangon as well as other cities and towns, many offering excellent service. Below are listed several agencies which are particularly recommended.

Abercrombie & Kent, Myanmar
2nd Floor, The Strand Hotel Annexe, 92, Strand Road, Yangon
Tel (95-1) 373034 248980, www.abercrombiekent.co.uk/myanmar
This agency is also the representative office for internationally renowned Abercrombie & Kent (A&K).

Asian Trails Tour Ltd
73, Pyay Road, Dagon Township, Yangon. Tel (95-1) 211212 223262
Highly recommended; Asian Trails cover all of South East Asia with Swiss efficiency but catering to an international clientele.
www.asiantrails.travel; res@asiantrails.com.mm

Diethelm Travel
6th Floor Centre Point Tower, 65, Corner of Sule Pagoda Road and Merchant Street, Kyauktada Township, Yangon. Tel (95-1) 373937 376801–4
Diethelm's head office is in Bangkok and it has years of experience in sending clients to Myanmar. www.diethelmtravel.com or info@diethelmtravel.com

Exotissimo Yangon
12th Floor MMB Tower, 166 Upper Pansodan Street, Mingalar Taung Nyunt Township, Yangon. Tel (95-1) 377801–8, www.exotissimo.com; mayanmar@ exotissimo.com. The head office of this agency is in Paris and it is very popular with French travellers.

Khiri Travel Myanmar
5/9 Bogalay Zay Street (lower block), first floor (behind Myanmar Red Cross building), Botahtaung Township, Yangon
Tel (95-1) 97313 49241; Email: myanmar@khiri.com; www.khiri.com

Myathiri Travels and Tours
Tel (95 1) 526593 525609; myathiri@gmail.com
Contact Joshua. This is a good small agency.

Myanmar Tourism Federation
No.3(A), Corner of Waizayandar Road & Thanthumar Road, Thuwanna, Thingangyun, Yangon, Myanmar. Tel (95-1) 8551012–3, www.myanmartourismboard. org; infomyanmartourismboard.org

Myanmar Voyages
No.133/B-2, Mawyawaddi Lane, (5) Quarter, 8 Miles, Mayangone Township, Yangon, Myanmar. Tel (95-1) 650206, 667342, www.myanmarvoyages.com;tlt@ myanmarvoyages.com.mm, jackietoh@gmail.com

Snowland Travels and Tours Ltd
139/1, Thanthumar Road, Thuwanna, Yangon, 11072, Myanmar. Tel (95-1) 541769, 570890, www.snowlandmyanmar.com; snowland@mptmail.net.mm, rakwipung@gmail.com

RIVER JOURNEYS

For those wanting to join a cruise along the Ayeyarwady River, and when the depth of water allows, along the Chindwin River, contact the boat operators listed below:

R/V Pandaw & R/V Paukan
www.ayravatacruises.com www.paukan.com
For reservations: res@ayravatacruises.com

R/V The Road to Mandalay & R/V Orcaella
Orient Express, 35/39 Taw Win Road, Dagon Township, Yangon
Tel (95-1) 229 860/229 861, www.orient-express.com

Amara River Cruise
6, Tayza Road, Minglardon Township, Yangon
Tel (95-1) 652 191, amara@myanmar.com.mm

RV Yandabo
402 Shwe Kabar Housing, Mindama Street, Mayangone Township, Yangon
Tel (95-1) 655 228, www.yandabo.com; reservation@yandabo.com

R/V Sanctuary Ananda (Scheduled Winter 2014)
Sanctuary Retreats Myanmar Ltd., 2nd floor Citymart Building, Aung San Stadium Northern Wing, Joe Phyu Road, Mingalar Taung Nyunt Township, Yangon
Tel (95-1) 255 954; www.sanctuaryretreats.com

Shwe Keinnery Vessels, GEC Building 35th Street, between 91st & 92nd Street, Mandalay. Tel 09 3311 5588, mmaihkamdy@gmail.com

NB: There are many private boats for hire on the Ayeyarwady and Chindwin Rivers, contact your travel agent for information. In the Mergui Archipelago several charter companies operate, they are all based in Thailand including 'Burma Boating' info@burmaboating.com.

HOTELS

During the past few years the hotel situation has changed dramatically in Myanmar. Yangon now boasts an increasing number of excellent hotels. The traveller who would like to feel that he or she is really in Myanmar, and not in a regular five-star hotel anywhere in the world, should try one of Yangon's new boutique hotels. Both the Savoy and the Governor's Residence are old buildings which have been modernized and converted to the highest of standards. Their interiors have been designed and decorated with great flair incorporating the best of Burmese artefacts. The dining rooms serve delicious food and have both Asian and Western menus. The swimming pools at both hotels are a joy to behold.

In fact Myanmar has got all its new hotels just right. Even the big ones that are part of international groups, such as Traders, have paid great attention to their interiors. They display a real feeling for the country—huge bunches of fresh flowers tumble out of vast lacquer bowls, and much of the furnishing incorporates Burmese design. The hotels listed below possess modern requirements such as gyms, business centres and so on. Satellite television is available in the rooms, and most carry both CNN and the BBC World Service television. Something that is very noticeable in these new hotels is the quality of staff; they are well trained and usually incredibly attentive.

Up-country and away from Yangon the local and overseas hoteliers have also been busy. The standards are not so high but some of the hotels have tremendous style and comfort. As you approach the renovated Bagan Hotel for instance, it looks as if you are visiting one of Bagan's pagodas. The entrance to the hotel is through an old red brick gate, similar to the Sarabha Gateway at the entrance to the Bagan site. Next door is the Thande Hotel at the centre of which stands a 1922 house constructed for the visit of the then Prince of Wales's visit. Visitors dine under a huge canopy of Accacia trees looking out over the Ayeyarwady River. The Inle Lake, Mandalay, Kalaw, Mrauk U and Ngapali all boast beautiful hotels—full of style.

PRICES

A very limited number of quality hotel rooms in Yangon means high prices even for less than luxurious accomodation. Below is a very approximate guide to prices. And bargains can be found, even in Yangon, if you make careful use of the appropriate websites; whilst away from Yangon quality rooms often go unsold especialy in the rainy season, so look carefully if you are making your own travel plans.

A=US$200–$500
B=US$120–$200
C=Usually below US$120

YANGON

Chatrium Hotel Royal Lake   A
40 Natmauk Road, Tamwe Township. Tel (95-1) 544 500, fax (95-1) 544 400
www.chatrium.com; info.chry@chatrium.com
This hotel overlooks Kandawgyi Lake and some rooms offer fine views of the
Shwedagon Pagoda.

Governor's Residence   A
35 Taw Win Road, Dagon Township. Tel (95-1) 229 860, fax (95-1) 228 260
www.governorsresidence.com; reservations@governorsresidence.com
A colonial-style house formerly used as the Kayah State guesthouse. This 45-room
hotel is located in a quiet residential area. The hotel is entered through a large
garden with a bridge leading over a moat. On closer inspection the moat
turns out to be a swimming pool on one side, and lotus pond on the other. The
bedrooms are in a new section at the back of the main house. Well designed with
remarkable stone baths, a little like a small pond. Beside the telephone the
management leave their guests a little wise advice: 'Kindly note overseas calls from
Myanmar are very expensive and no bargain accepted by the government'.
Telephone and fax charges are astronomical throughout the country so beware.

After an early-morning visit to the Shwedagon, enjoy breakfast on the terrace,
or a delicious dinner there in the evening. Sip your after dinner drink upstairs in
the open-air Mindon Lounge with the sound of frogs and crickets filling the air.
The Governor's Residence has been beautifully converted and is a romantic place
to stay.

Hilton Yangon   A
65 Sule Pagoda Road. www.hilton.com
Opening 2014 with 300 rooms, three restaurants, a lobby lounge and a sky bar
with unique panoramas of the heart of 'Old Rangoon'. This brand-new addition to
Yangon's luxury accomodations is strategically located in the centre of Yangon's
Heritage District, where Sule Pagoda Road and Merchant Street meet.

Inya Lake Hotel   A
37 Kaba Aye Pagoda Road. Tel (95-1) 662866 628 579, fax (95-1) 655 537
www.inyalakehotel.com; reservation@inyalakehotel.com
For many years the Inya Lake and the Strand Hotel were the only hotels where
foreign groups would be accommodated. Now the 240 rooms have been
refurbished to a high standard, as have all the public rooms.

Kandawgyi Palace Hotel   A
Kan Yeik Tha Road, Mingalar Taung Nyunt Township
Tel (95-1) 399 341/2, fax (95-1) 280 412; www.aureumpalacehotel.com

Built beside the Kandawgyi Lake (Royal Lake) this hotel of 200 rooms has undergone an extensive renovation and rebuilding programme. On a beautiful site near the Shwedagon Pagoda, it has a stunning, tiered swimming pool running down to the lake.

The Savoy Hotel   A

129 Dhammazedi Road, Bahan Township. Tel (95-1) 526 289, fax (95-1) 524 891
www.savoy-myanmar.com; generalmanager@savoy-yangon.com
Originally a private house, it has been converted into a boutique hotel with 30 rooms. This comfortable and well-run hotel is decorated with great charm, incorporating local lacquerware and antiques. While enjoying a delicious meal in the first-floor dining room, the visitor can marvel at the magic of the Shwedagon Pagoda as it shimmers across the trees—a superb view especially at night when floodlit.

Sedona Hotel   A

1 Kaba Aye Pagoda Road, Yankin Township. Tel (95-1) 666 972–7, fax (95-1) 666 911
A hotel with 366 rooms. Although large it manages to display some national character. The swimming pool is very well designed.

The Strand   A

92 Strand Road. Tel (95-1) 243 377, fax (95-1) 289 880
This grand old hotel (see page 123) has now been extensively restored with great style and with no expense spared. The Strand like many other hotels in Yangon is about to expand and will renovate the back section of the hotel which is presently given over to offices and shops.

Traders Hotel   A

228 Sule Pagoda Road, Pebedan Township. Tel (95-1) 242 828, fax (95-1) 242 800
Another hotel dating from the 1990's with some 500 rooms—again this hotel is expanding. For a big hotel Traders manages to have plenty of character. The interior designer has cleverly incorporated Burmese themes, so there is no doubt about what country you are in—so often not the case in hotels owned and managed by international groups. The various restaurants all serve good food with the ground-floor coffee shop serving a mixture of Asian and Western food, including excellent mohingha at breakfast. One of the great selling points of this hotel is its location right at the heart of the city.

Winner Inn   C

42 Than Lwin Road, Bahan Township, Yangon
Tel (95-1) 535 205/524 387; www.winnerinnmyanmar.com
For those who do not want to spend a lot of money on a hotel this centrally located—it is very near the Savoy Hotel—is very well run and a homely place to stay.

MANDALAY

There are four comfortable large hotels along with several boutique hotels in this city and a vast choice of small fairly basic guesthouses.

Rupar Mandalay Resort   A

Corner of 53rd & 30th Street, Chan Aye Thar Zan Township, Mandalay
Tel (95-2) 61555; www.ruparmandalar.com; ruparresort@myanmar.com.mm

A teak building in the Myanmar style very well designed this small hotel with some 20 rooms is pleasing to the eye. A stunning swimming pool and wherever you look much well thought out detail. All the modern amenities are available—for those wanting to relax this is the perfect place.

Mandalay Hill Resort   A

9 Kwin Street, Mandalay Hill
Tel (95-2) 35638, fax (95-2) 35639; mdyhill@mptmail.net.mm

As claimed in the sales brochure, "the most exciting location in Mandalay". The hotel sits at the foot of the Mandalay Hill, so has spectacular views both up the hill and down at the Mandalay Palace and moat. The 206 rooms are uninspiring but the public areas of the hotel have been interestingly designed, a fine mixture of East and West, with Burmese overtones. A good spa and the shops carry different and interesting goods. The swimming pool is outstanding—after a long hot day's sightseeing relax in one of the comfortable chairs and sip a cool refreshing lime soda. The large pool is surrounded with Burmese-style follies, which during the day can be used to shelter from the sun. By night they are beautifully lit and meld in with the pagodas behind on Mandalay Hill.

Sedona Hotel   A

26th and 68th Street, Chanayetharzan Township
Tel (95-2) 36488, fax (95-2) 36499
www.sedonamyanmar.com; sales.shm@sedona.com.mm

Built on the best site in Mandalay just at the south-east corner of the moat around the Mandalay Palace. The view from the hotel is of the pink Palace walls and straight up the moat to the pagoda-covered Mandalay Hill. There is a Burmese flavour to the exterior of the building with its tiered roofs. Inside it is a standard international hotel with 247 rooms, comfortable but with boring décor. The coffee shop, Café Mandalay has a nice terrace—a perfect place for breakfast—which overlooks the large swimming pool, garden and tennis courts.

Mandalay Swan Hotel   B

26th and 68th Street, Chan Aye Tha Zan
Tel (95-2) 31591, 31625, 35678, fax (95-2) 35677

Yangon office tel (95-1) 211 595

This medium-sized hotel with 106 rooms is a renovation of the old Mandalay Hotel. Now greatly improved, with air-conditioning and plumbing that works and even a nice swimming pool. The location of this hotel is good, just opposite the south wall of the Mandalay Palace, beside the Sedona Hotel. It is surrounded by a five-acre garden and is a pleasant place to stay.

Hotel by the Red Canal   B

No 417 corner of 63rd & 22nd Street, Aung Myae Tha Zan Township, Mandalay
Tel (95-2) 61177; www.hotelredcanal.com; info@hotelredcanal.com
This charming boutique hotel with 26 rooms built around a pool has a true Myanmar style—good looking teak furniture and detail.

Mandalay View Inn   B

17/B 66th Street between 26 & 27 Street, Chan Aye Tha Zan Township
Tel (95-2) 61119; www.mandalayviewinn.com; mandalayview@mandalay.net.mm
The sister hotel to Red Canal though not as pleasingly designed. It is small with only 12 rooms and all the facilities a traveller would need.

Mandalay City Hotel   B/C

80th Street, Between 82nd & 83rd Street, Chan Aye Tharzan Township
Tel (95-2) 535535 61700; www.mandalaycityhotel.com
For those who like the buzz of the city this is for them—you drive off a noisy main thoroughfare and into a courtyard. Built some 7 years ago the rooms are nice and plain, service is friendly, a swimming pool surrounded by interesting planting and the food is good.

There is a host of cheap guesthouses in Mandalay which charge around US$15–30 per night, for a basic bedroom with communal washing facilities. These hostelries come and go at great speed so the best way to find the current 'good' ones is to ask fellow travellers.

PYIN OO LWIN

Governor's House   A/B

www.aureaumpalacehotel.com; aureumpalace@myanmar.com.mm
There are two sections to this hotel, the former Governor's house which has been renovated to a high standard with the large reception rooms much as they were, except an indoor swimming pool has been added beside the dining room. In the house itself are 5 large bedrooms. The remainder of the 35 rooms are to be found in bungalows dotted around the garden.

For travellers planning to go by train to the Gokteik Viaduct this is a good stopping off point for the night, as the train leaves the Pyin Oo Lwin station at 8 in the morning—whereas if you stay down in Mandalay the train leaves at 4 am.

BAGAN

There is a selection of excellent hotels in and around Bagan; the remainder are guesthouses. The bedrooms in many of the guesthouses have their own bathrooms attached, but they will not serve any food.

Bagan Thiripyitsaya Sanctuary Resort   A/B
Bagan Archeological Zone, Old Bagan. Tel (95-61) 60048/60049
www.thiripytitsaya-resort.com; thiri@myanmar.com.mm
In a wonderful situation on the banks of the Ayeyarwady River and surrounded by pagodas and temples, this bungalow-style hotel has been running for years. All the bungalows have recently been renovated and are now comfortable. The garden is nice with a large swimming overlooking the river, but the food still leaves a lot to be desired (colonial/Indian cuisine, consisting of tough old curries) but like many hotels in Myanmar their fresh bread is delicious

Bagan Hotel River View   A
Near Archeological Museum, Old Bagan. Tel (95-61) 60316 60317
A stunning medium-sized hotel (108 rooms) sandwiched between the Gawdawpalin Temple, the Museum and the Ayeyarwady River. Built with great sensitivity and style. Their brochure boasts 11th-century history with 20th-century service. In the garden stand two 11th-century pagodas. The beautiful landscaping includes a large terrace and swimming pool.

Bagan Thande Hotel   A
Old Bagan City. Tel (95-61) 60025 60031
www.hotelbaganthande.com; thandeoffgyn@myanmar.com.mm
Another hotel on the banks of the Ayeyarwady, this is a truly lovely place with comfortable bungalows which have been built around the 1922 colonial house where the then Prince of Wales stayed. Enjoy a rum sour on the huge terrace under a canopy of spreading 'acacia leucophloca', these beautiful old trees are subtly lit at night. Most evenings a soft breeze comes off the river carrying the gentle noise of passing fishermen chatting in their small craft. The sun sets behind the hills on the opposite side of the river.

Aureum Palace Hotel—Resort   A
Min Nan Thu Village. (95-61) 60046 60047
www.aureumpalacehotel.com; sales-aureum@myanmar.com.mm
As you approach this luxurious hotel (of 114 rooms) it appears you are entering a village as the brick and teak buildings dot the 27 acres demesne. This hotel is built in the middle of the archeological site so the views from the various bungalows or the restaurants are incredible. The main axis of the site is to the west and the Ayeyarwady River. From the brick Lobby building you look across the

swimming pool to the plain of pagodas—the setting is breathtaking. For those who wish to watch the sunset from 'on high' a 60 metre viewing tower is part of the hotel complex.

Myanmar Treasure Resort   B
New Bagan. Tel (95-61) 60445
www.myanmartreasreresrts.com; newbagan@myanmar.com.mm
This sister hotel to the Aureum Palace again built in the style of the Bagan temples and in red brick. A much smaller hotel with 92 rooms, comfortable and good looking.

Both New Bagan, Old Bagan and Nyaung U have cheap guesthouses on offer. The rooms some with shared bathroom are basic but clean, most serve breakfast and many have a roof-top terrace, a useful asset as it is forbidden to climb many of the pagodas to watch sunrise and sunset.

Popa Mountain Resort   B
Popa Mountain, Kyauk Pa Daung Township
Tel (95–62) 70140, fax (95-62) 70140
Yangon office tel (95-1) 246 636, fax (95-1) 240 377
Perched on top of a volcanic peak looking across at Mount Popa, the home of the nats, this hotel with nine bungalows is a wonderful addition to the Bagan area. If visiting Mount Popa from Bagan it makes a perfect overnight stop. Beautifully decorated bungalows dot the site, there is a swimming pool with a dazzling view of Popa and the food is good. The hotel is in the Mount Popa Wildlife Reserve and so specialises in arranging trekking, riding, bird and butterfly watching.

INLE LAKE REGION

When visiting the Inle Lake there are three neighbouring towns in which you can conveniently stay. There is the cool, though sometimes rather damp, hill station town of Taunggyi (see page 226). This is roughly one hour's drive from the Lake itself. The large village of Nyaung Shwe at the northern end of the lake is another option and there are many hotels on the lake itself to choose from and frankly that is the best way to enjoy the beauty of the lake.

TAUNGGYI

Hotel Paradise   C
157 Khwanyo Road, Pyidawthar Quarter. Tel (95-81) 22009, fax (95-81) 22009
A nice, newish, small guesthouse in the northern quarter of the town. The rooms either have shower cubicles or private bathrooms in the 'superior' rooms . All rooms have mini-bars and satellite television—if there is no power cut. There is a restaurant which serves Chinese and Burmese food with a few European dishes.

Khermarat Guest House   C
48 Bogyoke Aung San Street. Tel (95-81) 222464
Another clean, new and well-run guesthouse. The cheaper rooms have a shared bathroom but the larger doubles have their own bathroom.

Taunggyi Hotel   C
Shun Yaw Khynn Street, Forest Quarter
Tel (95-81) 21601/21127, fax (95-81) 21601
The town's only hotel as such is an old colonial-style mansion, with an atmosphere to match, surrounded by a large garden. This nice hotel has recently undergone refurbishment so the rooms now have bathrooms attached and the telephones work. Until fairly recently the telephone was a wind-up machine, and as soon as the mists came down, which they often do in Taunggyi, the lines went dead—as did the electricity. The hotel is situated near the centre of town so the bar and main reception areas are quite jolly of an evening.

NYAUNG SHWE
This bustling town has many small guesthouses and hotels, but nothing smart.

Gold Star Hotel   C
Phaung Daw Pyan Road. Tel (95-81) 21635
This small, clean hotel, each room with its own shower, is part of a chain, with hotels in both Mandalay and Bagan.

Hu Pin Hotel   C
66 Kantar Quarter, West of Bazaar
Tel (95-81) 29291; www.hupinhotelmyanmar.com
A hotel which has expanded greatly, it started as a small guesthouse and now has some 60 rooms divided into three different buildings, with a fourth under construction. Good no-frills rooms with showers, and the perfect spot for photographers who want to catch the early morning market next door. The stall holders start arriving and setting out their wares as dawn breaks. They also have a roof terrace from which you can watch the sun set over Inle Lake. The hotel restaurant serves delicious Chinese food with a few local specialities, such as fried bean curd crackers.

Inle Inn   C
Yone Gyi Road, Nan Daw Won Quarter
Tel/fax (95-81) 21347; Yangon office Tel (95-1) 291 746
An old favourite which has been substantially upgraded over the years. There used to be one bathroom at the end of the Nissen-hut type building. Now there are showers attached to the rooms. The building has been extended and refaced with plaited mat panels and there is now a courtyard garden at the back of the hotel where visitors can order drinks.

Innlay Khaungdaing Hotel   C
Yangon office tel (95-1) 660 563/282 278, fax (95-1) 666 879
A sister hotel to the Inle Inn situated on the northern shore of the lake. Some rooms are housed in the main two-storey buildings with a few bungalows also available. It is fairly basic but nice. The local entrepreneur who owns and runs these two hotels under the banner of the EYE Hotel Group also owns and runs the Princess Resort on the lake itself. The group has recently taken over the management of the old colonial-style hotel in Kalaw (see page 218), 'a tranquil summer resort'. This can be a nice overnight stop on the way from Thazi down to the lake.

HOTELS ON INLE LAKE

In the past few years many hotels have sprung up along the eastern bank of the Inle Lake roughly a 25 minute speed boat ride from Nyaung Shwe. Apparently permission has just been granted for a new group of hotels to be built along the western banks of the Lake.

Inle Princess Resort A/B
Magyiain Village, Inle Lake, Shan State. Tel (95-81) 209055
www.inleprincessresort.com; inleprincess@myanmar.com.mm
As the speed boat roars along the main canal it suddenly darts off to the left along a narrow waterway—if in October the wild ginger flowers are in bloom. Suddenly the noisy engine is turned off as you near a boathouse where a leg rower jumps on board and the boat is rowed in to the hotels landing stage so as not to disturb the guest's peace—a charming touch. This hotel is beautifully laid out with simple teak chalets either along the lake-front or facing onto the internal pond—excellent planting. The rooms are very comfortable with the added delight of an outside shower. The restaurant with a lovely terrace overlooking the lake, serves delicious Shan dishes alongside other Asian and Western food.

Inle Resort A/B
Nyaung Shwe Township, Shan State
Tel (95) 09 5211555; www.inleresort.com; revinle@myanmar.com.mm
Another very good looking hotel built on the eastern shore of the lake. The traditional teak main buildings house the reception areas with the bedrooms in separate bungalows with their private terraces facing the lake. Again the restaurant serves a varied menu to suit all tastes.

Myanmar Treasure Resort A/B
Maing Thauk Village, Inle Lake, Shan State. Tel (95-81) 29481
www.myanmartreasureresorts.com mtinle@myanmar.com.mm
More of the same—these three hotels are all extremely good looking, well designed using the best of Myanmar traditional style and a pleasure to stay in.

Perfect for relaxing after a day's sight-seeing, unwind with a session in the spa, enjoy a pre-dinner drink on the terrace and watch the sun go down the other side of the lake—Inle is not a place one wants to leave.

Golden Island Cottages   B/C

Taunggyi office: 18 Myo Pat Road, Taunggyi, tel (95-81) 22224

Yangon office: 969/28 Aungbawga Street, North Dagon, tel (95-1) 584 593

As the boat whisks along the southern end of Inle Lake a collection of wooden cottages built on stilts comes into view. The Golden Island Cottages Hotel, a co-operative run by the Pa-O ethnic group, was the first of the hotels to be built on the lake and is full of charm. Built in a horseshoe shape, the reception area and dining room form the centre, with the cottages built around the arc—a series of traditional-style wooden bridges and walkways lead to the rooms. Each cottage has a simple bedroom, complete with mosquito net, its own fairly basic but clean bathroom—with hot water, very important after a day on the lake, which can be quite cold and damp in the winter. Each cottage has two little terraces, one from which to watch the sun rise, the other the sun set. If the weather is good a delicious dinner is served on the terrace outside the dining room. Some evenings the staff perform a charming 'cultural show'. The only hazard of this hotel is that it can be quite noisy during the early hours of the morning. Boats driven at maximum throttle rush past, while the tuneless prayers of devotees from the nearby village herald the dawn.

KALAW

For those planning to trek from Kalaw down to the Inle Lake there is now a fine hotel in this former hill station town.

Amara Resort

10 Thida Road. 10 Quarter, West Bogone, Kalaw, Shan State

Tel (95-81) 50470; amara@myanmar.com.mm

An old colonial house built around 1909 and restored in 2002 the hotel has 10 double rooms all with open fires as it is quite cold during the winter evenings. In true hill station style the gardens are full of antirinums and the like.

SITTWE

Noble Hotel

45 Main Road, Maw Keik Quarter, Sittwe. www.noblehotelsittwe.onestopdeals.com

Right in the centre of town this eleven year old hotel with 20 rooms is fine if you have to overnight in Sittwe on the way to or from Mrauk U. Across the road is the River Valley Restaurant a good place to eat.

MRAUK-U

Mrauk Oo Princess Resort   A/B

Aung Tat Yat, Mrauk U. Rakhine State. Tel (95-43) 50232 50235
www.mraukooprincessresort.com; mprinfo@myanmar.com.mm
An oasis of comfort and delightful design in an area barren of hotels, though in the town there are plenty of guesthouses. This is the sister hotel to the Inle Princess (Inle Lake) and is every bit as well managed and pleasing to the eye. Built in the Rahkine style the teak bungalows have lovely views across the gardens to the river. The piéce de résistance is the main teak building which is decorated with huge paper lights reminiscent of local fishing nets.

Royal City & River Valley

Minbar Gyi Road, Mrauk-U. Tel (95 43) 24200
www.rivervalleyrestaurantsittwe.com
This is both a guesthouse with some individual bungalows and regular rooms—all clean plain and simple with bathrooms. Then across the street is their restaurant which serves good local and western food. The guesthouse is situated in the middle of the little town of Mrauk-U beside the main boat dock.

NGAPALI

There has been an explosion of new hotels in Ngapali in recent years and more are being built. To date they have been developed with great sensitivity so are not disturbing the pure beauty of the beach. These hotels are the perfect place to end a two week trip around Myanmar—sight-seeing can be exhausting so here is the antidote, and there are direct flights from Yangon and Heho.

Bayview—The Beach Resort   A/B

Ngapali Beach, Thandwe District
Tel (95) 1504 471. www.bayview-myanmar.com; hotel@bayview.com.mm
One of a number of beautifully designed resort hotels. Built right beside the beach the bungalows are surrounded by a palm shaded garden. Enjoy evening drinks overlooking the Bay of Bengal and the setting sun. This award winning resort has two restaurants, the Catch and the Sunset Bar.

Sandoway Resort   A/B

Ngapali. Tel (95-43) 42233
www.sandowayresort.com; reservation@sandowayresort.com
Another lovely beach side hotel, very comfortable these bungalows have a slight Swiss chalet feel. Again a marvellous terrace for meals, all the amenities are on hand.

Amara Ocean Resort   A/B
Gaut Village, Ngapali. Tel (95-9) 8515480
www.amara-group.com; sales@amara-ocean.com
At this beach-side hotel there are 28 bungalows well designed, comfortable with good private terraces. The food in all these hotels is fine but not imaginative whereas in the road behind the hotels are several excellent local restaurants, well worth a visit. Just behind this hotel is the Silver Star Restaurant where the fresh sea food is 'out of this world' served with a variety of different sauces. Further along the road to the west is Min Thu again excellent food and a jolly place of an evening.

Thande Beach Hotel   A/B
Ngapali. Tel (95-43) 42278, 42279, www.thandebeachhotelmyanmar.com
frontoffice@thandebeachhotelmyanmar.com
This hotel is larger and older but in a wonderful position on the beach—it has 38 bungalows and some are two-storey. Comfortable but in a slight need of an upgrade, but the staff are charming. In all these hotels it is a good idea to request a sea front bungalow so you can enjoy the full magic of the beach.

MAWLAMYINE

The Mawlamyaing Strand Hotel   B
Strand Road. Tel (95-57) 25624
www.mawlamyaingstrandhotel.com; info@mawlamyaingstrandhotel.com
This hotel opened in 2012 so is very new and has a prime position on Strand Road. A four-storey building with Myanmar style roofs the spaces inside are well designed but perhaps could be better finished—one has the feeling it was built in a great hurry. Tables are set out on the grass of an evening so a delightful place for dinner overlooking the bay.

The name of this hotel just underlines the problem of transliteration in Myanmar—the town spelt in two different ways.

Cinderalla   C
21 Baho Road, Sitkei Gone Quarter. Tel (95-57) 24411
www.cinderellahotel.com; hotel.cinderella@gmail.com
A charming rather wacky hotel very brightly coloured a lot of mauve with a bright orange dining room. Up the hill away from the Strand the hotel has all modern amenities.

Attran Hotel   B
Strand Road. Tel (95-1) 251623, www.attranhotel.com; smileworld@mptmail.com
The Attran is the other hotel in a prime position looking out across the rivers, boasting the best terrace in town for an evening drink and dinner.

Nay Pyi Taw

Aureum Palace Hotel   A/B
1 Yar Zar Htar Ni Road. Tel (95-67) 42074650
sales-aureum@myanmar.com.mm
A 40-bed hotel with bungalows built around a pear-shaped lake, a member of the well-run Aureum group. Decorated in traditional style to a high standard of design and comfort. All the extras of a modern hotel are available including a 'nature spa'—a perfect leisure and business hotel.

The Hotel Amara   A/B
11 Yarza Thingaha Road. Tel (95-67) 422201–13
reservation@thehotelamara.com
As their website suggests 'a celebration of Myanmar creativity'. The 131 rooms and public areas are decorated in Myanmar style with a fine degree of comfort.

Mingalar Thiri Hotel   B/C
Yarza Thingarha street, Dathkhina Thiri City, Hotel Zone. Tel (95-67) 422140–59 (20 lines), hot line: (95-67) 422155; enquiry.mingalarthirihotel@gmail.com

Mount Pleasant Hotel   A/B
Pho Zaung Hill, Oattara, Thiri City. Tel (95-67) 431155–70 (16 lines); enquiry@ mountpleasanthotelmyanmar.com; www. mountpleasanthotelmyanmar.com

Royal Kumudra Hotel   B/C
10 Yaza Thingaha Road. Tel (95-67) 414187
A nice comfortable 42-room hotel, one of eight now in the hotel zone. As with all these new hotels it offers every amenity for, as its website proclaims, 'the most savvy and passionate traveller'.

Royal Naypyitaw Hotel   B/C
5 Yar Za Thin Ga Ha Road. A rather quirky interesting design this 92 bed hotel is also beside a lake, so many of the rooms have lakeside views. Again it possesses all modern amenities.

Putao

Malikha Lodge   A
Tel (95-1) 513300, www.malikhalodge.com; myn-treasure@myanmar.com.mm
To date the only hotel 'in style' in the north of Myanmar is Malikha Lodge—developed with no expense spared with every detail taken care of. Amazing views of the river and surrounding forest from the main Lodge which itself has comfortable reception areas with open fires. The bungalow rooms are very comfortable, with open fires and large baths in the middle of the room—strange but great looking. Good varied menu and charming staff.

A MALODOROUS DELICACY

There are few articles of food which meet with more energetic denunciation than the favourite Burman condiment, ngapi, which means literally pressed fish. The frogs of France, the rats and puppy dogs of China, the diseased liver of the Strasburg pâtés, the "ripe" cheeses of most European countries, and the peculiar character of game in England, with its occasional garniture of "rice," all meet with condemnation from those who dislike such dainties. The smell of ngapi is certainly not charming to an uneducated nose, but the Backsteiner or Limburger cheese of Southern Germany is equally ill-calculated to evoke approbation on a first experience. An old herring barrel smells strong, but there is nothing in nature that more than ngapi hath an ancient and a fish-like smell. Travellers on the steamers of the Irrawaddy Flotilla Company are wont to rail in no measured terms at the fish-paste which forms an invariable and obtrusively evident part of the cargo, yet no Burman would think a dinner complete without his modicum of ngapi, and it is a noteworthy fact that one form of the condiment is of frequent appearance on English dinner-tables in the East, under the name of balachong, a term borrowed from the Straits Settlements, but which designates nothing more nor less than a specially prepared variety of ngapi. In the same way there are equally various opinions with regard to the celebrated Durian, a fruit found as abundantly in the Tenasserim province as in the islands of the East Indian Archipelago, and equally highly prized by Burmans. Some Englishmen will tell you that the flavour and the odour of the fruit may be realised by eating a "garlic custard" over a London sewer; others will be no less positive in their perception of blendings of sherry, noyau, delicious custards, and the nectar of the gods, while a somewhat objectionable smell is regarded as doing no more than suggest, or recall, a delightful sensation. I am not aware that any Englishman has been equally enthusiastic with regard to balachong, but there is no doubt that ngapi seinsa ["raw-eaten fish-paste," so called because it is fit for consumption without being cooked] is identical with this much-used substitute for anchovy sauce, and is often brought direct from the Burman bazaar by Madrasi butlers, who declare it has come all the way from Penang, and charge correspondingly.

Shway Yoe, The Burman: his life and notions, 1882

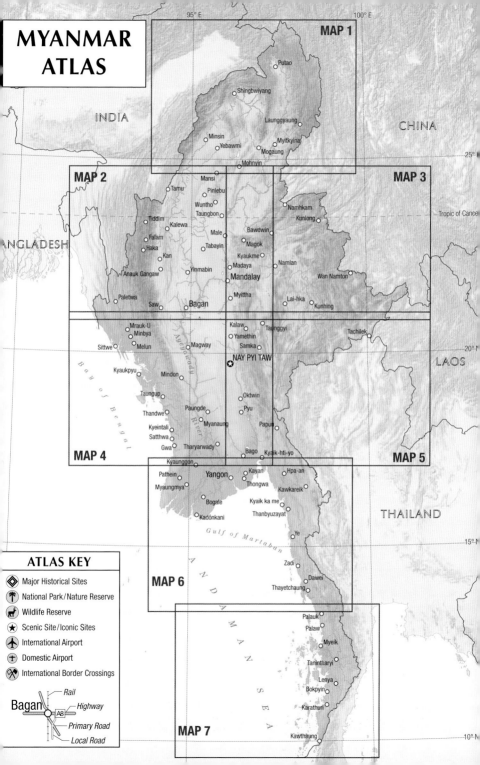

MYANMAR ATLAS

MAP 1

MAP 2

MAP 3

MAP 4

MAP 5

MAP 6

MAP 7

INDIA

CHINA

LAOS

THAILAND

BANGLADESH

95° E
100° E

Tropic of Cancer

25°

20° N

15° N

10° N

Places

Putao
Shingbwiyang
Launggyaung
Minsin
Yebawmi
Myitkyina
Mogaung
Mohnyin

Mansi
Tamu
Pinlebu
Wuntho
Taungbon
Namhkam
Kunlong
Tiddim
Kalewa
Bawdwin
Falam
Male
Magok
Haka
Tabayin
Kyaukme
Kan
Namlan
Anauk Gangaw
Yinmabin
Madaya
Paletwa
Mandalay
Wan Namton
Saw
Myittha
Bagan
Lai-hka
Kunhing

Mrauk-U
Minbya
Kalaw
Taunggyi
Tachilek
Sittwe
Melun
Magway
Yamethin
Samka
Kyaukpyu
Mindon
NAY PYI TAW
Taungup
Oktwin
Thandwe
Paungde
Pyu
Kyeintali
Myanaung
Papun
Satthwa
Gwa
Tharyarwady
Bago
Kyaik-hti-yo
Kyaunggon
Pathein
Yangon
Kayan
Hpa-an
Myaungmya
Thongwa
Kawkareik
Bogale
Kyaik ka me
Kadonkani
Thanbyuzayat
Ye
Zadi
Dawei
Thayetchaung
Palauk
Palaw
Myeik
Tanintharyi
Lenya
Bokpyin
Karathuri
Kawthaung

Bay of Bengal
Ayeyarwady River
Gulf of Martaban
ANDAMAN SEA

ATLAS KEY

- ◈ Major Historical Sites
- ⊕ National Park / Nature Reserve
- 🐾 Wildlife Reserve
- ★ Scenic Site / Iconic Sites
- ✈ International Airport
- ⊕ Domestic Airport
- ✷ International Border Crossings

Bagan
— Rail
— Highway
A8
— Primary Road
— Local Road

MAP 1

0   50   100

kilometers

Lambert Conformal Conic central meridian 96.5° west, sp15°N and 23°N
Scale 1:2,150,000
1cm = 21.5 kilometers

elevations in meters

0 50 100 200 300 1,000 1,500 2,000 3,000 5,881

INDIA

Dibrugarh

95° E

Jorhat

Ngalung Ga

SANGPAWNG BUM

Sake Hi

Shingbwiyang

HUKAWNG VALLE

Miku

Sela Nok

Sinlung Ga

Kawlum

Hukawng Valley
Tiger Reserve

Nritu

Lahe

Maingkwan

Tsawlaw

Janhtang

Lawng-ngaw

Kawala

Historic
Burma Road

Hwekum

River

Singkanng Hkamti

Shaduzup

Tinmaung

Shirang

Hpawngtut

Saramati
3,825m

Kaunghein

Kohima

Yawpami

Sagaing

Kamai

Layshi

Minsin

Kadonyat

Thunghkung

Somra

Nampagan

Sezin

Loipaw

PATKAI BUM

Chindwin

Kadonyat

In-daw-gyi Lake
Wildlife Sanctuary

INDIA

Yebawmi

In-daw-gyi
Lake

Tamanthi
Wildlife Reserve

25° N

Maungkan

Kawya

Namhta

Bilmyo

Hopin

Imphal

Gwedaukkon

Nawngpu-awng

Saingkyu

Meza

Mohnyin

Nawngsansaing

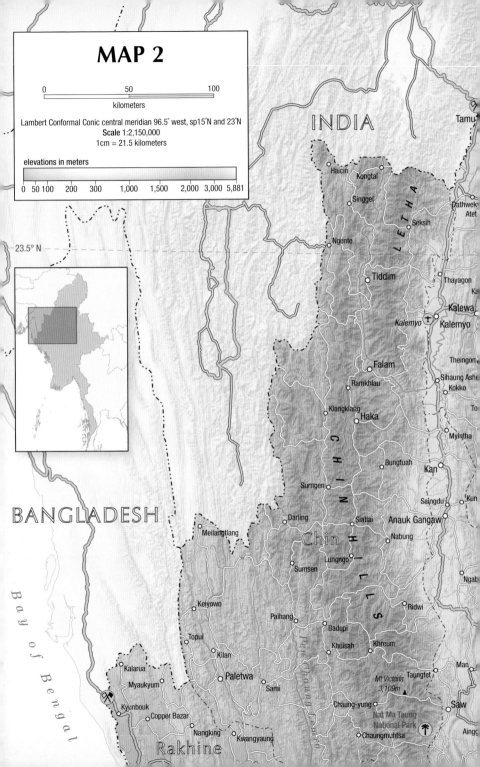

MAP 2

0   50   100
kilometers

Lambert Conformal Conic central meridian 96.5° west, sp15°N and 23°N
Scale 1:2,150,000
1cm = 21.5 kilometers

elevations in meters

0 50 100   200   300   1,000 1,500 2,000 3,000 5,881

23.5° N

INDIA

Tamu

Haicin
Kongtal
Singgel
Dathwek
Atet
Ngente
Seksih
L E T H A
Tiddim
Thayagon
Ka
Kalemyo
Kalewa
Kalemyo
Falam
Theingon
Ramkhlau
Sihaung Ashe
Kokko
Klangklang
Haka
To
Myintha
Bungtuah
Kan
Surngen
Saingdu
Kun
Darling
Siatlai
Anauk Gangaw
C H I N
Meilangtlang
Nabung
Chin
Lungngo
Sumsen
H I L L S
Ngab
Keiyowo
Ridwi
Paihang
Badupi
Topui
Khuisah
Khreum
Kilan
Man
Kalarua
Peu Chaung Daung
Myaukyum
Mt Victoria
3,109m
Taungtet
Kyunbouk
Paletwa
Sami
Chaung-yung
Saw
Copper Bazar
Nat Ma Taung
National Park
Nangking
Kwangyaung
Chaungmuhtsa

BANGLADESH

Bay of Bengal

Rakhine

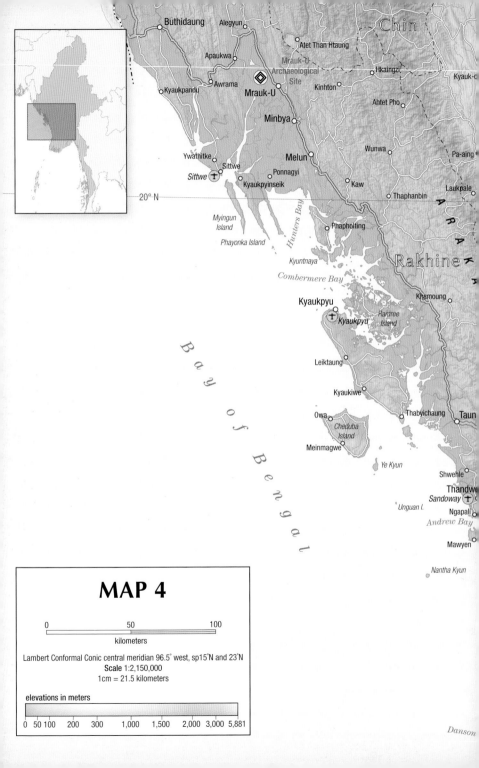

Buthidaung
Alegyun
Atet Than Htaung
Apaukwa
Mrauk-U
Archaeological
Site
Hkaingzi
Kyauk-o
Kyaukpandu
Awrama
Kinhton
Mrauk-U
Ahtet Pho
Minbya
Wunwa
Pa-aing
Ywathitke
Melun
Sittwe
Ponnagyi
Kaw
Laukpale
Sittwe
Kyaukpyinseik
Thaphanbin
20° N

Myingun
Island
Phapholting

Phayonka Island

Kyuntnaya
Rakhine

Combermere Bay

Kyaukpyu
Khamoung

Kyaukpyu
Ranree
Island

Leiktaung

Kyaukiwe

Owa
Thabyichaung
Taun

Cheduba
Island

Meinmagwe

Ye Kyun

Shwehle

Thandwe
Sandoway
Ngapali

Unguan I.
Andrew Bay

Mawyen

Nantha Kyun

Chin

A
R
A
K
A

Bay

of

Bengal

MAP 4

0   50   100
kilometers

Lambert Conformal Conic central meridian 96.5° west, sp15°N and 23°N
Scale 1:2,150,000
1cm = 21.5 kilometers

elevations in meters

0 50 100   200   300   1,000   1,500   2,000 3,000 5,881

Danson

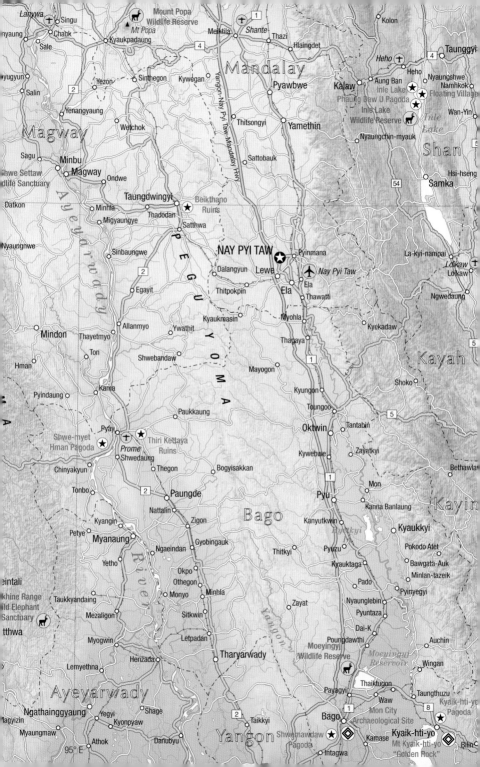

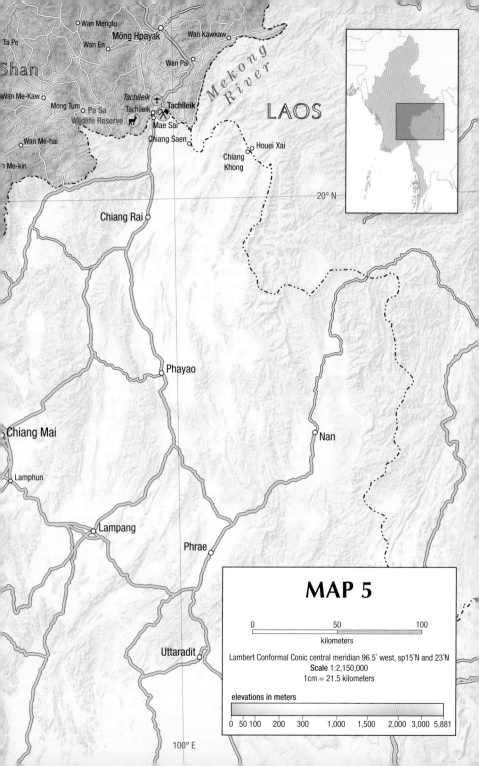

Ta Pe

Wan Menglu

Möng Hpayak

Wan En

Wan Kawkaw

Wan Pai

Shan

Wan Me-Kaw

Mong Tum

Pa Sa
Wildlife Reserve

Tachileik

Tachileik

Tachileik

Mae Sai

Wan Me-hai

Chiang Saen

n Me-kin

Houei Xai

Chiang
Khong

Mekong River

LAOS

20° N

Chiang Rai

Phayao

Chiang Mai

Nan

Lamphun

Lampang

Phrae

Uttaradit

100° E

MAP 5

| 0 | 50 | 100 |

kilometers

Lambert Conformal Conic central meridian 96.5° west, sp15°N and 23°N
Scale 1:2,150,000
1cm = 21.5 kilometers

elevations in meters

| 0 | 50 | 100 | 200 | 300 | 1,000 | 1,500 | 2,000 | 3,000 | 5,881 |

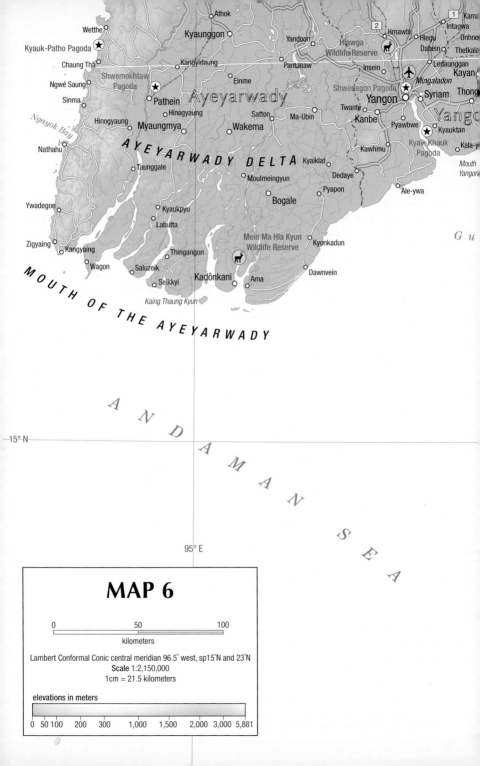

Athok
Wetthe
Kyaungon
Kyaup-Patho Pagoda
Yandoon
Hlawga
Hmawbi
Hlegu
Intagwa
Onhne
Kama
2
Wildlife Reserve
Dabein
Thetkala
Chaung Tha
Kangyidaung
Pantanaw
Insein
Ledaunggan
Kayan
Shwemokhtaw
Einme
Shwedagon Pagoda
Mingaladon
Ngwe Saung
Pagoda
Twante
Yangon
Syriam
Thong
Sinma
Pathein
Hinogyaung
Satton
Ma-Ubin
Kanbe
Yangc
Hinogyaung
Myaungmya
Wakema
Pyawbwe
Kyauktan
Nathahu
Kyaik Khauk
Kala-y
AYEYARWADY DELTA
Kyaiklat
Pagoda
Taunggale
Kawhmu
Mouth
Moulmeingyun
Dedaye
Yangor
Ywadegon
Kyaukpyu
Pyapon
Ale-ywa
Bogale
Labutta
Mein Ma Hla Kyun
Zigyaing
Kangyaing
Thingangon
Wildlife Reserve
Kyonkadun
G u
Wagon
Saluzeik
Kadônkani
Dawnvein
Seikkyi
Ama
Kaing Thaung Kyun

M O U T H   O F   T H E   A Y E Y A R W A D Y

A N D A M A N   S E A

15° N

95° E

MAP 6

0   50   100
kilometers

Lambert Conformal Conic central meridian 96.5° west, sp15°N and 23°N
Scale 1:2,150,000
1cm = 21.5 kilometers

elevations in meters

0 50 100   200   300   1,000   1,500   2,000 3,000 5,881

95° E

A
N
D
A
M
A
N

S
E
A

MAP 7

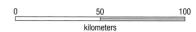

0	50	100

kilometers

Lambert Conformal Conic central meridian 96.5° west, sp15°N and 23°N
Scale 1:2,150,000
1cm = 21.5 kilometers

elevations in meters

0 50 100   200   300   1,000 1,500   2,000 3,000 5,881

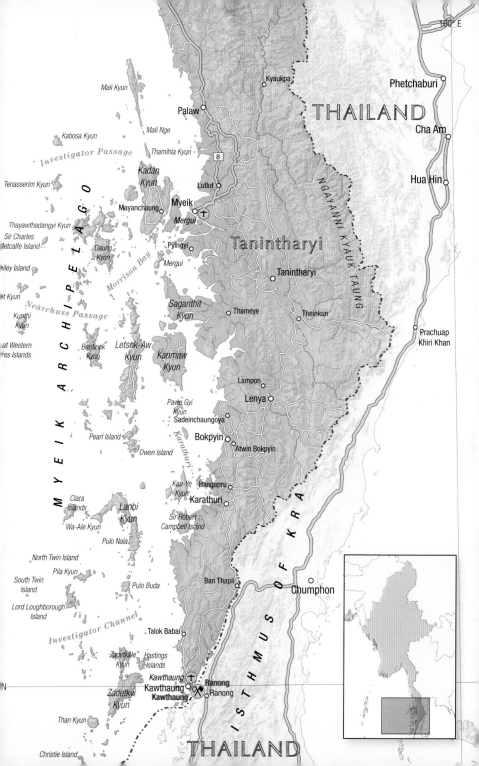

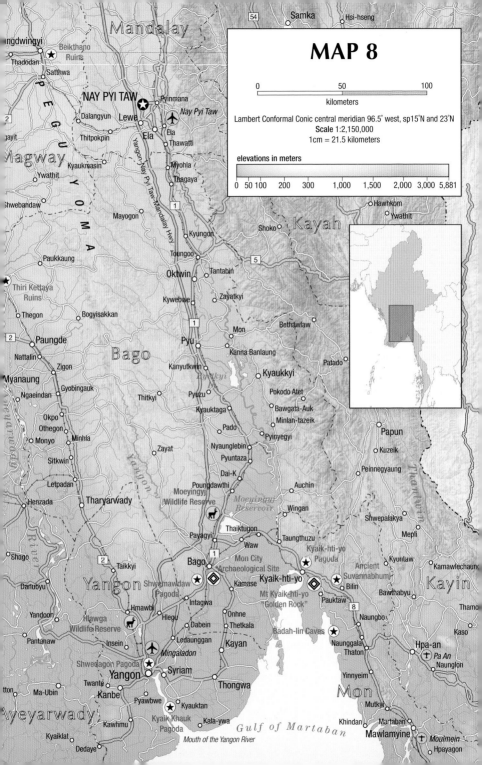

MAP 8

Samka   Hsi-hseng
54

ngdwingyi   Beikthano
            Ruins
Thadodan ★
   Satthwa

NAY PYI TAW ⊛   Pyinmana

   Dalangyun   Lewe   Nay Pyi Taw
      Ela   ✈
Thitpokpin   Ela
            Thawatti
   Kyaukmasin   Myohla
Ywathit   Thagaya
                          Hawhkom
Shwebandaw   Ywathit
         Mayogon
                   Kyungon   Kayah
                              Shoko
Paukkaung   Toungoo
                             5
  Thiri Kettaya   Oktwin   Tantabin
     Ruins
   Thegon   Bogyisakkan   Kywebwe   Zayatkyi
                                        Mon
2   Pyu   Kanna Banlaung   Bethawlaw
Paungde
 Nattalin   Zigon   Kanyutkwin   Patado
Myanaung Gyobingauk   Kyaukkyi
   Ngaeindan   Pyuzu   Pokodo Atet
      Thitkyi   Bawgata-Auk
   Okpo   Kyauktaga   Minlan-tazeik
  Othegon   Minhla   Pado   Papun
   Monyo   Zayat   Nyaunglebin   Pyinyegyi   Kuzeik
  Sitkwin   Pyuntaza
   Letpadan   Dai-K   Peinnegyaung
Henzada Tharyarwady   Poungdawthi   Thanlwin
                Moeyingyi   Auchin
                Wildlife Reserve   Moeyingyi   Wingan
                             Reservoir   Shwepalakya
                  Payagyi   Mepli
              Thaiktugon
Shago   Waw   Taungthuzu
2   Taikkyi   Kyaik-hti-yo   Kyunlaw
Danubyu   Bago   Pagoda   Ancient   Kamawlechaung
              Shwemawdaw   Mon City   Suvannabhumi
Yandoon   Hmawbi   Pagoda   Archaeological Site   Bilin   Kayin
         Intagwa   Kamase Kyaik-hti-yo
Pantanaw   Hlegu   Onhne Mt Kyaik-hti-yo Pauktaw Thamo
   Hlawga   Dabein "Golden Rock"   8
   Wildlife Reserve Thetkala   Naungbo   Kaso
Insein   Ledaunggan   Kayan Badah-lin Caves   Naunggala   Hpa-an
      Mingaladon   Naunggala   Thaton   ✈ Pa An
Shwedagon Pagoda Syriam Yinnyeim   Naunglon
   Yangon   Mon
 Twante   Thongwa
Kanbe   Pyawbwe   Kyauktan
   Kyaik Khauk   Kala-ywa   Mutkyi
   Pagoda   Gulf of Martaban Khindan   Martaban
Kyaiklat Mouth of the Yangon River   Mawlamyine   ✚ Moulmein
Dedaye   Hpayagon

RESTAURANTS

As with the hotels, there has been an explosion of good new restaurants in the major tourist destinations within Myanmar. All the new hotels have good restaurants serving both Asian and Western food. There is always a heavy emphasis on Chinese dishes, though most menus will contain one or two Burmese specialities. For Western food the hotel restaurants are the best. If eating in streetside stalls make sure that the food is freshly cooked and drink only bottled drinks, with no ice. Karaoke has found its way to Myanmar, particularly in the Mandalay restaurants. Throughout the country new restaurants appear all the time so ask your guide—here are a few tried and tested favourites.

YANGON

Green Elephant Restaurant
33 Thrimingalar Lane (Attia Road), Kamayut Township. Tel (95-1) 537 706
This restaurant has recently moved to another old colonial house—basically the shop (see page 98) and restaurant have been separated, although there are still some lovely things at the restaurant for sale that might catch your eye as you go to your table. The food served is authentic Burmese 'home cooking', delicious with plenty of choice. Some tables are inside but the covered terrace area is a fine place to eat—all the tables are covered in marvellous plaid clothes woven in the Shan State.

Monsoon
85-87 Theinbyu Road, Yangon
Tel (95-1) 295 224, Monsson-ygn@myanmar.com.mm
Downtown Yangon so a perfect place for lunch after a hot morning looking at the city's fantastic stock of heritage buildings, visiting the book market and so on. Itself in an old colonial house the menu is a mix of Asian cuisines and all delicious.

Pandonmar Restaurant
105/107 Kha Yae Bin Road, Ahlone Road, Yangon. Tel (95-1) 538 895
In an old house on several floors there are many different rooms to choose from in which to eat. On a nice night the best place is in the pretty front garden lit by lanterns swinging in the breeze; delicious food specializing in Myanmar and Thai dishes.

Signature
Near U Htaung Bo Roundabout Kandawgyi Relaxation Zone
Tel (95-1) 546488
On the edge of the Kandawgyi Lake this restaurant, a fine Myanmar style building,

has a lovely big terrace to eat out on or if too hot retreat to the cool of air-conditioning in the pleasant inside dining rooms. They have a varied menu of both Myanmar and western food.

Le Planteur

22 Kaba Aye Pagoda Road, Yangon. Tel (95-1) 541 997
www.leplanteur.net; info@leplanteur.net
One of Yangon's many colonial residences has been well converted to house Le Planteur. This restaurant serves exclusively French food. The meats such as dried ham and salami are cured on the premises, and the home-made terrines and rillettes are delicious. Vegetables are grown in the garden, so the fresh salads are tasty. Other specialities are the charcoal-cooked meats. Enjoying dinner in the beautifully lit garden is a real pleasure.

Union Bar and Grill

42 Strand Road, Bohtataung. Tel (95-9) 3101 8272; info@unionyangon.com
Provides a relaxed atmosphere to check your e-mails, grab a bite for lunch or dine and enjoy their expertly made cocktails in the evening. Complete with a large, extensively stocked central bar, comfortable seating, intimate dining and a lounge, Union Bar and Grill blends authentic Myanmar with the West.

MANDALAY

As in Yangon all the good hotels serve a good mixture of cuisines, but if going out to see the marionette or dance shows try one of these restaurants.

Green Elephant

3 Block 801 27th Street, Aung Daw Quarter, Mandalay
Tel (95-2) 612 37 742 73; greenmdy@mail.mandalay.net.mm
Another of the excellent Green Elephant restaurants, again tables covered with the pretty Shan plaid cloth, lovely silk lanterns giving a gentle light in the evening. Food is always of a high quality.

A little Bit of Mandalay

Aung Taw Quarter, 413B, 65th Street between 27th & 28th Mandalay
Tel (95-2) 61295
A nice simple wooden framed terrace, good food with jolly atmostphere.

Pakokku-Daw Lay May

73rd Street between 27th & 28th
For a real Myanmar food experience this is the place, but only at lunch time. Choose what type of curry, meat, fish or vegetable and then along with the curry different vegetable dishes of the day plus a soup and rice will be served. All delicious and very clean.

Royal Lake Café and Restaurant
Near Royal Barge, West Kandtawgyi, Mandalay. Tel 09-2009445
On a very hot day a good place to stop for a cooling lunch or light meal is the Royal Café on the shores of the Royal Lake. This area is now a delightful park, before the river was dammed there was only a lake here during the rainy season but now it is a permanent lake.

Golden Duck
192 Corner of 80th and 16th Street. Tel (95-2) 36808
A popular noisy Chinese restaurant where the food is good—as the name would suggest, duck dishes are its speciality.

BAGAN

Here as in Yangon and Mandalay the restaurants serve a mixture of Myanmar and Chinese dishes.

Sarabha Restaurant
Sarabha Gateway, Old Bagan. Tel (95-62) 70194
Located just beside the Sarabha city gates, this well-established restaurant has the majority of its tables set up under a mat shed in a pleasant garden. It specializes in Burmese food such as coconut rice and fish curry.

Sarabha Two
Under the trees near the Ananda Pagoda
This is a real Bagan experience, in the middle of a field a collection of tables shelter under spreading tamarind trees. A family restaurant with an open kitchen, on offer will be a delicious curry of the day, or crispy fried chicken served along with vegetables, rice and some wonderful condiments, pounded ginger and garlic, mashed eggplant.... an experience not to be missed. It is very clean but as a precaution wash your spoon and fork in the hot tea—mouthwatering jaggery (from toddy palm) fudge for desert.

Sunset Restaurant
Riverside in New Bagan
A little way downstream or south is this stunning family restaurant. Drive along the road from Thiripysaya Hotel, soon after the village of Myinkaba, on the right-hand side of the road, will be a sign to Sunset Restaurant. Follow the little lane and at the end is the restaurant. You walk through a beautifully landscaped garden, the way lit by lights in huge terracotta pots. The tables used to be either under the stars or underneath a rattan shelter, now they have built more permanent structures, still a very romantic place to dine. On each table is a huge bunch of fragrant frangipani flowers. The view over the river is magical with the illuminated Lawkanada Pagoda reflected in the water.

Green Elephant Nandawun
Tel 09 2043463
Further along the road in the Lawkanandar Park is the former River View
Restaurant now taken over by Green Elephant. Stunning view over the river the
restaurant has the same flair and good food as the other sister restaurants.

Green Elephant
Main Road, New Bagan. Tel 0973197142
This is recently opened in New Bagan—again excellent design with some lovely
old Myanmar pieces in the restaurant—the back-drop is an imitation of a Bagan
temple wall, cleverly done. The same good food is on offer.

INLE LAKE REGION

For colonial food go to the Taunggyi Hotel, otherwise some of the best food in
town is to be found at the stalls beside the market (see page 218). Shan food is
delicious, particularly the noodles (soup noodles are called khauk swe) and these
are in plentiful supply at the stalls—as always just make sure they are either
cooked in front of you or steaming hot. Other restaurants come and go at a great
rate, so ask around for the favourite of the moment.

For restaurants in Nyaung Shwe ask in your guesthouse which ones they
recommend. If you stay at the Hu Pin Hotel, it has a good restaurant and the Inle
Inn will produce some food if warned in advance. As always there are stalls around
the market. The following restaurants are on the lake itself.

Golden Seagull
Opposite Phaung Daw U Pagoda
An option for lunch on the lake, it is a large and rather impersonal restaurant—
stick to the fried rice or noodles.

Inn Thar Lay
Beside Phaung Daw U Pagoda
This is a perfect place to stop for lunch after visiting the Phaung Daw U Pagoda.
The food is basic but delicious and while you wait for lunch nibble their crispy
fried bean curd chips. The first floor open restaurant is a perfect spot from which
to watch the leg-rowing races in October during the Inle Lake Festival.

Inthar Heritage House
Inpawkhon Village, Inle Lake. Tel 09 525 1232; www.intharheritagehouse.com
If visiting the southern end of the lake stop off at this beautiful old teak building
a former rice mill. Lunch is served on the terrace, the food is all organic and the
recipes mostly come from the owner's Intha grandmother, crispy fresh vegetables,
delicious noodles and much beside.

For beverages, there are several brands of locally brewed beer, one of the most popular is Myanmar Beer. Imported beers are also on sale. There is also Mandalay Rum and Brandy, the former when mixed with fresh lime makes a delicious rum sour cocktail. In most hotels and restaurants foreign brands of spirits are available—even in restaurants off the beaten track you are likely to find Johnny Walker whisky. Locally made and imported soft drinks are everywhere, as is bottled water. Myanmar grows its own tea and coffee, which are excellent, and there is also plenty of what is called British Tea, in other words, Lipton's.

Fresh vegetables and fruits on sale at the daily morning market at Kaing Tong Township

THE MYSTERY OF THE LONG-LOST SPITFIRES

The most extraordinary tale is unfolding—a tale in which one might expect either Bulldog Drummond or Sherlock Holmes to be prowling around. It is alleged that shortly after August 1945 (it could be as late as 1946) as World War 11 came to an end in Asia, and the Japanese surrendered in Burma there were a number of unassembled crated Spitfires in the county. South-East Asia Command decided that this formerly precious cargo was too bulky to ship home to Britain so they were hidden—the Spitfires were buried in their wooden crates for possible use at a later date, but seemingly no official record of their whereabouts was kept.

For the past twenty years rumours have swirled around that the planes are there but where? Sixteen years ago a UK Spitfire enthusiast David Cundall decided to try and find them. By now of course their value is way beyond their original cost of £12,000 per plane—today there are some fifty Spitfires in flying condition worldwide. As well as Mr Cundall a group from Israel have also been on the trail of the planes.

Mr Cundall travelled back and forth to Burma, he interviewed as many people he could find who might know their whereabouts, he got in touch with some American 'Seabees' (Construction Battalion) former members of the US Navy who during WW11 had specialised in building temporary runways. They were able to give Cundall first-hand information as to where the planes are buried. So armed with that information together with the help of some ground penetrating imaging, he was able to identify what may turn out to be the illusive treasure. All of this had to be done of course with the agreement of the Myanmar government as technically the buried planes belong to them.

Now the story hots up—the research stage for Mr Cundall had been an expensive mission but to dig them up was going to be extremely costly so he searched for an investor. Another Spitfire enthusiast and successful businessman came onto the scene a Mr Steve Boultbee Brooks. He was happy to bank-roll the recovery of the planes and immediately flew to Myanmar in the spring of 2012 where it so happened the British Prime Minister David Cameron was making an historic visit to the country.

Unfortunately at this point the two gentlemen, Mr Cundall and Mr Boultbee Brooks could not agree a deal on the 'way forward' or to the division of the spoils.

As so often in Myanmar the weather intervened—during the rainy season it would be virtually impossible to dig up the said crates, this interlude gives time for the three factions to mediate and come to an agreement together with the Myanmar government as to how this should proceed.

Along with most good mysteries this story has several intriguing questions. For instance why where the planes buried rather than bulldozed into the ground? As by the end of World War 11, Spitfires were already being overtaken by the first generation of jet planes. Why were their whereabouts not overtly recorded? How had the crates arrived in the first place, were they transported over the dangerous Ledo Road? Indeed there are many possibilities as to how they got to Myanmar including flying in... If so to ship the planes back to Britain would have been easy...but not cost effective with so many surplus Spitfires in the UK in the late 1940s. Perhaps once opened the crates will reveal all.

Expert read by Peter Arnold
e-mail: spitfire@dial.pipex.com

Seabees are members of the United States Navy construction battalions. The word **Seabee** is a proper noun that comes from the initials of **Construction Battalion**, (CB) of the United States Navy. The Seabees have a history of building bases, bulldozing and paving thousands of miles of roadway and airstrips, and accomplishing a myriad of other construction projects in a wide variety of military theaters dating back to World War II.

*8-MV483 Spitfire Mk VIII of 155 Squadron
operating in the Burma campaign 1944–1945*

MYANMAR'S ABUNDANT FLORA AND FAUNA

No other country delights the eye so constantly as Myanmar. Its magnificent spreading trees, glorious flowers, and wealth of animal species combine with its monuments and countryside to make it visually unique.

Three basic factors underlie the richness of Myanmar's wildlife. First the country's geographic circumstances—contained by mountains and sea, bisected by the Tropic of Cancer, and irrigated by the noble Ayeyarwady—have created the perfect hothouse. Secondly Burmese culture and particularly its predominant religion, Buddhism, celebrate all natural life. (Burmese fishermen do not kill their prey—they rescue them from drowning!) Thirdly a less happy reason: Myanmar has avoided the worst of developing Asia's environmental horrors because, while its neighbours have been galloping ahead economically, it has stood still.

Flowers are everywhere. Throughout the year trees, shrubs and vines bloom—together with the occasional antirrhinum or aster, a hang-over from colonial times, and many varieties of gorgeous roses. Along a dusty village road brilliant bourgainvillea cascades over a wooden fence, noble Tamarind trees punctuate the rice paddy, the scent from the Neem tree flowers takes your breath away as you walk into a pagoda precinct. Enter the shady stairways leading up to the Shwedagon Pagoda in Yangon and the Sabai (*jasminum Samac*) aroma fills the air.

Burmese ladies love to wear flowers in their hair. The brilliant white star-shaped Sabai flowers are either threaded onto strands of cotton, or made into posies. Older ladies often coil their hair into a *sadone* (a cylindrical top-knot) with the petals hanging down: or a young girl will simply tuck a little bunch elegantly into the nape of her neck. Sometimes this same flower is used as a conditioner—the long black hair is shampooed, combed through then, with a cascade of Sabai flowers clipped on to imbue its scent, left to dry in the sun. Sabai flowers, so pristine white and fragrant, are considered auspicious. The choicest strands are twined around the Buddha image in the family shrine or offered on a *Kalat* (small three-legged lacquer stand).

At the bustling market great hampers of flowers are unloaded at dawn onto flat baskets ready to sell. In the little market restaurants each table is decorated with a seasonal posy. Look on the hawkers' trays: there again, with bags of nuts or cigarettes, will be small flower posies. These are not just decoration but to appease the business *nat* or spirit who, if kept happy, will encourage sales. Again strands of flowers hang from the driving mirrors of cars, buses and lorries, or a bunch on the bow of a river boat— to ensure that the travel *nat* will protect one during the journey.

In every market are stalls piled high with neatly sawn sticks from the *Thanaka* tree. The wood is ground on a flat stone, a little water added to make a smooth paste. This is then applied to the skin—sometimes circles on the cheek or a star pattern—and acts as both a cosmetic (its astringent quality tightens the skin) and as protection from the sun.

Many of Myanmar's flora, (catalogued in the 'List of Trees, Shrubs and Principal Climbers' by Chit Ko Ko and Hundley) have medicinal uses. The juice from the leaves of various jasmines is used to cure colds, fever and laryngitis and also pounded and applied as a poultice to swollen joints. In April along the road-side near Mount Popa, ladies sit behind huge baskets filled with the delicate pale yellow Magnolia flowers. Behind the stall are little glass bottles containing the whole flowers in liquid—a marvellous perfume. Of course a darker side of Myanmar's 'medicinal' flora is the opium poppy grown in worryingly large quantities in the Shan hills.

The profusion of flowers and an absence of chemical fertilisers results in a mass of butterflies. Great black velvety ones, almost as big as a bird and with a bold splash of turquoise, settle on the gangaw (Mesua ferrea) to feed. Or little bright yellow or blue dots dance around a bush of gardenias.

Myanmar boasts huge reserves of hard woods. Around half of the country's nearly 700,000 square kilometres remain covered with tropical forests which today produce around three-quarters of the world's teak. These majestic straight trees with their great flat leaves are seen all over the country—not just in the jungle areas. The *pyingado* tree or 'iron wood', so called due to its density and weight, grows some 50 feet before it puts out any branches. Elephants and buffaloes are still used for felling and hauling the great trunks to the river, for the journey south to the sawmills. Indeed animals are an essential part of daily life in non-automated, agrarian

Myanmar. The ox cart with its stately, soothing rhythm is the elegant symbol of the countryside. Practically no tractors are available so ploughing with oxen is a frequent and pleasing sight—though I suspect the farmer himself would have it otherwise.

Myanmar's jungles still shelter an exciting diversity of wild mammals—to name but a few, elephants, tigers, civet cats, several species of deer, tribes of monkeys, mithans (wild buffalo), Sumatran rhinoceri and wild boar. Today there are some 30 Wildlife Sanctuaries and designated National Parks throughout the country, some date back to the 1890s. These come under the umbrella of the Ministry of Forestry aided by FREDA (Forest Resource & Development Conservation Association) a local NGO concentrating on involving the community in environmental conservation and sustainable forest management. One of the first foreign NGO's to work in Myanmar in this field was the Wildlife Conservation Society (WCS). In 1993 they set up a 'long-term programme in Myanmar. We conduct biological surveys, monitor the population of key wildlife species, aid in the establishment of protected areas, and assist protected area staff with landscape management'. The world's largest tiger reserve in the Hukuang (Hukawng) Valley is the achievement of one of their number, Alan Rabinowitz and the local team he worked with. Alan has written a page-turning account of this project in 'Life in the Valley of Death' (see page 289).

Alan first heard of the Hukuang Valley, 'wild and beautiful with a savage heart' when he arrived in Myanmar to work for WCS in the 1990s. In modern history the Valley has a grim persona, for it was along the tribal paths through this valley that many thousands of men, women and children made their escape into India in 1942 as the Japanese army advanced up the country. However it proved to be a ghastly and difficult route with a multitude dying of malaria and hunger—a cursed trail as many locals believed. Alan Rabinowitz knew that the valley was supposed to be home to tigers but if WCS was going to help protect the big cat's habitat he had to find them, as well as their main predators, hunters and gold miners—the area is rich in gold and other minerals. Then he and his team had to forge some kind of compromise so that all parties could live and prosper in harmony. It is a gripping story of hardship but ultimate success when in 2004 the Myanmar government gazetted the 8,500 square mile landscape as the Hukaung Valley Tiger Reserve.

Sailing on the Ayeyarwady River one sometimes sees small, pale river dolphins playing in twos or threes around the bows. Another WCS initiative in partnership with the Myanmar government is a 43-mile protected section of the river and home to the dolphins, some 4 hours north of Mandalay. The river dolphins and the local fisherman have an extraordinary bond whereby the dolphins herd fish into the fishermen's nets. The river conservation programme also protects the endemic turtles. Snakes—many harmless but kraits and cobras too—are mostly found further south in the dry zones. They enjoy sunning themselves in crevices of Bagan's brick temples, or coiled around a carved wooden figure on Mandalay's teak Shwenandaw Monastery. A journey anywhere in the country reveals the richness of bird life—kingfishers and egrets in the paddy fields, colourful parakeets swooping onto the *jacaranda* trees, or exquisite humming birds hovering to collect nectar from *hibiscus* flowers. On a Yangon street corner a man sits among little birdcages. For a few *kyats* you can buy some of their occupants, release them and so improve your *karma*.

As in so many other aspects of Myanmar, good data on her fauna is hard to come by. So their survival prospects cannot be assessed with authority. Nevertheless with her forest and hill peoples under such intense economic and political pressures, the 'miracle cure' poachers are almost certainly at their terrible work as are the miners and lumber merchants. But there is good news too: with enterprising souls having managed to set up a number of nature reserves and bird sanctuaries all of which are being policed, plus the public awareness of conservation is increasing.

Myanmar has had to endure such disasters but remains an oasis of spiritual calm and human warmth. Living in harmony with the natural world is so deeply imbedded in the way of this ancient land: that surely is the best reason to feel optimistic about the future of one of the world's richest legacies of flora and fauna.

GLOSSARY

betel	the Areca nut, which along with lime is wrapped in a leaf and chewed, giving a mildly intoxicating effect
chinlon	Burmese game played with a small rattan ball, in which the ball must be kept in the air and not touch the hand
chinthe	mythical lion who guards a pagoda entrance
daw	title of respect for an older woman
eingyi	blouse worn with the *longyi*
hinthe	mythical bird resembling a duck with an up-turned tail, also known as a *hamsa*
hti	golden umbrella at the summit of a pagoda
jaggery	the sugar made from the toddy palm
jataka	the stories of the Gautama Buddha's former lives
karaweik	royal bird that carried the god Vishnu and is a symbol of royalty—for instance, the royal barge was the shape of the bird
karma	a person's fate due to his actions in a previous incarnation
kyat	Burmese currency
kyaung	Buddhist monastery
kyeizu pyu	please
kyeizu tin ba de *or* chei-zu tin-bar-te	thank you
kyi-waing	the circular gongs, an important part of the Burmese orchestra
lapet	pickled tea
longyi	sarong worn by both sexes
mingalaba	good morning/hello
minthani	female dancer at a *pwe*
mohingha	Burmese breakfast of noodles and soup

mudra	the different hand positions of the Buddha portrayed in works of art
myo	city or town
nadwin	the ear-piercing ceremony or initiation into the Buddhist faith for girls
nat	a spirit
ngapi	paste made from fermented prawns
Nirvana	the state of perfect enlightenment, of release from the cycle of birth, suffering and death
Pali	the language of the texts of Theravada Buddhism, including the Tripitaka, the Buddhist canon
pandal	platforms from which the water is thrown during the annual Water Festival
ponna	Brahman astrologer
pwe	an entertainment
pyongyi	Buddhist monk
saing-waing	circle of drums used in the Burmese orchestra, in the middle of which sits the musician
sawbwa	a Shan prince
shin-pyu	initiation ceremony into the monkhood for boys
shwe	gold, golden
taunggya	slash-and-burn method of farming
Thakin	a founder member of the pro-independence movement spearheaded by Aung San
thanaka	tree whose bark is ground into a cosmetic
Thingyan	annual Water Festival
Tripitaka	Buddhist scriptures
U	title of respect for an older man
viss	unit of measure, equal to approximately 1.6 kilograms (3.5 pounds)

RECOMMENDED READING

History and Travellers: Many of the empire-builders and adventurers, priests and merchants, and other motley travellers that Burma, as Myanmar was then called, has attracted have written about the country, often with style, perception and, not infrequently, wit.

As in the case of India, colonialists (disciplined, enquiring, keen-eyed types) have provided some of the most useful as well as enjoyable accounts. Two such were Sir Henry Yule and Sir George Scott—both quintessential men of the Victorian British Raj. Yule, who joined the Bengal Engineers in 1840, travelled to Burma as secretary to Colonel Arthur Phayre's Mission to Ava in 1855. His 380-page *A Narrative of the Mission to the Court of Ava in 1855* (Smith, Elder, and Company, 1858; Oxford in Asia Historical Reprints, Oxford University Press, 1968) both chronicles the mission voyage up the Irrawaddy to the court of King Mindon and provides a penetrating social study. The facsimile edition has an informative introduction by Professor Hugh Tinker. The copious and often beautiful illustrations include drawings and watercolours by the mission's official artist, Colesworthy Grant, as well as by the author, helpful maps and photographs by Linneus Tripe. A positive cornucopia of a book.

Sir George Scott joined the Burma commission in 1886 and proceeded to build an immensely distinguished career, notably as Superintendent for the Northern, and later Southern, Shan States. Also known by the name Shway Yoe, Scott wrote prolifically and with great insight and sensitivity about the country and its people. In particular, *The Burman, His Life and Notions* (Macmillan and Sons, 1910) and *Burma As It Was, As It Is and It Will Be* (George Redway, 1886) remain, with minor exceptions, accurate descriptions of daily rural life, a century after they were written.

In the late 19th century, the ship on which Rudyard Kipling was travelling made a brief stop in Rangoon and then Moulmein (modern day Yangon and Mawlamyine). He records this short interlude in Volume I of *From Sea to Sea* (Doubleday McClure, New York, 1899 and Macmillan, London, 1900). In these few days he managed to imbibe the feeling and beauty of the country and its occupants. Burma also features in several of his poems and the much quoted *Mandalay* is most conveniently found in the *Oxford Dictionary of Quotations* (Oxford University Press, Fifth Edition, 1996).

Another brief but perceptive visitor was Somerset Maugham. He describes his voyage up the Irrawaddy in *The Gentlemen in the Parlour* (Heinemann, 1936), now re-published by Vintage Classics. Two more modern travellers have written lively accounts of their Burmese adventures: *Golden Earth* by Norman Lewis (Eland Books, London and Hippocrene Books, New York, reprinted 1984) and *The Great Railway Bazaar: by Train Through Asia* by Paul Theroux (Random House, 1975).

The historian and novelist, Maurice Collis, had in the 1920s been a member of the Indian Civil Service stationed near Mandalay in Sagaing and later in Rangoon. His *Land of the Great Image* (Faber & Faber Ltd, 1942) tells the remarkable tale of the Portuguese Jesuit Father Manrique's journey to, and three-year sojourn at, the Rahkine (Arakan) capital of Mrauk-U in the 1620s. Of his many other books on Burma, *Siamese White* (Faber & Faber Ltd, 1951 and D D Books, Bangkok, 1982) and *Trials in Burma* (Faber & Faber Ltd, 1938) are the most interesting. All are now re published by Faber Finds.

As for history books, the most helpful and interesting include: *The Pagoda War* by A T Q Stewart (Faber & Faber Ltd, 1972), which deals with the Anglo-Burmese conflicts of the mid-19th century; *Stilwell and the American Experience in China* by Barbara Tuchman (Macmillan, 1971); *The Making of Burma* by Dorothy Woodman (Cresset Press, 1962); *The Stricken Peacock* by the Burmese historian, Dr Htin Aung (Martinus Nijhoff, 1965); and *A History of Modern Burma* by J F Cady (Cornell University Press 1958). For an account of the 1988 uprising read Bertil Lintner's *Outrage: Burma's struggle for democracy* (White Lotus, 1990) or his excellent pamphlet, *Aung San Suu Kyi and Burma's Unfinished Renaissance* (White Lotus, 1991).

Many of the above books are available in Myanmar in the various Yangon bookshops, good quality facsimile copies have been printed.

For a modern political travelogue read *Finding George Orwell in Burma* (Penguin 2005) by Emma Larkin. This presents the country as it was during the years of the military junta, Larkin knows the country well so it is extremely perceptive. Also by Emma Larkin is a spine-chilling account of the aftermath of Cyclone Nagris, *After the Flood: The Untold Story of Disaster under Burma's Military Regime* (Granta Books 2009) and also published as *Everything is Broken: A Tale of Catastrophe in Burma* (Penguin, 2010).

The historian Dr Thant Myint-U has recently produced *Where China Meets India* (Faber and Faber 2011) a study of the cultural history of *Burma and the New Crossroads of Asia* as its sub-title proclaims. This book was published just as Aung San Suu Kyi was released from house arrest but before the recent political changes really began so the author ponders what will happen next and states "progress in Burma would be a boon for the region". Dr Thant Myint-U is also the author of *A River of Lost Footsteps; A Personal History of Burma* (Faber and Faber 2007). Using the evocative Rudyard Kipling quote for the title the book takes the reader from the fall of the last King in the 1880s to modern times.

Novels: George Orwell was another English writer who found himself stationed in Burma in the 1920s. He portrays the stilted Raj life in *Burmese Days* (Penguin, 1982) with acid disdain. His subsequent short stories on Burma, *A Hanging in Decline of the English Murder* (Penguin, 1983) and *Shooting an Elephant in Inside the Whale* (Penguin, 1982), are particularly moving.

Perhaps one of the best English novels set in Burma is F Tennyson Jesse's *The Lacquer Lady* (Virago Press Limited, 1979), a beautifully written and spell-binding reconstruction of the extraordinary true story of Fanny Moroni at the court of King Theebaw and Queen Supayalat, and how her love affair literally precipitated annexation of Mandalay and Northern Burma by the British. Miss Tennyson Jesse's *The Story of Burma* (Macmillan 1946), though lacking the surrealist romance of the *The Lacquer Lady*, is nevertheless an excellent historical study of Burma up to World War II. (Written while the Japanese were still in occupation, the final chapter asks 'What next?')

E C V Foucar lived in Burma as a child and later, until the Japanese invasion in 1942, as a barrister. Of his extensive writings about the country, *Mandalay the Golden* (Dobson, 1963) is perhaps his most lively.

A novel brimming with mystery is *The Piano Tuner* by Daniel Mason (Vintage Books 2003) which tells the story of Edgar Drake a piano tuner travelling up into the darkest jungles of 19th century Burma to tune the piano of the Surgeon General—this has been made into a film. The historical novel *The Glass Palace* by Amitar Ghosh (Harper Collins) is also full of intrigue. It tells the tale of the fall and exile of the Burmese royal household.

Biography: There is one biography which stands on its own, Leslie Glass's *The Changing of Kings—Memories of Burma 1934–1949* (Peter Owen Publishers, 1985). This touching, funny and very perceptive book spans, as the title implies, the years immediately leading up to World War II, experiences during those troubled years and then the final period of British colonial rule.

Of the numerous biographies written on *World War II, The Road Past Mandalay* by John Masters (Michael Joseph, 1961) and *A Hell of a Licking: the Retreat from Burma 1941–2* by James Lunt (Collins, 1986) are excellent.

Burma Railway: Images of War is a book of the drawings and diaries of POW Jack Chakler (Mercer Books 2007) whilst working on the Burma Railway, a moving account.

The last few years has seen several new biographies of Aung San Suu Kyi, Peter Popham's *The Lady and the Peacock* (Rider Books 2011) is a fine and fascinating portrait of an extraordinary woman.

Two books which afford the reader a unique insight into Burmese family life and philosophy are by the renowned Burmese authoress, the late Mi Mi Khaing. The first, *The Burmese Family* (Longman, 1946, A M S Press, New York, 1984) is dedicated to her 'Father and Mother', who have 'shown to five children the shining path of moderation that is the Middle Way,' so through her sensitive and lyrical prose Mi Mi Khaing reveals the path of the Middle Way to the reader. In the second book *Cook and Entertain the Burmese Way* (Mi Mi Khaing, 1975, available in Myanmar) the secrets of the Burmese housewife are vouchsafed. The last book published by Mi Mi Khaing before her death, not a biography as it dealt with the role of women in Burmese society. It is entitled *The World of Burmese Woman* (Zed Books, 1984)—again available in Yangon bookshops.

A reviewer had this to say of Maureen Baird-Murray's biography, *A World Overturned* (Constable & Co, 1997): 'This wholly delightful book belongs on the shelf beside that other classic of childhood, Mi Mi Khaing's *The Burmese Family*.' This touching and fascinating account of life in Burma just before World War II and during the Japanese occupation, is a perfect paperback to travel with.

While under house arrest Aung San Suu Kyi kept herself busy by writing a collection of essays, *Freedom from Fear* (Penguin, 1991) and a biography of her father, *Aung San of Burma* (Penguin, 1991). Since then she has written *Letters from Burma* (Penguin, 1995) and *The Voice of Hope* (Penguin, 1997).

One of the most extraordinary recent biographies, *From the Land of the Green Ghosts* by Pascal Khoo Thwe (Flamingo 2003) is the story of a young political refugee from the Padaung tribe who finds himself studying English literature at Caius College Cambridge.

Praise for *'Life in the Valley of Death'* (Island Press 2008) by Alan Rabinowitz is powerful. 'As a general rule, books by saints are best avoided...the guy's halo is green, bright and fully deserved'. This story of how the world's largest tiger reserve came to be in the jungle of the Hukuang Valley, or as the author puts it in the land of 'guns, gold and greed', is exciting and very well written.

Travel Books: Most of the usual suspects are out of print at present though are bound to be back on the market soon so check with Amazon. Meanwhile a new edition of the Lonely Planet *Myanmar (Burma) 2011* is available both in and out of Myanmar.

Several interesting books for the traveller are published in Myanmar, including: *The Pictorial Guide to Bagan*, compiled by the Director of Myanmar's Archaeological Survey; *The Golden Glory: Shwedagon Pagoda*, compiled by the Directorate of Information; and *Historical Sites in Myanmar* by Aung Thau.

For the business traveller who wants something to pop into their briefcase Odyssey Publications has produced a detailed physical map of the country with 27 cultural boxes of text, '*Myanmar: Featuring the Ayeyawady & Year Round Tourist Attractions*', available both in and out of Myanmar.

André and Louis Boucaud provide a rare insight into the country's notorious opium producing region in their book *Golden Triangle*, published by Asia 2000 (see literary excerpt on page 255).

In 1988 a small private publishing house, Kiscadale, was launched in Britain—its list comprises both reprints and new books on Myanmar and caters to all tastes and interests. It is the brainchild of Paul Strachan, who himself has written an excellent book entitled, *Pagan: Art and Architecture of Old Burma* (Kiscadale, 1989). Amazon carries the Kiscadale publications.

For the lacquerware enthusiast, there is a beautiful book entitled *Burmese Lacquerware* by Sylvia Fraser-Lu (Tamarind Press, Bangkok, 1985). One of Myanmar's renaissance men, U Myint Thein, or Uncle Monty as he was lovingly known, wrote a charming book of poems. Throughout his long career he was a diplomat, politician and lawyer, serving as the Chief Justice of Burma from 1957 until 1962. The book, entitled *When at Nights I Strive to Sleep*, was published by The Asoka Society, Oxford in 1971. Finally, there are Dr Htin Aung's excellent handbooks which help one get under the skin of Burmese culture. Some of these have recently been republished in Myanmar, including *Burmese Law Tales*, *Burmese Folk Tales*, *Burmese Drama*, and *Folk Elements in Burmese Buddhism*.

Hot off the press comes a book on the colonial-era buildings of Yangon, *30 Heritage Buildings of Yangon: Inside the city that Captured Time* produced by the Association of Myanmar Architects (Serindia Publications 2012). Published in both English and Burmese it tells the story of 30 buildings in peril. Dr Thant Myint-U historian and founder of the Yangon Heritage Trust warns the reader "If Yangon's architectural heritage is destroyed, a big part of its legacy as a cosmopolitan, multi-faith and multi-ethnic city will be lost."

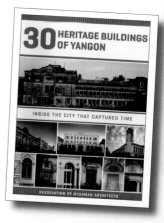

Elephants ford a river in the Hukawng Valley. For more information on Panthera's conservation work visit www.panthera.org where you can peruse their gorgeously illustrated brochure

BURMA AND THE MAN WHO FORESAW THE CRISIS OF ECONOMICS

Andrew Sheng, President of the Fung Global Institute, Feb 2012

Note: For anyone disillusioned with the failures of mainstream economics, a book by E.F. Schumacher first published in 1973 is a must read, says Fung Global Institute President Andrew Sheng. With no-nonsense analysis, Schumacher described how economic theory often ignores the way the real world works—and emerges the worse for it.

Today, amidst great awareness that mainstream economic theory is seriously flawed, many of us are looking for alternative modes of economic thinking. I have in my collection a book by the late English economist E.F. Schumacher called *Small is Beautiful*, first published in 1973. Having not read it until last month, I was overwhelmed by its brilliant and unconventional approach to economic thinking.

The book became almost cult reading when it came out 40 years ago, in the aftermath of the first energy crisis. The author was a Jewish refugee from Germany to England who studied at Oxford and Columbia universities. He became economic advisor to the British National Coal Board and was sent in 1955 to work in Burma as an economic development advisor. It was from his experience there, including staying in a Buddhist monastery, that he evolved a highly non-Western way to consider human development, such as living within the limits of natural resources and using appropriate "intermediate technology" that is a middle way between high tech and basic. This explains why Chapter 4 of the book was called Buddhist Economics.

The book is actually a collection of essays written at different times. Like his teachers, John Maynard Keynes and John Kenneth Galbraith, Schumacher wrote in elegant and striking prose:

"One of the most fateful errors of our age is the belief that the problem of production has been solved. The illusion...is mainly due to our inability to recognise that the modern industrial system, with all its intellectual sophistication, consumes the very basis on which it has been erected. To use the language of the economist, it lives on irreplaceable capital which it cheerfully treats as income."

He immediately plunges into an attack on the whole philosophy of modern economics that reduces everything into monetary values as measured by GDP, arguing that the logic of limitless growth is wrong:

"...that economic growth, which viewed from the point of view of economics, physics, chemistry, and technology, has no discernable limit must necessarily run into decisive bottlenecks when viewed from the point of view of the environmental sciences. An attitude to life which seeks fulfilment in the single-minded pursuit of wealth—in short, materialism—does not fit into this world, because it contains within itself no limiting principle, while the environment in which it is placed is strictly limited."

Being a system-wide thinker, he deplored the narrowness of economics:

"Economists themselves, like most specialists, normally suffer from a kind of metaphysical blindness, assuming that theirs is a science of absolute and invariable truths, without any presuppositions."

He was probably the earliest to recognise that the concepts of GDP ignored the costs of depletion of natural resources and the high social damage through pollution: "It is inherent in the methodology of economics to ignore man's dependence on the natural world."

Most recent reviewers of his book commended him on the accuracy of his forecasts, made all those years ago, on population and the rate of consumption of energy resources. Some reviewers considered that the book brilliantly explained the "why" of the need to conserve, but not the "how". I think he went deeper than that.

Schumacher was not just a social philosopher but a practical observer of large-scale social organisations, particularly bureaucracies. The realist side of him can be found in this quote: "An ounce of practice is generally worth more than a ton of theory."

Indeed, he was very insightful about the importance of smallness in a large organisation. This was because as organisations become larger and larger, they become more impersonal. He recognised the inherent contradictions within large organisations that have alternating phases of centralising and decentralising. Here, he noted that the solution is not either-or, but the-one-and-the-other-at-the-same-time. In other words, contradiction and illogical situations are inherent in large systems.

This is because all organisations struggle to have "the orderliness of order and the disorderliness of creative freedom." Every organisation struggles with the orderly administrator versus the creative (that is, disorderly) entrepreneur or innovator.

From this basic contradiction, Schumacher had a theory of large-scale organisation divided into five principles, which would be worth researching further.

The first principle is subsidiarity—which holds that the upper authority should delegate to the lower level powers where it is obvious that the lower levels can function more efficiently than the central authority.

The second principle is vindication—namely, governance by exception. The centre delegates and only intervenes under exceptional circumstances which are clearly defined.

The third principle is identification—the subsidiary must have clear accounting in the form of balance sheets and a profit and loss account.

The fourth principle is motivation—here, he recognised that the lower levels of large organisation has little motivation if everything is directed from the top. This is where the values of the organisation become critical in addition to rewards in terms of money.

The fifth is the principle of the middle axiom. He notes that "the centre can easily look after order; it is not so easy to look after freedom and creativity".

The word "axiom" means a self-evident truth. The principle of the middle axiom is "an order from above which is yet not an order". In practical terms, you set out an objective, but do not detail and direct how that objective is to be achieved, giving some degree of innovation and freedom for the subsidiary levels of the organisation to achieve the objectives.

What is amazing is that 40 years ago, Schumacher quoted Chairman Mao for the best formulation of the necessary interplay between theory and practice: "Go to the practical people, learn from them; then synthesise their experience into principles and theories; and then return to the practical people and call upon them to put these principles and methods into practice so as to solve their problems and achieve freedom and happiness".

All these sound very simple, but are actually quite hard to practise. Schumacher has certainly convinced me that there are good alternatives to current conventional economic thinking.

Shwedagon Pagoda

HISTORICAL-CULTURAL CHRONOLOGY CHART

	MYANMAR	ASIA	EUROPE AND THE WESTERN WORLD
BC 3500		Earliest Chinese town; Long Shan culture.	Invention of wheel and plough (Mesopotamia) and sail (Egypt).
3000			
2500	Legendary lists of Kings of Arakan begins (c.2666).	Use of bronze in Thailand. Growth of civilisation in the Indus valley (c.2750).	Old Kingdom, or Pyramid Age, of Egypt begins (c.2685 to 2180 BC).
1500		First urban civlsation in China; Shang Bronze Age culture (c.1600); Evidence of writing in China (c.1500); Development of Brahma worship in India. Composition of Vedas begins (c.1450).	Beginnings of Mycenaean civilization in Greece (c.1600).
750		Sanskrit religious treaties (c.800–400).	Homer's Iliad and Hesiod's poetry first recorded (c.750).
500		Death of Siddhartha Gautama, founder of Buddhism (c.486); Death of Confucius (c.479).	Period of Greek classical culture (c.479–338).
300	Pyu civilisation established in upper Burma (200).	Ashoka, Mauryan emperor (273–236) converted to Buddhism (c.262); Shi Huang Di of Qin Dynasty unites China (221); Construction of the Great Wall.	Alexander the Great invades Asia Minor, then reaches India (329).
100	Visit of Zhang Qian, emissary from Han China (c.128).	Opening of Silk Road across Central Asia. Trade with Rome (c.112).	
AD 50			Jesus of Nazareth crucified in Jerusalem (c.30). Roman invasion of Britain (43).
100	Founding of Pagan (c.108).		
150		Buddhism reaches China. Chinese Buddhist monks make pilgrimages to India.	

Date	Burma	Asia / World	Europe
200	Mahamuni Buddha image probably cast in Arakan.		
300	Original stupa built at Shwedagon Pagoda site by the Mon people.	Founding of Constantinople (330).	Huns, Visigoths, Vandals ravage western Europe (c.370–410).
500			Death of St. Benedict (543).
600		Death of Muhammed (632).	
700		Printing in China (c.730); Paper making spreads from China to Muslim world and eventually Europe in 1150.	
800			Charlemagne crowned emperor in Rome.
1000	Dagon (later Yangon) is founded (c.1028) by the Mon; Anawrahta succeeds to throne at Pagan (1044) and establishes the First Burmese Empire.	Moveable type printing invented in China (1045).	Norman conquest of Britain (1066).
1100		Angkor Empire (Cambodia) at greatest extent (c.1180).	The Song of Roland (c.1100).
1200	Mongols invade Burma ending First Burmese Empire (1287); Mons establish Talaing Empire at Martaban (1287).	Mongols under Genghis Khan begin conquest of Asia (1206); Emergence of first Thai kingdom (c.1220); Kublai Khan founds Yuan Dynasty in China (1279).	Magna Carta: King John makes concessions to English barons (1215). Death of St. Francis of Assisi (1226).
1300	Sagaing founded as capital of independent Shan kingdom (1315); New Shan Dynasty (Thedo Minya) establishes capital at Ava (1364); This dynasty of 17 kings survives until 1554.	Ming Dynasty founded in China (1368).	Black Death from Asia invades Europe (1348).
1400		Vasco de Gama: first European sea voyage to India and back (1498).	Columbus reaches America (1492).
1500	Portuguese establish trade ports in Arakan and Syriam (1519); Second Burmese Empire established at Pegu (1541); King Bayinnaung expands empire to include Chiangmai and Ayuthaya (1550–81); First British trader (Ralph Fitch) visits Burma (1586).	Babur conquers Kingdom of Delhi and founds Mughal Dynasty (1526).	Italian Renaissance; Tobacco first introduced to Europe (1559).
1600	Felipe de Brito impaled in Syriam after 13 years as Governor (1613).	Manchus found Qing Dynasty in China (1644).	Foundation of British and Dutch East India Companies.

	MYANMAR	ASIA	EUROPE AND THE WESTERN WORLD
1700	King Alaungpaya founds Konbaung Dynasty (1752); Alaungpaya captures Dagon (1755) and renames it Yangon, later to be called Rangoon by the British; Alaungpaya defeats the Manipuris to the west and invades Siam to the east, where he dies in a retreat from Ayutthaya (1760).	Taj Mahal at Agra completed (1653); Foundation of Calcutta by English (1690). Greatest extent of China's empire, under Emperor Qian Long.	Puritans land in New England (1620); English Civil War begins (1642); New Amsterdam taken by British from Dutch (later renamed New York) (1664). French Revolution begins (1789); George Washington becomes first President of U.S.A. (1789).
1810		Britain defeats Marathas and becomes effective ruler of India (1818); British found Singapore as free trade port (1819).	Napoleon defeated at Waterloo (1815).
1820	Burmese invade British India (1824) leading to First Anglo-Burmese War; (Assam, Arakan and Tenasserim annexed by Britain (1824–1826); Treaty of Yandabo (1826).		First passenger steam train, Stockton to Darlington (England) (1825).
1830			
1840		Opium War; Britain annexes Hong Kong (1842).	First electric telegraph (Britain) (1838). Communist Manifesto issued by Marx and Engels (1848).
1850	Second Anglo-Burmese War, Lower Burma annexed (1852); King Mindon comes to throne of Ava (1853); Mindon establishes Mandalay as the capital (1857). It is to be Burma's last royal capital.	Taiping Rebellion in China (1850–64); Indian Mutiny (1857).	Darwin publishes The Origin of Species (1859).
1860		End of Tokugawa Shogunate in Japan (1868).	
1870	Burmese mission to Europe; received by Queen Victoria (1857); Fifth Buddhist Synod in Mandalay (1871–72); Mindon dies and is succeeded by Theebaw (1878); potential heirs to the throne are massacred.		American Civil War. Slavery abolished in U.S.A. (1861–5); Emancipation of Russian serfs (1861); Suez Canal opens (1869). Emergence of Impressionist school of painting (1874).

	World events	Asia events	Burma events
1880			King Thebaw negotiates treaty with the French (1884); Third Anglo-Burmese War (1885–1886); formal annexation of Burma as a province of British India (1886); Thebaw exiled to Ratnagiri, India (1886).
1890	Boer War begins (1899).	Sino-Japanese War. Japan occupies Formosa (1894–5).	
1900		Boxer Uprising in China.	
1910	Outbreak of First World War (1914); Russian Revolution (1917); League of Nations established (1919).	Chinese Republican Revolution: Sun Yat-sen first President (1911).	
1920	Wall Street stock market crash (1929).	Gandhi's non-cooperation movement in India (1921–2).	Montagu-Chelmsford reforms in India; (diarchy) extended to Burma (1923).
1930			Burma separated from British India and given Legislative Council (1937).
1940	Outbreak of Second World War (1939); Development of penicillin (1939). Defeat of Germany and end of Second World War (1945).	Japan attacks U.S.A. at Pearl Harbour (1941); Civil war in China (1946); India and Pakistan become independent nations (1947); Communists come to power in China (1949).	Japan invades Lower Burma (1941); the Burmese Government together with Aung San's Burma Independence Army declare Burma independent (1943); Rangoon recaptured. Japanese surrender (1945); Assassination of Aung San and all but three of his Cabinet (1947); Union of Burma becomes independent, with U Nu as Prime Minister (1948).
1950	Fifth Republic in France. De Gaulle first President (1958).	Bandung Conference of Third World leaders (1954).	Sixth Buddhist Synod held in Rangoon (1954–6); Ne Win heads caretaker government (1958).
1960	East Germans build the Berlin Wall (1961); Cuban missile crisis (1962); First man on the moon (1969). President Nixon resigns following Watergate Affair (1974);	Escalation if U.S. involvement in Vietnam War (1964); Cultural Revolution in China (1966). Vietnam unified under the communists (1975); Death of Mao Tse-tung and fall of Gang of Four in China (1976); Khmer Rouge holocaust in Cambodia (1977);	U Nu regains power in elections (1960); Ne Win heads successful military coup (1962).
1970			Socialist Republic of the Union of Burma created (1974); Major earthquake in Pagan (1975).

	MYANMAR	ASIA	EUROPE AND THE WESTERN WORLD
1980		Vietnamese capture Phnom Penh during invasion which ousts Khmer Rouge (1979), Soviet Union invades Afghanistan (1979).	Egypt and Israel sign peace treaty at White House (1979).
1981	Ne Win retires from Presidency but retains Chairmanship of the Burma Socialist Programme Party (1981).		Debates on nuclear disarmament; Ronald Reagan is elected President of the United States; murder of John Lennon. First orbital flight of the Space Shuttle.
1982 1983		Discussions between Britain and China on the future of Hong Kong (1983); Independence of Brunei (1983).	Falklands War.
1984		Sino-British Joint Declaration agrees to hand Hong Kong back to China on 30th June 1997.	
1985			Mikhail Gorbachev becomes President of Soviet Union; First use of DNA fingerprinting; Live Aid concert.
1986		End of dictatorship of Ferdinand Marcos in the Philippines.	Space ship and Chernobyl disasters; Assassination of Olof Palme.
1987 1988	After the popular uprising, a military coup leads to the establishment of a 21-member military regime known as the State Law and Order Restoration Council.		World population reaches 5 billion. Perestoika begins; End dictatorship Augusto Pinochet; Pan Am Flight 103 blown up over Lockerbie.
1989	The military regime changes the official name of the country to Myanmar; all place names and geographical features are changed from English to Myanmar.	Tiananmen Square Massacre in Beijing; End of Soviet invasion of Afghanistan; Death of Emperor Hirohito; Fatwa issued against Salman Rushdie.	Fall of the Berlin Wall; Collapse of the Soviet Bloc.

Year	Myanmar	Asia / Regional events	World events
1990	Aung San Suu Kyi placed under house arrest; NLD (party lead by Aung San Suu Kyi) wins 82% of seats in election; the government refuses to honour election result.		Sir Tim Berners-Lee invents the World Wide Web; Reunification of Germany; launch of Hubble Space telescope; Gulf War begins.
1991	Aung San Suu Kyi wins the Nobel Peace Prize.		Gulf War ends; Dissolution of the Soviet Union.
1992			Bill Clinton is elected President of United States.
1994			End of apartheid in South Africa and election of Nelson Mandela as President.
1995			Establishment of World Trade Organisation.
1996	Trade sanctions imposed by USA and EU.	Taliban government takes control of Afghanistan.	USA and EU impose sanctions.
1997	Myanmar is admitted to ASEAN.	Transfer of sovereignty over Hong Kong from United Kingdom to China.	Diana, Princess of Wales is killed in a car crash in Paris.
1998		Osama bin Laden publishes a fatwa against the West; North Korean famine kills some 2.5 million people.	
1999		Fourth Indo-Pakistan War; Crisis in East Timor leads to around 1400 deaths.	Euro introduced; World population reaches 6 billion (1999).
2000			George W Bush is elected President of the United States; Vladimir Putin becomes President of Russia; International Space Station begins operations (2000).
2001		Afghan War begins; President Joseph Estrada of the Philippines impeached.	9/11 attacks destroy the World Trade Centre in New York and damage the Pentagon in Washington DC; War on Terror declared (2001); Chechen rebels seize theatre in Moscow; Guantanamo Bay detention camp is established (2002).
2002		Bali bombings; Independence of East Timor.	
2003	Prime Minister Khin Nyunt unveils military regime's seven-point roadmap for a transition to democracy. It leads to the adoption of a constitution after a referendum and in 2010, to the country's first general election in more than 50 years.		Iraq War begins triggering worldwide protests; the Human Genome Project is completed; Space Shuttle Columbia is destroyed on re-entry into the atmosphere.

*With British Prime
Minister David Cameron*

With US President Barack Obama

With His Majesty King Harald of Norway

*With Singapore President
Dr. Tony Tan Keng Yam*

With Hillary Clinton when she was Secretary of State

With Deputy Prime Minister of Japan, Taro Aso

With Chinese President Xi Jingping

With Thailand Prime Minister Yingluck Shinawatra

	MYANMAR	ASIA	EUROPE AND THE WESTERN WORLD
2004	Prime Minister Khin Nyunt, the Military Intelligence chief, is arrested and the entire MI organisation purged, with dozens of officers sentenced to long jail terms.	Boxing Day Tsunami in Indian Ocean kills about 230,000 people; First free election in Afghanistan.	
2005	The military regime moves the capital to Nay Pyi Taw.	Tulip Revolution in Kyrgyzstan; 80,000 killed by earthquake in Kashmir.	IRA end military campaign in Northern Ireland; 7/7 attacks on London Underground; Angela Merkel becomes Germany's first women Chancellor; Hurricane Katrina kills some 2000 in the Gulf of Mexico; The Kyoto Protocol comes into effect; Pope John dies succeeded by Pope Benedict.
2006		The Baiji, the Yangtze river dolphin, becomes functionally extinct.	
2007	Anti-government protests lead by monks suppressed by military regime.	Assassination of Benazer Bhutto.	
2008	Cyclone Nargis kills about 138,000 people; referendum approves new constitution, which reserves 25% of seats in the hluttaw (parliament) for the military.	End of monarchy in Nepal.	Barack Obama is elected President of the United States; Gaza War begins.
2009		Formation BRICS economic bloc.	Gaza War ends; Gaza blockade continues; Formation of BRICS economic bloc.
2010	Pro-government USDP party victorious in general election; Aung San Suu Kyi released from house arrest; the military regime changes the national flag and the country's official name is changed to Republic of the Union of Myanmar.	Tensions arise between North and South Korea.	Earthquake in Haiti kills 230,000; Largest oil spill in US history occurs in Gulf of Mexico.

2011	First session of Parliament convenes; Thein Sein, a former general and Prime Minister, becomes President; Work suspended on a dam on the Ayeyarwady River being built and financed by China; President Thein Sein meets Aung San Suu Kyi; US Secretary of State Hillary Clinton and other foreign dignitaries visit; the USA and the EU relax sanctions.	Earthquake in Japan triggers tsunami that results in 16,000 deaths and the meltdown of Fukushima nuclear power plant; floods in Pakistan, Thailand and the Philippines kill about 2500 people; deaths of Osama bin Laden, Gaddafi and Kim Jong Il.	Arab Spring; Iraq War ends; World population reaches 7 billion.
2012	The NLD wins 43 of 45 parliamentary seats in a by-election; Aung San Suu Kyi becomes a Member of Parliament; Aung San Suu Kyi makes her first trip abroad in 27 years, visiting Thailand, Norway, Ireland, Britain, France, USA and India; visit of President Barack Obama; President U Thein Sein addresses United Nations General Assembly.		Diamond Jubilee of Queen Elizabeth 11 of UK and Commonwealth; Greek debt crisis; Arab Spring continues; After 244 years Encyclopaedia Britannica discontinues its print edition; A pastel version of Edvard Munch's The Scream is sold for US$120 million in NYC; Tortoise Lonesome George dies in Galapagos making species extinct; Cern announces the discovery of a new particle after experiments at the Large Hedron Collider; 2012 Summer Olympics held in London; Series of attacks against USA diplomatic mission, in Libya US Ambassador Christopher Stevens is killed.
2013	Irrawaddy literary Festival (February); World Economic Forum (June); Southeast Asian Games (27th December); First Congress of National League for Democracy (March); Myanmar authorities and Kachin generals in Peace Talks (Spring 2013).	North Korea third nuclear test; UN imposes further sanctions (February); Xi Jinping becomes President of China (March); Philippines General Election (May).	Inauguration of President Barak Obama'as second term (January 2013); Syrian civil war continues; Second anniversary 2011 revolution, more protests in Tahrir Square (January); Pope Benedict resigns, Pope Francis elected, first Jesuit and South American to be Pope (March). US Government shut down (October).
2014	Myanmar holds Chairmanship of the Association of Southeast Asian Nations		

INDEX

User's Note: The alphabetical arrangement of index entries is word-by-word. References to the text inside the front and back covers are denoted by use of the letters **FC** and **BC**, respectively. Subjects mentioned in the captions for photographs and illustrations have also been indexed. The page references for these are in **bold** type.

For references to captions used in the photo essays, the page number preceding the photo essay is given before the individual page reference, which is in roman numerals. For example, **240 iv**.

Certain place names and features that appear on the eight map pages of the Myanmar Atlas that follows page 272 have also been indexed. The references are given in bold type, as follows: **272 (Map 1)**. Place names on the Atlas Key map have not been indexed.

The heading 'Burma' is used for references prior to the change in the country's name in 1989, after which references are entered under 'Myanmar'. For geographical places, references have been entered under the current name, with a 'see' reference from the former place name.

As 'U' is a title and not part of a person's name in Myanmar, this has been inverted in the name entry, viz: for 'U Thant' in the text, the index entry is 'Thant, U'.